SOVEREIGNTY & SUSTAINABILITY

SOVEREIGNTY & SUSTAINABILITY

INDIGENOUS LITERARY STEWARDSHIP IN NEW ENGLAND

Siobhan Senier

University of Nebraska Press
LINCOLN

Portions of chapter 2 were previously published in "The Continuing Circulations of New England's Tribal Newsletters," *American Literary History* 29, no. 2 (May 2017): 418–37, used with permission of Oxford University Press; and "Rethinking Recognition: Mi'kmaq and Maliseet Poets Re-Write Land and Community," MELUS: *Multi-Ethnic Literature of the U.S.* 37, no. 1 (2012): 15–34, used with permission.

Portions of chapter 4 were previously published in "Bowman Books: A Gathering Place for Indigenous New England," *Studies in American Indian Literatures* 27, no. 1 (Spring 2015): 96–111, 129, used with permission of University of Nebraska Press.

Library of Congress Cataloging-in-Publication Data
Names: Senier, Siobhan, 1965– author.
Title: Sovereignty and sustainability: indigenous literary stewardship in New England / Siobhan Senier.
Description: Lincoln: University of Nebraska Press, [2020]. | Includes bibliographical references and index.
Identifiers: LCCN 2019025462
ISBN 9780803296770 (cloth)
ISBN 9781496219923 (epub)
ISBN 9781496219930 (mobi)
ISBN 9781496219947 (pdf)
Subjects: LCSH: Indian literature—New England—History and criticism. | American literature—Indian authors—History and criticism. | American literature—New England—History and criticism.
Classification: LCC PS153.I52 S46 2020 | DDC 810.9/8974—dc23
LC record available at https://lccn.loc.gov/2019025462

Set in Questa by Mikala R. Kolander.

Contents

Illustrations

Preface

I started writing this book while working on another, *Dawnland Voices: An Anthology of Indigenous Writing from New England* (2014). That book—the first published collection of Native American literature from the northeastern United States—took nearly ten years to complete. It involved almost a dozen tribal community editors from ten distinct tribal nations, over eighty living authors, and countless descendants and relatives of authors who have passed. The book showcases a wide variety of literary forms, from the earliest known political petitions, letters, and speeches, to contemporary blog entries and children's poetry. It is close to seven hundred pages long.

I wanted to publish a regional anthology because, as a teacher in New England public universities, I felt a strong obligation to represent local literatures. However, regional Native American writers were surprisingly difficult to find. Initially, I assumed that "recovering" this literature would depend on my own assiduous archival work. I was wrong. Native people themselves know who their writers are, and they know dozens of them, dating back centuries. Many of these writers go out of print the moment they are published; some never make it into formal publishing mechanisms at all. Some are archived only in tribal offices or individual family homes. And yet tribal communities maintain robust accountings of their own literary histories. Narragansett people know stories about Princess Red Wing, who edited the *Narragansett Dawn* in the 1930s, even if they do not have their own copies of that magazine. Wampanoag people recite poetry by Mabel Avant at public events, even though she appears never to have been published outside of her community on Cape Cod. Penobscot people, years before Duke University Press "recovered" Joseph Nicolar's 1891 *Life and Traditions of the Red Man*, were selling Xeroxed copies of that book out of local gas stations up near Old Town, Maine. Abenaki people cherish their lovingly used copies of nineteenth-century language primers by Joseph Laurent and Pier Pol Wzokhilain, and they circulate them as part of their current language revitalization work.

Dawnland Voices only scratched the surface of these vibrant literary traditions. The tribal editors had much more writing than we could reasonably include between the covers of a single volume. They also had fascinating conversations about that literature, about what to include or leave out, and about how to contextualize it. The book felt like it was only the beginning, so we began expanding the anthology into a website, dawnlandvoices .org, which has two sides. *Dawnland Voices 2.0* is a biannual literary magazine open to new and established regional Indigenous writers. Where *Dawnland Voices* originally took its name from many New England tribes' histories of referring themselves as, for instance, "people of the first light" (Wampanoag), the online magazine now includes writings from Indigenous relations in what are now New York and the eastern seaboard, as well as from Indigenous people who either have moved out of New England or are Indigenous to other places and have put down roots here. The other side of the website, *Indigenous New England Digital Collections*, includes a variety of electronic exhibits: one on baskets, one on tribes' efforts to digitize their own collections, and a growing collection of digitized tribal newsletters.

The book at hand is intended partly as a companion to the print anthology and the website, to provide teachers and readers with a little more context for what they find therein. Beyond that, this is primarily a book about how Native American communities have kept their literary traditions alive—how they have remembered them, promoted them, and adapted them.[1]

Indigenous people keep close tabs on their most important writers, books, and newsletters. They do so through a complex mix of formal and informal, written and oral practices. Elders save letters and newspapers in their own filing cabinets; tribal offices make copies of old books and pamphlets; history buffs point each other to bibliographies and local institutional archives; and relatives *tell stories* about who wrote what, how they wrote it, and what they said. Tribal communities celebrate, argue about, quote, and reprint their writers, effectively maintaining their own local, flexible, yet enduring literary canons. They do all of this with or without acknowledgment and support from outside communities, with or without conventional publishing mechanisms or markers of literary prestige.

I focus on New England, where Native American writing continues to be marginalized not only within the larger American literary canon but even within the field of Native American and Indigenous studies. Scholars in that field have built a robust conversation around writers of the early colonial period like Samson Occom (Mohegan) and William Apess (Pequot), but we seem to stop republishing, teaching, and talking about regional writers after about 1830. This unfortunately contravenes the argument that so many ethnohistorians and Indigenous people have made so forcefully: that New England's Indigenous cultures and communities are *continuously present*. In this book, then, I focus on the twentieth and twenty-first centuries, where we can see New England's Native communities not only *surviving* through five centuries of colonialism but *thriving* as historians, editors, novelists, poets, publishers, and bloggers.

In the course of writing this story I kept running up against a constellation of terms inside and outside of Native American and Indigenous studies. No one these days can discuss Indigenous literature without some address to *sovereignty* or the political status of Indigenous groups as self-determining *nations*. In thinking about sovereignty, it is likewise difficult to avoid thinking about the profound interrelations between Indigenous lands and Indigenous culture—the "coupled human-natural systems" that many scientists now consider the centerpiece of discussions around *sustainability*. I will take up some of the many arguments around sovereignty and sustainability in my introduction, but I find that the persistent resurfacing of these terms in much Indigenous writing and thinking makes them impossible to ignore.

Native American literature can be read as an expression of tribal sovereignty; it also speaks frequently to sustainability, in both the ecological and cultural senses of that word. Further, literature is itself something that, as I suggested earlier, Indigenous communities work hard to sustain. Like other human communities, they make decisions about what to save, what to jettison, and what to adapt. To describe these interrelated processes—the ways that Indigenous people have sustained their cultures and their lands with and through literature—I have landed on the term "stewardship." This term suggests a duty of care toward land, community, and text, and it helps explain how these communities have been so successful at maintaining their literary canons over the very long haul, with disruptions from settler colonialism that in the final analysis are only temporary.

Whenever I read or teach northeastern Indigenous literature, I am overwhelmed, not just by how *much* Native people in New England have written but also by the many ways and forms in which they have written and by their compelling reasons for doing so. They have written under (or in defiance of) pressure from colonial authorities who wanted to convert them to Christianity or otherwise assimilate them. They have written when high school guidance counselors have told them they couldn't. They have published books when no for-profit publisher has cared to read their work, and they have cared for their tribal newspapers and grandmothers' letters when no major funding institution has helped them buy acid-free boxes or pay their archivists. They have cited each other's histories and recited each other's poetry, keeping it alive, often, through oral traditions—the very traditions assumed to be "replaced" by writing. Interweaving sovereignty, sustainability, and stewardship—as well as "New England," "Indigenous," and "literature"—I mean to push against the idea, promoted in so many other books about Indians in New England, that Indians have vanished or are irrelevant remnants. I mean to show that regional Native literature in fact looks to a dynamic future.

In writing this book I try to adhere to a citational practice modeled by such Indigenous scholars as Craig Womack, Robert Warrior, Jace Weaver, Daniel Heath Justice, Zoe Todd, and many more: a citational politics that deliberately elevates the work of Indigenous thinkers. Justice encourages us to think about "citational relations," calling our footnotes and bibliographies "relational [practices], acknowledgements of intellectual genealogies from which we all benefit and which require expansive diversity to remain healthy and transformative" (241–42). In the case of sustainability studies, we might note that there is plenty of scholarship quoting Aldo Leopold and David Orr; in literary history and archival studies, plenty of scholars will quote Jacques Derrida. Academic readers already know these voices, but too many remain ill acquainted with the many Indigenous intellectuals, past and present, whose work enriches and sometimes even anticipates them. I hope that my subsequent chapters can introduce scholars and teachers in American literary studies, ecocriticism, periodical studies, archival studies, and even digital humanities to the rich, long-standing conversation about these topics among Indigenous scholars and writers.

Acknowledgments

True to the image of the sustainability feedback loop that is so central to this project, this book owes much to a wide network of friends, colleagues, and mentors. Individual chapters and the book as a whole have been greatly improved by conversations with Joan Tavares Avant, Judy Battat, Lisa Botshon, Lisa Brooks, Jesse Bruchac, Margaret Bruchac, Cari Carpenter, Monica Chiu, Linda Coombs, Janet Dean, Julie Dinger, Dawn Dove, Jessica Fish, Robin Hackett, Rebecca Herzig, John Christian Hopkins, Nicola Imbracsio, Paulla Dove Jennings, Joan Lester, Anthony Lioi, Donna Roberts Moody, John Moody, Brandon Morgan, Melinda Plastas, Denise Pouliot, Paul Pouliot, Rick Pouliot, Eve Raimon, Cheryl Savageau, Donald Soctomah, Lorén Spears, Cristina Stanciu, Lisa Walker, Edward Whitley, and Melissa Tantaquidgeon Zobel. At the University of Nebraska Press, Matt Bokovoy has been a smart and steadfast shepherd of both this book and the anthology that preceded it. Four anonymous external readers made this manuscript much stronger.

The James H. and Claire Short Hayes Chair in the Humanities supported much of the research here and in *Dawnland Voices*, as well as the building of dawnlandvoices.org. University of New Hampshire librarians Eleta Exline and Meredith Ricker contributed immeasurably to that website's electronic and human infrastructures. After her retirement, Meredith continued to be a friend and collaborator on the digital project;

her knowledge, attention to detail, and openness to learning from and with Indigenous people were profoundly *sustaining*. Shortly before I was ready to send this final manuscript to Nebraska, and much too soon, Meredith passed away. I dedicate this book to her memory.

SOVEREIGNTY & SUSTAINABILITY

Introduction

One night
my father brings in a book.
See, he says, Abenaki,
and shows me the map
here and here and here
he says, all this
is Abenaki country.
I remember asking him
what did they do
these grandparents
and my disappointment
when he said no buffalo
roamed the thick new england forest
they hunted deer in winter
sometimes moose, but mostly
they were farmers
and fishermen.
—Cheryl Savageau (Abenaki), "Looking for Indians"

In lowercasing the place we now call New England, Cheryl
Savageau slyly reveals two realities about this region: one,
it is a colonial construct imposed on a geographic area with
its own biocultural history—hunting moose, planting, fishing—

that transcends current state and national borders; and two, Indigenous people have survived this construct, often adapting to its new economic realities (e.g., working in factories, using print atlases), and just as often by remembering and continuing their oldest ways of being in this place.

New England's Indigenous writers understand full well the violence enacted upon them by the idea of the region. There is no natural or inevitable reason that Maine, New Hampshire, Vermont, Massachusetts, Rhode Island, and Connecticut should be clustered together in a single identity. Yet the idea of New England—home of freedom-seeking Pilgrims, hardy self-made Yankees, Boston accents, and clam chowder—remains powerful. This is perhaps especially true for the region's original inhabitants, insofar as they are expected to have vanished from this place; as Jean O'Brien (Ojibwe) has explained, New England historiography has spent centuries making white settlers the region's "first" people, while describing Indians, inevitably, as the "last" of their tribes. Thus while there may be no natural or inevitable reason to consider Wampanoag, Mohegan, Abenaki, and Passamaquoddy people all together, these disparate tribal nations do share some things, not least of which is that they are often treated as illegitimate presences, as somehow less than Indian because they do not hunt buffalo or look like the Apaches on Savageau's TV.

Stereotypes and vanishing-race mythologies are hardly peculiar to New England, but they do exercise special force here. For historical reasons, and unlike their counterparts out west, many tribes in this region lack large (or any) reservations or long-standing relations with the federal government, often making them geographically and politically invisible. Simultaneously they have had some of the longest histories of interaction in the United States with colonial settlers and colonial institutions, and so many Native individuals may appear less visible, culturally and even phenotypically, to outsiders. Where New England's Indigenous communities do have substantial property, or where they make any bids for self-determination, they can attract horrible vitriol, from violent face-to-face racism to state policymaking that abrogates their right to fish, hunt, and run their own affairs. Indeed, for all that New England is a construct, it is no less real for the ways that it affects people's lives and imaginations.

And yet, as Savageau's lowercasing suggests, Indigenous people not only predated this region but also expect to outlive it. "Looking for Indians" is a continuous-present construction, not just an ironic description of a young child's mindset but a longer commitment to finding traces of what the Dakota historian Philip Deloria might call "Indians in unexpected places," traces of their endurance within the modernity that is supposed to have eliminated or assimilated them. Savageau makes a similar point in "The Illusion of Ownership," a quilt rendered in birchbark patterns and soft leafy greens, indicating Abenaki people's cultural, spiritual, and economic affinities with trees (Center for New England Culture). The quilt has strips of fabric in a stone-wall-like pattern that are pinned on, so they can be easily removed. Stone walls—usually considered a fixed feature of the New England landscape—become utterly ephemeral in this setting, suggesting that what endures are in fact the trees and Abenaki people's stories about them and relationships to them. Northern Native people, Savageau shows, work in factories; they watch television; and at the end of the day, they still know who they are. They sustain and are sustained by their ever-evolving traditions, whether in the form of fishing or poetry, planting or quilting.

Sovereignty and Sustainability is a study of how Native American writers in New England have written their continuous presence in this place and remembered those writings, despite the most concerted efforts of regional and canonical literary histories to disavow them. When Savageau's father took out that atlas and showed her the contours of her homeland, he was acting on very old patterns of community and land stewardship. The Abenaki literary historian Lisa Brooks has said that, in earlier times, Abenaki people used birchbark maps to indicate their territories and their movements, and that these mapping practices continue into current Abenaki literary practices—that in fact the very word for "birchbark map," *awikhigan*, eventually came to mean "book." Birchbark and paper, maps and books: these have been vital tools that northeastern Native people have used, continuously, to maintain their relationships to their land and to each other. This is what I am calling *literary stewardship*, in a double sense: on the one hand, Indigenous people have used literature to sustain their long-standing ethics of care and indeed their sovereign political rights over their homelands and their communities; on the other, they have understood this literature itself as something to be cared for and treasured. Indigenous people in New England have been remarkably persistent and successful in remembering who their historic writers are and honoring their present ones. They recite and re-cite their maps, dictionaries, and newsletters; they craft and share new stories and lyrics about these conversations; and they reimagine and re-place themselves within their traditional territories and among their past and future kin.

The persistence of Indigenous literary traditions over the disruptions of settler colonialism is a matter of great interest in the field of Native American and Indigenous studies, as the historians Lisa Brooks, Kristina Bross, Matt Cohen, Drew Lopenzina, Philip Round, Hilary Wyss, and others have helped us conceptualize Indigenous "literature" in the broadest possible ways, as textual production that has included nonalphabetic literacies like wampum and baskets as well as poetry and political petitions. This literary persistence was also a central concern of *Dawnland Voices: An Anthology of Writing from Indigenous New England* (Senier 2014), which I had the privilege of compiling with eleven tribal editors and to which this monograph is a companion. *Dawnland Voices* runs almost seven hundred pages and took almost ten years to complete, and when it was done, its sheer heft surprised even me and many of the authors who believed—who knew—that Native American people in New England have been writing at least since so-called contact with Europeans and that they have continued to write despite all manner of attempts to deny or bury their writing and their history.

I suppose that when I started that anthology I imagined myself, like many other literary historians, delving into archives and making dramatic discoveries (with all of the irony that "discovery" entails, in the context of a non-Native scholar researching Native history). But it was seldom I who found this writing. Almost everything I learned about Native literary history I learned by talking with tribal community members. It was Melissa Tantaquidgeon Zobel who told me about the many Mohegan women (Emma Baker, Fidelia Fielding, Gladys Tantaquidgeon) who came before her. It was Joan Tavares Avant who told me about her grandmother Mabel Avant, whose poetry is still recited at Wampanoag community events today. It was Lisa Brooks who told me, matter-of-factly, that many Abenaki people had read Joseph Laurent's 1880 dictionary, and that, by the way, the poet Cheryl Savageau lived close by in New Hampshire, and I could invite her to read at my university.

Many if not most of these writers are either out of print or unpublished or published only in small community booklets and newsletters. Yet tribal communities remember them and talk about them and recirculate their words. This is the question that has come to fascinate me and that I consider in this book: how communities without access to so many of the resources commonly associated with literary prestige and preservation nevertheless manage to remember and cherish their writers and their words. I don't mean this in any romantic or totalizing way: not every Passamaquoddy person has read every word of Lewis Mitchell, any more than every Irish person has read every word of Yeats. Still, many, many Passamaquoddy people know about Lewis Mitchell, about the speeches he made to the Maine state legislature in the late nineteenth century, and about his recording of Passamaquoddy traditions, often in Passamaquoddy. They know about him even though there has never been any major edition of his works, no spot for him in the *Norton Anthology of American Literature*, no academic conferences devoted to the celebration of his work. In this context— this (neo)colonial context—tribal stewardship of tribal literary traditions is nothing short of revolutionary.

The book at hand is a series of stories about how tribal communities in New England, among the least visible of all Indigenous people in the United States, have sustained their own literary histories. Sometimes they have done that by gravitating toward particular genres and forms, like historic timelines and community newsletters (the subjects of chapters 1 and 2), which help them care for and recirculate the writings and oral traditions that have come before. Sometimes they have availed themselves of small presses and self-publishing to write and share their fiction and poetry (chapters 3 and 4). These days they are certainly leveraging online publications, social media, and electronic archives (chapter 5). No matter the genre or the medium, though, Indigenous people have remembered and stewarded their tribal literature as part of much broader networks, drawing on oral traditions, sacred places, heritage sites, and communities of humans and other-than-humans. They have seldom treated "Literature" as a separate domain, isolated from other cultural and human (and even nonhuman) production. Rather, they have used literature to help sustain their lands, communities, and other cultural institutions, in turn letting those same lands, communities, and other institutions sustain the literature.

I use the word "sustain" deliberately, as a secondary goal of this book is to reexamine the idea of sustainability through the framework of Indigenous sovereignty. Both terms are often overused and misunderstood, now contested in many circles, academic and popular, Native and non-Native. In most legal and scholarly formulations, *sovereignty* refers to the political status of American Indian people: they are nations, with their own governments, territories, and rights to self-determination. That is the political definition of sovereignty; more broadly, sovereignty is often invoked when Indigenous people seek to exercise self-determination in a variety of arenas. Thus Native people will talk of cultural sovereignty, linguistic sovereignty, and, yes, literary sovereignty. Sovereignty can be a contentious term because it has come to evoke a range of colonial political gambits, including the demand for tribes to win "acknowledgment" from settler nation-states—and indeed the very idea that the nation-state is the sine qua non of legitimate tribal existence. At the same time, it remains a useful term for reminding settlers that Native Americans are not simply ethnic groups but political entities, with specific legal rights to self-determination.

Sustainability, likewise, has come to bother many people who feel tired of corporate marketing strategies and shallow ideas of "green" development. But the term has a deeper and more complex history in international policy circles, as well as among environmental historians, cultural heritage professionals and Indigenous activists. To these groups, sustainability signifies the thorough interdependence of ecological and cultural survival, the latter being what Gerald Vizenor (Anishinaabe) has famously called "survivance," or the "active sense of presence, the continuation of native stories, not a mere reaction" (vii). Vizenor's characteristically pithy coinage suggests Indigenous survival, resistance, and adaptation, all hinging on the power of Indigenous words, in all of their oral, published, and semipublished forms. Similarly, Taiaiake Alfred (Kahnawake Mohawk), an often-cited philosopher on questions of Indigenous sovereignty, has pointed specifically to the value of Indigenous writers' "strong words about ways to reconnect to our lands, cultures and communities . . . how to survive and be Indigenous" (qtd. in L. Simpson 10).

As some of the longest-colonized peoples in the United States, the Native people of New England have some of the longest histories of writing "strong words" that "reconnect" them to their territories and each other. In my reading, this long literary history shows that sustainability cannot be uncoupled from sovereignty, or what Indigenous activists call "free prior and informed consent"—consent before anything is done on and to their lands or with and to their cultural heritage. This reading puts Indigenous intellectual traditions—not "folklore" and not "lifeways"—at the center of discussions of environmental and social justice. Reading this literature, we see how communities with historic, practical, and spiritual ties to particular land bases have collectively determined and debated the best ways to continue living on and with those lands, and with each other. We see, in turn, how they have sustained that writing itself, circulating it, archiving it, quoting it, and talking about it. What I am calling literary stewardship indicates that Native people's care for their own literary traditions is inseparable from their care for their lands and communities. It indicates that, for these writers, ecological and cultural sustainability are not simply parallel or analogous but one and the same.

The New England Context

"New England" is a fiction; there is nothing natural about grouping these six states—or indeed any other states—under one identity. But its constructedness unfortunately does not make it any less powerful. Native people in New England are among the most marginalized and invisible Indigenous groups in the United States, culturally and politically, owing much to New England's (and the nation's) understanding of this place as the seat of national origins, a place from which Indians vanished centuries ago. The most obvious and cherished regional myth is also national: every November, countless schoolchildren don construction-paper feathers to celebrate the Pilgrims' arrival and mourn the Indians' demise. Wampanoag people are now looking with some trepidation toward the four-hundredth anniversary "celebration" of this event. In the words of the late historian Patrick Wolfe, however, invasion is "a structure not an event" (2). Without denying that colonization is punctuated by and narrated through historic events—the *Mayflower*'s arrival in 1620, King Philip's War in 1676—Wolfe reminds settlers that their continued presence produces continued violence in Native space.

As third-graders' annual Thanksgiving reenactments suggest, colonialism requires considerable work to maintain. Historiography has played its part here, as Jean O'Brien (Ojibwe) has shown in *Firsting and Lasting: Writing Indians out of Existence in New England*. Surveying local histories from the seventeenth to the twentieth centuries, O'Brien finds that European settlers have never given up narrating and renarrating themselves as the "first" Americans, while marking individual Indians as the "last of the ____ ." So dogged have historians been about eulogiz-ing Native elders with numerous grandchildren, in O'Brien's witty assessment, they wound up creating a landscape "thickly populated by last Indians" (113). Invasion also continues in the form of direct legislation. In 1880, for instance, the state of Rhode Island "detribalized" the Narragansett, declaring them officially extinct and auctioning off their public lands. In 2009 the U.S. Supreme Court ruled that the Narragansett (still very much in existence) could not take "new" lands—thirty-one acres that the tribe had basically repurchased—into trust for tribal elderly housing.[1] More recently the Maine state attorney gen-eral declared that while Penobscot people own islands in the main stem of the river for which they are named, they do not own the water surrounding them: a move to which Penobscot people have responded with the refrain, "When the river's gone we are gone."[2] Rulings like these—attempts to legislate Indians out of existence—are still happening, all over New England, and they give the lie to any notion that conquest is a done deal.

With the relentless repetition of such neocolonial laws and tropes, it is little wonder that many New Englanders believe that (real) Indians don't live here anymore. Indeed another neocolonial tool that has worked quite deliberately against New England Indigenous people, with their longer histories of inter-marriage with Europeans and African Americans, is the idea of blood quantum. Whether on- or off-reservation, dark-skinned or blond and blue-eyed, Native people in the Northeast have daily to confront (at best) bizarre questions about "how much" Indian they are or (at worst) outright hostility from neighbors who think they are scamming outlandish per-capita payments off honest taxpayers.[3] Blood quantum has been thoroughly cri-tiqued as a measure of identity. It is known to be purposefully restrictive, designed expressly to reduce the total number of Indians who could make land claims; compare it, for instance, to the infamous "one-drop rule" of African American iden-tity, which claims that even the most remote African ancestry "makes" a person black. Still, blood quantum ideologies are perniciously stubborn, and in New England, where Indigenous people have survived invasion for the longest time, they face constant insinuations that they don't "look Indian"—that they are not brown enough or (alternately) that they are too brown.

Finally, Native people in New England face what Amy Den Ouden and Jean O'Brien have dubbed "the Connecticut effect": a virulent backlash against the economically successful Pequots that has spread throughout the region in the form of questions about Native authenticity and special entitlements (2–3). Since 1983, when the Mashantucket Pequot tribe in Connecticut successfully petitioned the federal government for recognition and subsequently opened the Foxwoods Casino, New Englanders have been bombarded with racist stereotypes of Indians as cash-grubbing frauds. J. Kēhaulani Kauanui, an American studies professor at Wesleyan University, has parsed some typical comments in local newspapers. For example, settlers write, "The recognition of tribes is unconstitutional because all Indians are American citizens and no law should treat them differently"; "Tell me again how 'All men are created equal'? I want to open my own casino!" This is what Mark Rifkin calls "settler common sense"—a form of white entitlement predicated on the notion that conquest is finished, and an erasure of how contemporary political legal structures continue the work of invasion and dispossession. As Kauanui puts it, "The question of tribal sovereignty is misread through a twisted notion of racial equality that denies settler colonialism" (7).

Twisted notions of racial equality are hardly unique to New England, nor are blood quantum myths, neocolonial legislation, and bad historiography. Indigenous people face these phenomena across the United States and around the world. But such notions conspire to keep New England Native people persistently invisible, and that goes for the way professional literary historians have conducted their work as well. Even though the field of Native American literature has been acknowledged for only a few decades as a discrete body of work by some of the most powerful conferrers of literary value (university curricula, academic scholarship, and the shelves at Barnes and Noble), a canon of Great Native American Writers has already coalesced.

It includes contemporary authors like Sherman Alexie (Spokane/Coeur d'Alene), Louise Erdrich (Turtle Mountain Ojibwe), Joy Harjo (Muscogee), N. Scott Momaday (Kiowa), and Leslie Marmon Silko (Laguna) and historical writers such as John Milton Oskison (Cherokee) and Zitkala-Sa (Dakota). There is even a modest industry now in Native American literary recovery, in which scholars "revive" authors who have been forgotten or otherwise ignored. But all of this good recovery effort has brought very little attention to writers from the Northeast. While many anthologies do include the eighteenth-century minister Samson Occom (Mohegan) and the nineteenth-century minister William Apess (Pequot), this only perpetuates the idea that New England Indians are few and far between, that they are remnants of the past.

This is puzzling, because New England tribes have had some of the longest surviving and richest literary traditions, traditions revealed not only in *Dawnland Voices* but also in the works of scholars such as Lisa Brooks, Kristina Bross, Drew Lopenzina, Philip Round, and Hilary Wyss. The first Bible printed in America (1660) was printed in the Massachusett language. Christian missionaries undoubtedly imported alphabetic literacy as a tool of colonialism, an instrument for Indian conversion, but as Brooks and other scholars have shown, Native people quickly embraced and adapted these technologies for their own ends. In colonial Massachusetts, Wampanoag people were using a Roman-style alphabet to produce Wampanoag-language documents as early as the 1640s—very often for wills and deeds, tribally specific documents meant to keep tribal lands in tribal control, that is, to maintain sovereignty.[4] Moreover there is a documented history of nonalphabetic writing among Indigenous people prior to colonization: the Mi'kmaq, for instance, were seen by Jesuit missionaries using hieroglyphic writing, which they still use today as a form of cultural sustainability.[5]

A technology meant to expropriate Indigenous lands and eliminate Indigenous people—writing—is thus appropriated by Indigenous people and used to fight to retain those lands and preserve and promote their own traditions. In the region now called New England, Native people have been engaged in this fight through the written word for four centuries. Though regionalism has a long history in American literary studies, it is only relatively recently that the field of Native American and Indigenous studies has begun to turn its attention to regional frameworks. In the hands of Lisa Brooks, Tol Foster, Christine DeLucia, and other scholars, regionalism has emerged as a critical lens that can account for kinship and other networks that have predated and survived colonial settlement, while constructing the very imperial formation of the region itself. It helps us understand, as Foster puts it, "the relation between Native and America in a way that privileges the local and the tribal" (268). In the study at hand, a regional focus shows how, in the U.S. context, Indigenous people have produced and cared for (stewarded) literature to exercise their self-determination (sovereignty) on and in relation to their traditional land bases over the very long haul (sustainability).

Sovereignty

Sovereignty is a subject of considerable discussion among Indigenous intellectuals and leaders. While everyone agrees on the goals of self-determination and survivance, most also recognize that the formation of nation-states themselves have caused mighty trouble. Taiaiake Alfred argues that "Native leaders have a responsibility to expose the truth and debunk the imperial pretense that supports the doctrine of state sovereignty and white society's dominion over Indigenous nations and their lands" (59). He grants that sovereignty has had rhetorical usefulness, insofar as it has helped Indigenous communities challenge the hypocrisy of the settler state; nevertheless he is emphatic that the ultimate goal is not a particular governmental paradigm but the restoration of traditional Indigenous values, which "challenge the destructive and homogenizing force of Western liberalism and free-market capitalism [and] honour the autonomy of individual conscience, non-coercive authority, and the deeper interconnection between human beings and the other elements of creation" (61). From the early twentieth century on, most tribal governments in the United States and Canada have been constituted in conformance with the demands of the settler states: organizing, for instance, around individual (often male) leaders or around branches (such as a judiciary, police, and council) that are intelligible in Euro-American terms rather than reflecting much older practices of self-governance, like matriarchy or consensus. That does not mean those older practices and values no longer exist in these contexts, only that there is frequently a tension between them and the pragmatic, strategic, or coerced forms of tribal governance.

In the New England context, Native communities fight to retain or reclaim their own historical paradigms of political agreement and negotiation within a federal system called recognition—which, just as the term implies, requires that Native systems be recognizable within the U.S. government system. For the past several decades, federal recognition has played an outsized role in regional Native politics, culture, and news coverage. Because the Northeast was colonized well before the United States even existed, tribes had fewer formal treaty agreements, or they made their agreements with more localized colonial governments. Brian Klopotek (Choctaw) describes historic nonrecognition as a "mixed blessing," arguing, "This arrangement allowed the tribes to remain in their home area, [but] . . . neither were they afforded the meager benefits and protections that the federal government developed for Indian tribes over the years" (11). Today a government-to-government relationship with what is now the United States provides benefits including the right to exercise control over hunting and fishing and over pollution; the ability to legislate adoption cases, prosecute perpetrators of domestic violence, and sell art as "Native"; the ability to access certain pots of federal money for health, education, and economic development; and the right to build and run a casino, though this is increasingly difficult and ever less lucrative than it was in the 1980s.[6]

In 1978, after some years of Native American activism around self-determination and civil rights, the U.S. government established a formal process for unrecognized tribes—that is, tribes that had not yet entered into treaties or other legal agreements with the federal government—to apply for recognition. It is a byzantine and complicated process that requires tribes to meet seven criteria, including these: "that a single Indian group has existed since its first sustained contact with European cultures on a continuous basis to the present; that its members live in a distinct, autonomous community perceived by others as Indian; that it has maintained some sort of authority with a governing system by which its members abide; that all its members can be traced genealogically to an historic tribe; and that it can provide evidence to substantiate all of this" (Quinn 152). Even a reader with the most rudimentary knowledge of the history of U.S. Indian removals—and of state actions like "detribalization," mentioned above—can probably start to imagine why these criteria might be problematic. In a compelling (and horrifying) reading of her people's case, the archaeologist Rae Gould (Nipmuc) finds that the Bureau of Indian Affairs relied for its decision to deny recognition on an error-ridden 1861 document rather than on extensive tribal knowledge. Tribes nevertheless continue to attempt this process, even though most fully understand, as Gould says, that the process is essentially an extension of the long "discourse of erasure concerning native people in New England" (215).

The first successful case in New England came with the Maine Indian Settlement Claims Act (1980), which extended federal recognition to the Penobscot, Passamaquoddy, and Maliseet. The Narragansett (Rhode Island) and Mashantucket Pequot (Connecticut) followed in 1983, and the Mohegans (Connecticut) in 1994. Despite the regional hysteria over casino-grubbing tribes, only the Pequots and Mohegans have established casinos; Rhode Island and Maine, conversely, have gone out of their way to thwart the exercise of tribal sovereignty for economic development of just about any kind.[7] Recognition may also be applied differently to groups or bands belonging to the same tribal nation. For example, the Aquinnah Wampanoag received federal recognition in 1987, but the Mashpee Wampanoag didn't win their case (an infamously protracted one, which I discuss in chapter 1) until 2007. Similarly, the Maine Indian Settlement Claims Act initially left out the state's fourth group, the Micmac, who did not win recognition until 1991.

As this spotty and capricious history might suggest, federal recognition does bring benefits, but it has also caused a good deal of strife between tribes and even within individual tribal nations. The process of applying is long, expensive, and debilitating; it can easily turn nasty, as states are not above exploiting internal differences among tribal members in order to win the state case. A negative decision can be extremely damaging for a tribe, in the eyes of other tribes and the general public, as well as demoralizing for tribal members themselves. Many tribes, including Gould's Nipmuc, remain unrecognized, the victim of long and so far unsuccessful battles. The Schaghticoke Tribal Nation in Connecticut was granted recognition in 2004, only to have it rescinded the following year.[8] The various Abenaki bands of Vermont and New Hampshire have pursued different paths to recognition, though none has yet been successful at the federal level. Some are unconvinced of the desirability of federal recognition, and it is not uncommon to hear members even in recognized tribes question the costs of their specific agreements. Recognition, in short, is a mixed bag. As Klopotek explains, "Recognition overflows with potential benefits," including new opportunities for economic development and a sense of community pride and well-being; at the same time, it "bears hidden risks to what might be called traditional tribal configurations," limiting tribes' exercise of self-determination within a federal framework of "domestic dependent nations" and sometimes even "exacerbat[ing] class stratification and tilt[ing] the focus of tribal members toward materialism and the kind of economic system that kept them impoverished in the past" (238).[9]

One of the most vocal and trenchant critics of the sovereignty paradigm, insofar as it has promoted that "kind of [materialist] economic system," is Glen Coulthard, a Yellowknives Dene political scientist at the University of British Columbia. In Canada as in the United States, tribes have had to pursue their rights to self-determination largely through legal land claims against the state. This situation has produced what Coulthard calls a "reorientation of Indigenous struggle from one that was once deeply informed by the land as a system of reciprocal relations and obligations (which in turn informed our critique of capitalism in the 1970s and early 1980s) to a struggle that is now largely for land, understood here as some material resource to be exploited in the capital accumulation process" (86). Against this formulation of sovereignty—a struggle for land and for acknowledgment or "recognition" from the state—Coulthard identifies a historical Indigenous pursuit of "political and economic relations that would foster the reciprocal well-being of people, communities and land over time" (86). This, to him, is an Indigenous discourse of sustainability.

Sustainability

Coulthard's analysis points to the inextricability of sovereignty and sustainability. The former is, at its heart, about the long-term survival of tribal communities, traditions, and land bases. The latter is irreducibly a political matter, contingent on the ability of those communities to keep their relations to their traditional territories and to each other. Joanne Barker (Lenape) has said that sovereignty is "historically contingent": "What it has meant and what it currently means belong to the political subjects who have deployed and are deploying it to do the work of defining their relationships with one another, their political agendas, and their strategies for decolonization and social justice" (50). We can say the same of sustainability.

   In many circles the very word "sustainability" elicits strong negative reactions. Critics tend to construe sustainability as an economic and ecological issue rather than a cultural and political one, and they bristle at corporate greenwashing and the equation of sustainability with economic development. Coulthard himself objects vociferously to state and corporate twisting of the idea of the term: "The longer the project lifespan of a proposed project—that is, the longer period that a project proposes to exploit a community's land, resources, and labor—the more sustainable it is said to be" (86). To be fair, the most widely invoked definition, that of the World Commission on Environment and Development (also known as the Brundtland Commission), describes sustainability as "meet[ing] the needs of the present without compromising the ability of future generations to meet their needs." This definition, and many subsequent rearticulations, yoked sustainability to development, and in the minds of many sustainability lovers and haters alike, development is what sustainability means. Thus ecocritics like Stacy Alaimo lament that "although the concept of sustainability emerges in part from economic theories that critique the assumption that economic prosperity must be fueled by continual growth, the term is frequently invoked in economic and other news stories that do not in any way question capitalist ideals of unfettered expansion" ("Sustainable This, Sustainable That" 559). The ecologists Julianne Lutz Newton and Eric Freyfogle are more damning: "Sustainability's popularity . . . provides telling evidence that conservation is on the rocks. . . . Conservationists need to get their act together, intellectually and morally" (24). To these critics, sustainability discourse is too humancentric and in practice too presentist, with the "present" seldom asked to forgo "meeting" its own "needs" for the sake of the future.

Sympathetic though these critiques may be, they elide some of the more complex histories and discussions of sustainability coming from sustainability science and from international policy discussions, particularly among activists from the Global South. Sustainability science is a relatively new field that addresses intractable and multivalent problems like climate change, species depletion, and poverty. Instead of discrete disciplines and methods, it emphasizes systems—not only specific systems like earth systems or biological systems but also systems thinking, an epistemology that stresses interrelatedness.[10] In this field's current parlance, sustainability is the study of "coupled human-natural systems." These scientists understand that they cannot address climate change, for example, without attending to cultural and social factors as well as environmental and economic ones. Many sustainability scientists are therefore radically committed to transdisciplinary work, including community-based participatory research. To take one regional example, scientists at the University of Maine have been working closely with Penobscot basket makers to prepare for the coming invasion of the emerald ash borer, an insect that has already destroyed large swaths of ash trees across the central and northeastern United States. The destruction incurs serious economic costs to landowners and municipalities forced to remove and quarantine diseased trees, but its impact on local Native people is arguably even greater, as the ash tree is a "cultural keystone species" critical to "the social, cultural and physical health of the tribal nations in Maine" (Ranco et al. 82). The sustainability scientists studying this issue with Penobscot basket makers are interested in conducting collaborative research (e.g., mapping ash stands and making policy recommendations); critically, they also "track the barriers to and opportunities for collaboration, recognition, and integration of different forms of knowledge and enacting policy" (82). In so doing, they are challenging the existing power structures that define sustainability and produce knowledge about it.

A similar challenge is being leveled by Indigenous philosophers and activists of the Global South, often in direct opposition to corporate and national interests. In these early decades of the twentieth century, we are witnessing what the Dakota activist Waziyatawin and others are calling a moment of Indigenous resurgence: the eruption of relatively large-scale, visible, and Indigenous-led movements against capitalist exploitation and planetary destruction, of which the 2016–17 Dakota Access Pipeline protests are perhaps the best known. To see this resurgence as an effective theorizing of sustainability is not the same thing as romanticizing or essentializing Indigenous people as somehow "one with the earth"; it is not to suggest that every Indigenous group throughout history has maintained thoroughly sustainable practices; nor is it to say that ancient, less impactful practices can necessarily be revived and transposed wholesale into late capitalist regimes. Rather it is to see that Indigenous people have long debated and renegotiated the very meanings of sustainability, designating particular values and practices as sustainable when they seem to help maintain long-term connections to Indigenous land bases, with all of their human and other-than-human relations. As Waziyatawin argues, Indigenous people were among the first to intuit the connections between human systems and ecological destruction, not because of any magical abilities but because of their position as the subjects of occupation (68).

One particularly useful concept that Indigenous activists have introduced in recent years is free prior and informed consent (FPIC), the demand for consultation with and approval of tribal communities on any projects affecting Indigenous territories and resources. FPIC is based on the understanding that the exploitation and destruction of Indigenous lands has gone hand in hand with the exploitation and destruction of Indigenous cultures. In effect, it amounts to the right to opt out of extractive colonialist projects and practices. This principle is enshrined in the United Nations Declaration on the Rights of Indigenous Peoples, whose often-cited Article 25 states, "Indigenous peoples have the right to maintain and strengthen their distinctive spiritual relationship with traditionally owned or otherwise occupied and used lands, territories, waters, and coastal seas and other resources and to uphold their responsibilities to future generations in this regard" (United Nations). This articulation of sustainability is striking, and strikingly unlike corporate articulations of that term. It clarifies the relations between coupled human and natural systems by binding people's collective identities and cultures to particular environments they have inhabited over millennia. In Jodi Melamed's excellent analysis, the United Nations Declaration describes "a structure of knowledge, based on the inextricability of culture/land, in which culture does not exist apart from its terrestrial embodiment and land does not exist apart from its cultural relations with human beings"; this is, she says, "an Indigenous understanding that culture is always located and is not solely anthropocentric but depends upon relations with terrestrially situated elements" (197–98). Think of the Penobscot line "When the river dies we die": when paper mills dump dioxins into the

Penobscot River, they make it impossible for Penobscot people to continue sustenance fishing, poison some of the grasses used in basketmaking, and destroy space used for gathering and ceremonial purposes. Thus the idea that "when the river dies we die" obtains even for Penobscot people living off-reservation or in urban spaces; the assault on that river is simultaneously an assault on them as Penobscot people. Penobscot culture, as Melamed would say, is located, dependent on "relations with terrestrially situated elements." More specifically, this relation is political. It cannot be understood apart from sovereignty.

Thus when the political scientist Jeff Corntassel (Cherokee) describes contemporary Indigenous people's approaches to sustainability, he frames them as "everyday acts of resurgence" that "reclaim, restore, and regenerate homeland relationships" (89). He cites the millennia-long Cherokee relationship to Kituwah mound in North Carolina, which has been violently disrupted by centuries of war with settlers, forced removal, and, more recently, resource extraction by Duke Energy. Yet to this day Cherokee people continue to bring ash and rocks (sometimes from their own homes and fireplaces) to rebuild the mound; they have conducted their ceremonies there and keep telling their stories, both traditional and contemporary, of their relationship to this place. "Our stories," Corntassel observers, "need to be retold and acted upon as part of our process of remembering and maintaining balance within our communities" (89). Similarly, when the biologist Robin Kimmerer (Potawatomi) writes about Indigenous plant knowledge, she is just as often writing about the importance of ceremonies, "reciprocal creations, organic in nature, in which the community creates ceremony and the ceremony creates communities." She reflects, "In a colonist society the ceremonies that endure are not about land; they're about family and culture, values that are transportable from the old country. Ceremonies for the land no doubt existed there, but it seems they did not survive emigration in any substantial way. I think there is wisdom in regenerating them here, as a means to form bonds with this land" (250). In Kimmerer's and Corntassel's assessments, Indigenous "relations to the land" are not somehow mystical; they are political and ultimately practical mechanisms for long-term, collective survival.

Indigenous intellectuals the world over have voiced this understanding over and over again. Recently, for instance, they have responded to the UN's 2015 Sustainable Development Goals, a resolution that follows the 2000 Millennium Development Goals. While applauding the UN Permanent Forum's stated commitment to eradicating global poverty, activists reiterate that poverty will not be eradicated for Indigenous people without "security of rights to lands, territories and resources," particularly "collective rights" (DeLuca). In a discussion at the 2017 UN High Level Political Forum, Janene Yazzie (Diné) forcefully criticized sustainability policies and development projects that depend on individual models of land tenure, saying that these "threaten our ability to collectively manage our traditional territories." As Indigenous activists have illustrated in their many recent protests against oil pipelines, water pollution, and other forms of border-crossing destruction, the implications of suppressing Indigenous collective rights go far beyond the borders of any reservation. Yazzie points out, for example, that "these Indigenous territories that we are protecting conserve 80 percent of the world's biodiversity" (DeLuca). Thus when Waziyatawin calls Indigenous resurgence a "paradox," she means that "just when liberation may be within our grasp, the ecological destruction may be so complete that Indigenous lifeways may be impossible to practice. In this context there is a simultaneous and urgent need for both the restoration of sustainable Indigenous practices and a serious defense of Indigenous homelands" (68).

That Indigenous people have something important to say about sustainability shouldn't be news, but unfortunately their intellectual contributions to these conversations rarely get their due. In both academic and popular discourse, this is a product of run-of-the-mill racism, coupled with anxiousness over romantic stereotyping. Ever since the anthropologist Shepard Krech famously debunked the trope named in the title of his 2000 book, *The Ecological Indian*, it has been fairly common to hear Native communities dismissed on the grounds that they have been no "better" for the environment than any other groups.[11] But the observation that, historically, Indigenous people may have engaged in environmentally destructive practices of their own is in the final analysis fairly banal and fails to account for the power dynamics of settler colonialism and late capitalism. In a response to Krech, the anthropologist Darren Ranco (Penobscot) has written, "It does not take a rocket scientist to understand that the idea of the ecological Indian fits well in the context of European and U.S. colonial practices, all of which have been designed to take and exploit the resources of Native American peoples. So, if social scientists want to know why Indians talk about land and assume the role of ecologists or conservationists, they have to understand that we see ourselves this way because of what we have witnessed others do" (37–38). In Ranco's own fieldwork, he finds that while Indigenous ecological self-representation is sometimes politically unsuccessful, it "is one of the few avenues for justice" open to Indigenous people in contemporary legal and material contexts (33). Before dismissing Indigenous claims to ecological stewardship on the grounds that Indigenous people have built a casino or seemed to have exceeded certain fishing quotas, it is more important to consider the specific political and economic conditions that may have led a particular Native community to engage in a specifically destructive behavior at a specific historical moment.[12]

However, it is seemingly always easier to cite settler scholars. A quick pass through Google Scholar shows Krech's *Ecological Indian* cited 1,084 times, while Winona LaDuke's (Anishinaabe) environmental treatise, *All Our Relations*, published that same year (1999), is cited only 463 times. Perhaps this explains the rage in Métis scholar Zoe Todd's excellent 2016 screed, "An Indigenous Feminist's Take on the Ontological Turn." Todd describes her disappointment at a lecture given by the famous philosopher Bruno Latour, who coined the term "nature-culture" to try to upend "the peculiar trait of Westerners that they have imposed, by their official Constitution, the total separation of humans and nonhumans" (104). "Here we were," Todd marvels, "celebrating and worshipping a european [*sic*] thinker for 'discovering' what many an Indigenous thinker around the world could have told you for millennia. The climate is a common organizing force!" As a field, environmental humanities has done eminently productive work: historians have detailed precisely how the very idea of nature as something separate from humans, that must be "preserved" apart from humans, is itself a human construct (Cronon); ecocritics have also shown how humans and other-than-humans are ultimately entirely porous, with constant exchanges (desirable or undesirable) among humans, nonhumans, toxins, and other agents (Alaimo, *Bodily Natures*). Yet in Native American and Indigenous studies circles, one can hear increasing frustration over the academic failure to take seriously Indigenous intellectual traditions that have articulated very similar observations. Todd's piece is well worth reading both as a peer-reviewed publication in the *Journal of Historical Sociology* (published in 2016) and in its original form in 2014 as a blog post that went viral. The blog allows Todd to capitalize on the affordances of the Web to cite Indigenous thinkers through video links—a virtual enactment of the Indigenous-centered citational politics for which she is calling.

The catch-22 for Indigenous people, then, is that while their lands and knowledge may be ransacked for materials that might somehow save settlers from themselves, they are themselves dismissed as playing to stereotypes when they assert the sustainability of their own traditions. As a strategy for occluding the "structure-not-an-event" that is settler colonialism, this dismissal is entirely purposeful, because many (if not most) of the most unsustainable environmental practices of the past half-century have in fact been predicated on abrogations of Indigenous sovereignty. In New England alone we could point to paper mills' dumping of dioxins into the Penobscot River over the objections of Penobscot people; the rapid overdevelopment of Cape Cod in the 1970s, which disrupted the Wampanoag community at Mashpee; or, for that matter, Connecticut state legislators' welcoming of Pequot and Mohegan casinos in hopes that the state would receive short-term economic benefits. Indigenous approaches to sustainability are not mere reactions, and they are not romantic anachronisms. They are, inconveniently for extractive settler economies, land claims and intellectual property claims. Sustainability asserts Native people's inherent rights to continue being who they are, in ways that they choose, on or in relation to their traditional territories—and to an understanding that they have done so for much longer than colonial states have existed.

Stewardship and Indigenous Literature

How can we think about the work of Indigenous literature in furthering sovereignty and sustainability? And—more specifically to the study at hand—how is it that Indigenous people, whose literary traditions have been so underresourced and marginalized, have managed to maintain their own deep literary histories along with their other forms of traditional knowledge? I am much taken with an idea of stewardship proposed by Kristen Carpenter (Cherokee), Sonia Katyal, and Angela Riley (Citizen Potawatomi), writing for the *Yale Law Journal*. They mean something quite different from the heavily Christian ideal of stewardship found in a good deal of Euro-American nature writing, which usually suggests that humans "use" land "gently" or "wisely" (Garrard 123). Carpenter and colleagues want instead to explain how Indigenous communities, over centuries, have continued to exercise a "fiduciary duty of care or the duty of loyalty" to territories and heritage even in cases where they may not hold legal title to particular places or items (1069). They never deny the possibility or desirability of Indigenous ownership, collectively or individually (they are emphatically not saying that "Indians don't want to own things"), and they are mindful of differences across tribes in governance and tenure models. They note that "while pervasive among Indigenous peoples, this kind of constitutive relationship with the land that is deeply experienced on a collective level is not widely reflected in domestic property theory with its emphasis on individual rights" (1052). In their formulation, stewardship "embodies a notion of mutual trusteeship—enriched by a view of the interdependence between present and future generations and between different peoples—that acknowledges the fact of global cohabitation and mandates a sense of shared responsibility" (1078).

Some of these ideas are echoed by other Indigenous thinkers: the insistence on reciprocal relations, on collectivity, and on the need to reclaim and redeploy very old practices and epistemologies amid contemporary realities. But Carpenter et al. go further, I think, in explaining how cultural productions function in maintaining these relations among Indigenous people and territories. Certain cultural property, they say, is "integral to the collective survival and integrity of Indigenous groups" (1046). This property may include "subsistence landscapes, water sources or ancestral remains that perpetuate tribal lifeways and peoplehood" (1068). We might add that it could include literature—story and language in all their forms, from traditional narrative to contemporary poetry, novels, and dictionaries. In Carpenter and her colleagues' reading, the importance of cultural practices and objects to collective survival makes them worthy of collective protection. This holds true not just for obviously collectively authored texts like oral narratives or newsletters but even for books and essays written by individual authors: cultural products are not considered matters of self-expression or individuation, or not only matters of self-expression and individuation.

Stewardship provides a little more traction for literary analysis, in my reading, than the phrase "cultural sustainability," which is generally approached in one of two ways. Environmental humanities scholars, for their part, often look at how specific cultural practices can advance the larger project of sustainability—for instance, through arts that engage people in or with "nature" or by analyzing literary works that comment on or otherwise try to intervene in planetary destruction. Anthropologists and historic preservation professionals, meanwhile, are concerned to protect heritage sites and "intangible heritage" like music, oratory, and dance from environmental and anthropogenic damage.[13] Important work has been carried out in these fields to push us beyond the idea that sustainability can ever be solely a matter of individual behaviors, like getting rid of your clothes dryer, or technocratic solutions, like imposing limits on carbon emissions. Sustainability may need those things, but, these scholars have shown, it has to be a matter of culture writ large. Still, the cultural-sustainability discussions have tended to cordon off evaluations of cultural production *as* sustainable (or not) from analyses of cultural productions *about* sustainability. Carpenter and colleagues, conversely, observe that "Indigenous people undertake cultural practices to restore relationships among tribal members and the natural world; in many cases, they require access to tangible and intangible resources to conduct such practices" (1051). In this view, we can see how something like a set of traditional narratives or tribal newsletters both describe Indigenous thinking about sustainability and are themselves resources that have been sustained or stewarded by the people and environments that have created them.

In the chapters that follow, then, I read Native literature as part of deeper networks of relations, considering it as producing and produced by its human and more-than-human communities and landscapes. That is a bit different from simply reading this literature as a direct expression of any particular sovereignty and sustainability ethos. People looking here for interpretations of how, for instance, a Narragansett magazine or a Mohegan novel reveals traditional ecological knowledge are bound to be disappointed. The broader question I am asking is this: How is it that New England Native people have survived four centuries of land dispossession, legislative chicanery, and outright racism with their tribal literary traditions, among other things, so remarkably robust? Kyle Powys White (Citizen Potawatomi) and his colleagues have observed that "Indigenous peoples are widely recognized as holding insights or lessons about how the rest of humanity can live sustainably or resiliently. Yet it is rarely acknowledged in many literatures that for Indigenous peoples living in the context of settler states such as the U.S. and New Zealand, our own efforts to sustain

our peoples rest heavily on our capacities to resist settler colonial oppression" (K. P. White et al. 1). In this spirit, I join a host
of other scholars—among them, Jean O'Brien, Colin Calloway,
and Lisa Brooks—who have elaborated on New England Indigenous peoples' continuous presence. To their work I add that
regional Indigenous people know who their writers are, and
they see these writers and their work as an indispensable part
of a large network of human and natural systems.

When I started "looking for Indians," as the Abenaki poet
Cheryl Savageau might put it, I was first aghast, then chastened. Aghast because they sometimes seemed, to my mind,
rather cavalier about protecting and promoting their writing.
Individual writers were sometimes skeptical about the desirability of reprinting, archiving, or even publishing their work.
Published authors didn't always keep copies of their own work,
or even remember when and where they had published. Community historians were keeping important documents in damp
garages or offices vulnerable to flooding and fire, sometimes
clipped from newspapers or books without noting the original
source. Many seemed hesitant to digitize any of this material
in the interest of preservation and access. Finally, of course, I
was chastened because I didn't understand, truly, the complete
lack of resources many such communities face, how they have
learned to survive without many material resources, and why
they might feel protective about sharing their work.

As a university-based humanities scholar, I am more or less
consumed by a constant rhetoric of crisis. It's the late age of
print! Publishers and bookstores are closing! People are tex-
ting instead of reading! And nobody wants to major in English
anymore. With all of my training in different media and historical production, and for that matter in Indigenous history
and racial politics, I had somehow not made the eminently
rudimentary connection that regional Indigenous communities have survived much bigger crises than the collapse of an
academic journal or the out-migration of undergraduates to
the business school. I had not really seen that Indigenous survival did in fact include their literary traditions, only in a differ-

ent way than I had been trained to recognize those traditions. I was somehow stubbornly wedded to the idea that literature needs university-trained professionals if it is to continue to be appreciated and remembered and to keep growing. And while I've certainly not given up on the value of professional literary training, I do wonder what we might learn from Indigenous literary stewards, who have not overinvested in any one medium at the expense of all others, who have not fetishized literature over all other forms of cultural production, even as they hold their "strong words" in perhaps even *higher* regard than do some non-Native professionals.

Carpenter and her colleagues' idea of stewardship suggests to me that literature is only one of many cultural practices that Indigenous people undertake to restore relations to their homelands and to each other. For this restoration, they absolutely do require tangible and intangible resources, but they might rank or value those resources differently. The land itself is paramount—the territory that provides both physical sustenance and the sacred space on which to hold ceremony and create verbal art in the first place. Important as well are the elders, the ancestors, and future generations. This stewardship is a fiduciary duty of care involving the whole community, in which literature is part of a living network. In Western canons, literature is often conceptualized as something apart from the rest of life, as something that depicts it and perhaps intervenes in contemporary events, but not necessarily as something that is in such vibrant and living dialogue with other heritage and life forms. If we consider seriously the interpenetration of ecological, social, and cultural systems, it is perhaps no accident that this "paradox of Indigenous resurgence" is happening in New England communities in literature, as well as in politics and activism (Waziyatawin). Native people here are writing, publishing, and disseminating their work like never before—or perhaps quite like before. Today, as in earlier times, they have bypassed some of the conventional mechanisms excluding them from mainstream publishing and literary prestige to sustain and steward their own literary heritage.

Chapter 1 focuses on Wampanoag authors because they were among the first people regionally to adopt alphabetic literacy and because Wampanoag people continue to be so central to the settler myth of Indian vanishing. Historiography is their genre of choice, particularly in the form of chronologies and timelines. While some readers might not consider these forms particularly literary, they allow Wampanoag writers to narrate Wampanoag people's continuous presence in Wampanoag territory. As we will see in the story of their federal recognition battle, timelines allow Wampanoag people to assert their sovereignty directly, as they contravene settler chronologies that imagine Indigenous disruption and disappearance. In the hands of Wampanoag writers, too, timelines illustrate sustainability, not only by conjoining knowledge of the past with visions for the future but also by collapsing time and space. These timelines articulate themselves to—and often appear physically on—Wampanoag heritage sites and sacred spaces. They steward those spaces, with all of their human and other-than-human agents, and they steward the Wampanoag literature that has come before, often folding in oral tradition, poetry, and other forms.

Chapter 2 is about periodical literature, an as yet untapped trove of writing by regional Native people. In 1935 the Narragansetts published what may have been the first Native magazine in New England, the *Narragansett Dawn*, which called on tribal people to reorganize and rebuild. This publication was followed by an effusion of other regional tribal newsletters, newspapers, and other occasional periodicals, often entirely unknown to those outside the tribe and containing a wealth of fascinating prose and poetry. These newsletters challenge two popular ideas about print culture: the idea that print is a cultural stage "after" orality and the idea that print culture created "imagined communities," opportunities for citizens who do not have regular face-to-face contact to feel themselves part of a shared polity. Tribal newsletters show a rather different, recursive path to sovereignty and sustainability, whereby the oral and the literate, the physical and the imagined, sustain and steward each other.

Chapters 3 and 4 consider the rise of professional and semi-professional Native authors and publishing in New England. Belletristic literature—novels, poetry, memoirs—is sometimes imagined as the pinnacle of literary progress, as though cultures need to work through the more direct forms (sermons, letters, diaries, newspapers) to get to the good stuff. I will argue, of course, that this isn't true, and that professionalizing Native writers retain (and sustain) many of the forms and practices of their forebears. In chapter 3 I look at the publishing histories of three highly successful novelists—John Christian Hopkins (Narragansett), Joseph Bruchac (Abenaki), and Melissa Tantaquidgeon Zobel (Mohegan)—who have worked as full-time writers and aspired to make a living through their craft. I narrow the focus of the chapter to consider the sustainability of the novel itself as an art form, and how Indigenous authors use the novel to speak to questions of sustainability. Chapter 4 looks more closely at the publishing work of Bruchac and his son Jesse, especially in their devotion to publishing and promoting the work of other New England Native authors.

Chapter 5 considers the future of regional literary sovereignty and sustainability via digital and digitizing literatures. The first decades of the twenty-first century are shaping into an exciting time for digital literatures, but unfortunately they are also replicating some patterns of literary history-making from earlier centuries. This chapter discusses "decolonizing DH" as a new facet of sovereignty and sustainability. As *Dawnland Voices* revealed, these literary traditions—if we are willing to consider "literature" in its broadest possible definitions—reach forward into the contemporary blogosphere, into YouTube video stories and hip-hop poetry. These apparently new or ephemeral productions participate in some of the longest Indigenous literary traditions in the United States, and they look forward to equally long futures.

ONE

"We're Still Here"

Wampanoag Timelines and the Stewardship of History

Wampanoag territory is a compelling place to start thinking about sovereignty and sustainability, not least because it is the place where Americans like to imagine that Indians vanished and a new nation was born. Every year Wampanoag people endure a variety of celebrations of the day they allegedly welcomed the Pilgrims and then stepped aside to make way for the new settlers. Americans like to imagine that conquest took place in the remote past, with the more multiculturally minded among us ruing the violence and disease that led to Indian disappearance. Few non-Natives are attuned to the *ongoing* exercise of settler colonialism, through education systems designed for assimilation, continued assaults on tribal governance and tribal land, cultural appropriation, and outright racism. Throughout such assaults, Wampanoag people have sustained their political identity, their land, and their culture on and beyond their two major reservations, one in Mashpee, on Cape Cod, the other at Aquinnah, on Martha's Vineyard. Their endurance is so remarkable, yet so often unremarked, that it serves as a kind of refrain among Wampanoag people: "We're Still Here" has appeared as a title and a call in Wampanoag museum exhibits, books, and films.[1]

Writing has been a critical tool for making this happen. Precisely because of their position as early subjects of occupation (and thus of efforts to "civilize" them through literacy), Wampanoags have one of the longest and richest histories of alphabetic literacy in North America. This history extends from the first Bible printed in North America, in the Massachusett language, to some of the most prolific Indigenous authors in the region today. Helen Attaquin, Joan Tavares Avant, Amelia Bingham, Linda Coombs, Helen Manning, Earl Mills Sr., Morgan James Peters (Mwalim), Paula Peters, Robert Peters, Russell Peters, and Chester Soliz have all published books about Wampanoag history and culture—and this is an incomplete list. They are mostly self-published or published by small operations in very limited print runs. Ignored by big-house publishers (who steadily produce best-selling but questionable books about Wampanoag history like *Caleb's Crossing* and *Mayflower*),[2] and rarely discussed in academic circles or reviewed in influential venues like the *New York Times*, Wampanoag writers have developed a rich literary history and some powerful forms of literary stewardship—using literature to exercise their "fiduciary duty of care or the duty of loyalty" to Wampanoag places, Wampanoag ancestors, and even to other Wampanoag texts (Carpenter et al. 1069).

One such form has been the timeline. Wampanoag writers are inveterate historians; we could even say they specialize in a particular historiographic genre or set of genres: the timeline or chronology. Chronologies might not seem particularly literary; to be fair, they can seem author-less and ancillary, whether they appear on a museum's wall or in a book's appendixes. But of course timelines *are* authored, by people with distinct conceptions of what was (and was not) important in history.[3] Like some of the other "seemingly utilitarian and thus often overlooked genres" studied by Kelly Wisecup—lists, vocabularies, and petitions—Wampanoag timelines constitute "literary histories that are not bounded by dispossession, narratives of vanishing, or settler colonial expansion, but by Native efforts to strengthen their communities" (31).

If you look over any number of Wampanoag writings, from the earliest land transactions to the Mashpee and Aquinnah websites, you will see that almost all of them employ some list of key dates—sometimes quite long lists, sometimes just one or two dates. They do not necessarily use actual *lines*—horizontally organized series of dates—or other visual tools, nor do they always narrate these chronologies fully. In some cases a simple date list is embedded in an essay; in others, a series of key dates organizes a larger, narrated chronicle. In almost every case, the chronology is juxtaposed with a variety of other forms, including traditional oral narrative, family photographs, maps, recipes, and block quotations of ancestors or relatives. Sometimes, in fact, the timelines are so deeply embedded in these other forms that they don't stand out, or they appear only as minute parts of the larger story. But directly or indirectly, almost every Wampanoag writer uses some form of chronology of Wampanoag and colonial history.

This makes enormous sense, given that Wampanoag people have been subjected to some vicious settler timelines. One particularly disastrous one was written in 1978, during the early years of the Mashpee tribe's long fight for federal recognition. The U.S. District Court for Massachusetts selected five separate dates, discussed below, to declare that Mashpee history was discontinuous, and that therefore the Mashpee Wampanoag could not legally be considered a tribe. That decision hinged on, and promoted, a profound misconception that "Indians can never be modern," as Jean O'Brien puts it,[4] that Indigenous communities and relationships to land must always yield to colonial "progress." And it cost the Mashpee Wampanoags several more decades and untold expense in finally being granted federal recognition in 2007.

Wampanoag chronologies can be read, on one level, as challenges to such judicial and legislative attempts to abrogate or deny tribal sovereignty and sustainability. In the hands of Russell Peters, Joan Avant, Linda Coombs, and others, chronologies insist on Wampanoag *continuity*, showing that Native people have always been here, that they remain here, and that they have a strong vision for the future. So in a very basic sense, timelines are a powerful way for Wampanoag people to narrate their own long history as a distinct community in a distinct place. But even more than that, timelines—which flag specific dates at which Wampanoags reasserted that connection to that land base and to their rights of self-determination—represent a sensibility that underwrites a variety of Wampanoag heritage forms, including spaces in the natural landscape. Timelines appear in and inform Wampanoag writings ranging from history to poetry and manifesto; they also appear in oral traditions, sacred spaces, historic markers, and cultural heritage sites. Just as they reaffirm the relationships between Wampanoag people and Wampanoag space(s), so too do timelines stimulate a consideration of the relations among different kinds of cultural production (written, oral, archaeological) and among different kinds of spaces (media, built, natural).

It's no accident that many of the writers discussed in this chapter have deep ties to cultural heritage institutions and sacred spaces. In a sense, heritage sites and sacred spaces themselves are also timelines: they collapse time into space, conveying particular notions of past and present, disappearance and continuance. The anthropologist Keith Basso has read Apache sacred places this way, as "geographical features [that] have served the people for centuries as indispensable mnemonic pegs on which to hang the moral teachings of their history" (62). But they are more than "mnemonic pegs" in local epistemology: they have agency of their own. As Marie Battiste (Mi'kmaq) and James Youngblood (Sákéj) Henderson (Chickasaw/Cheyenne) put it, "In Indigenous thought, ecologies are considered sacred realms, and they contain the keepers that taught Indigenous ancestors the core of Indigenous spiritual practices" (100). Wampanoags suggest a vast network of "mutual trusteeship" (Carpenter et al. 1078) in which humans, their writing, and their other-than-human relations all play a role in stewarding each other.

The authors discussed in this chapter have often cared for their intellectual and cultural traditions with next to none of the material support enjoyed by Euro-American collecting institutions and publishers: no hefty grants from the National Endowment for the Humanities, no major philanthropic or corporate donors, no state-of-the-art climate-controlled facilities and professional staff, no high-profile contracts and book tours with HarperCollins. From one point of view, this is part of their power. Leanne Simpson (Nishnaabeg) contends that "the beauty of our knowledge systems, even in a dominant, capitalistic, commodity-based reality, is that they do not cost capital to maintain" (*Lighting the Eighth Fire* 77). That doesn't mean, of course, that tribes and Native authors don't (or shouldn't) seek some of that capital. But the Wampanoag case—particularly the Mashpee Wampanoag sovereignty battle described below—highlights a paradox or double bind of sovereignty and sustainability: that tribes have often been cornered into expending exorbitant resources proving to settler colonial governments that they have in fact sustained and governed themselves for centuries, and that in so doing they have had to accommodate regimes that are obviously seeking to undermine their land claims and cultural persistence in the first place. In what follows, I argue that timelines are one of many low-cost, sustainable ways that Wampanoag people have written back against this colonial erasure. Chronologies are in effect a Wampanoag genre, one that stewards and is stewarded by tribal relations to traditional territories and homeland, to kin and community, and to cultural heritage.

Wampanoag Timelines and Federal Recognition

The 1978 Mashpee Wampanoag land claims case, *Mashpee Tribe v. New Seabury Corp.*, is widely written about. It resonated throughout Native America, as Indigenous leaders and scholars continue to parse the court's thorough, and arguably willful, misreading of Indigenous history and contemporary Native identities. The tribe initially sued to recover about thirteen thousand acres of its land that had been illegally sold during the nineteenth century. Unfortunately, by the 1970s Cape Cod had become wildly desirable real estate. Because colonial responses to Native identities and self-determination are so thoroughly dictated by settlers' desire for Native land, the court required the Mashpees to prove that, at key points in colonial history, they adhered to a particular legal definition of "tribe," one based on narrow, non-Native conceptions of racial identity and governance.[5]

The court decided that the Mashpees did fit the definition of "tribe" in 1834 and 1842, the years during which they were incorporated as the Indian District of Mashpee, then spelled "Marshpee." But the court found the Mashpees were *not* a tribe in 1790, the year so pivotal in many contemporary recognition battles, when the U.S. Nonintercourse Act declared that any sales of Indian land had to be ratified by Congress (as the Mashpee sales were not). Looking at 1869 and 1870, when Massachusetts lifted restrictions on sales of Mashpee Indian land and incorporated Mashpee as a town, the court came to the same conclusion: not a tribe. This is not an uncommon move in the adjudication of Indian claims: to declare that a tribe ceased to exist because, in a given year, a state declared it so.[6] In Judge Walter J. Skinner's final analysis, because the Mashpees were not *continually* a tribe, they had no rights to the land they were trying to retrieve.[7]

If this decision—that a community could be a tribe in some years and not others—sounds incomprehensible, it is.[8] And yet the general assumptions underlying the decision are unfortunately widespread today, especially in New England: that Native identity and community are somehow diluted over time, as Native people intermarry with non-Native people or adopt "non-Native" practices; that people who make particular claims for so-called Native entitlements must be ethnic frauds trying to hoodwink the state and their (settler) neighbors. The 1978 hearings were full of questions for contemporary Mashpee people about "how Indian" they were. The court determined that they failed the litmus test if, for instance, they wore modern bandanas instead of "Indian headbands" (Clifford, *The Predicament of Culture* 346). This line of questioning, which would be humorous if it weren't so damaging, prompted the anthropologist James Clifford to write a widely cited essay, "Identity in Mashpee," analyzing this static conception of culture, which assumes that ethnicity is something to which people either adhere or somehow abandon when they come into contact with other cultures. This concept of cultural authenticity is applied to no other group the way it is applied to American Indians, for the not-so-hidden reason that they own territory and resources that settler colonials want. Ever since Judge Skinner made his conclusions, articles and books have been published pondering this notorious decision.[9] It is now literally a textbook case in judicial racism, appearing in books like the college-level introduction, *The Social Construction of Race and Ethnicity in the United States* (2001), as a classic example of how racial classifications are maintained, whose interests they serve, and how they affect people's lives.

Of all the ink spilled on the Mashpee case, though, few have considered the voluminous writing produced by Wampanoag people themselves. Indeed one interesting byproduct of federal recognition cases throughout Indian Country is that they have prompted many tribal people to research and write their own histories. Brian Klopotek has explained that federal recognition cases are far from the only prompt for cultural revitalization; most tribes that have endured for any period have done so by responding to repeated prompts, both internal and external. In New England, though, the wave of federal recognition cases beginning in the late 1970s spurred a dramatic new output in Indigenous literary production. Many of the writers discussed in this book wrote specifically for their tribes' federal cases; others were prompted by the political situation to begin their own research and writing. At Mashpee and beyond, the land claims case helped generate a profusion of writing. And almost all of these authors include some list of chronological events in their books. Sometimes these appear as appendixes, annotated lists of major dates. Sometimes the chronology forms the backbone of the book.

A model is *The Wampanoags of Mashpee* (1987), written by Russell M. Peters during the heyday of the land claims case, during which time he was also president of the Tribal Council. Out of print but still well known and used among Wampanoag people and their allies, the book reads like one solid timeline. The pages are horizontally organized around a series of bold-face dates from 1620 to 1982, each with a short essay describing the Wampanoags' continuous tribal identity and continuous presence on their land.

1. Tribal historians document historical moments almost completely unacknowledged by settlers. Source: R. Peters, *The Wampanoags of Mashpee*, 46. Used with permission.

Along the way, Peters weaves in historic and contemporary photographs, maps, and the voices of other Wampanoag people in the form of poetry and essays. This layout effectively demonstrates that Wampanoag people *have* successfully sustained themselves and their land over time. And Peters lets readers know that the book is not simply an account of the past but a way to understand Wampanoags' *future* sovereignty and sustainability: "The Mashpees are [still] fighting for federal recognition as an Indian tribe, the rights to their museum and burial grounds, and for some land that would allow them to retain a spiritual and cultural identity that will last as long as the tides ebb and flow" (9). Peters argues what so many environmental historians have intuited: that sustainability requires knowledge of the past as well as a vision for the future. He articulates what we might think of as a Wampanoag approach to ecology, one that is mindful not only of the specific tracts of land and water that have so long sustained Wampanoag people, but also of the cultural heritage institutions (museum, cemetery) that Wampanoag people have built to tie themselves to that place, and of the cultural practices that sustain and are sustained by both those natural and human structures. *The Wampanoags of Mashpee* shows how Indigenous timeline writing can simultaneously describe and enact tribal sovereignty and sustainability.

Published after Judge Skinner's decision, but before the tribe resumed its federal recognition case in 1990, Peters's book is a clear response to the court's fixation on those five dates. And yet it is not beholden to the court's way of seeing history. Whereas Skinner began with 1790, the year of the federal Nonintercourse Act, Peters leaves that date out altogether: U.S. law will not be the beginning and end point of Wampanoag history. Though he does begin with the arrival of Europeans in 1620, he establishes this year not as the beginning of the end but as the beginning of a failed experiment in settler colonial domination: "The English settlers would make many attempts to gain access to [this land]" (11). Peters continues to show that process through the seventeenth and eighteenth centuries, what Jean O'Brien has called "dispossession by degrees." But whereas colonial historiography sees Native history as a story of continual attrition and loss, Peters keeps interrupting this narrative with essays on Mashpee spiritual thought, which show how "religion, kinship and land serve to maintain solidarity among the Mashpee Indians" (22). Mixing the timeline with traditional creation narratives, poems by his fellow tribal members, maps of the territory, and photographs of ancestors and family members, Peters's book rebuts the court's version of particular historical "facts" and its way of *seeing* history in the first place.

Wampanoag authors thus use chronologies to describe—and enact—continuous tribal identity and presence. But chronologies are not merely responses to a late twentieth-century land claim fights; they appear in the work of Wampanoag authors outside of Mashpee, well before the Mashpee trial, and arguably in the very earliest Wampanoag writings.[10] In their vast collection of Massachusett-language texts from the 1660s to 1750s, for example, Ives Goddard and Kathleen Bragdon describe a genre they call the "recorded oral land transfer." Required by the Massachusetts Bay and Plymouth Colonies, these were administrative documents produced by tribal leaders in the presence of witnesses, recounting land transfers that had happened much earlier. These directly quote the oral agreements, including their specific dates, indicating, as Goddard and Bragdon put it, "the continued validity of verbal agreements after the adoption of literacy" (14). Just as powerfully, they indicate that what shows up in the written timelines long preceded the advent of writing itself.

For example, in 1740 the Aquinnah sachem Mittark recalled how his sachemship dealt with a challenge from his older brother:

> This is what happened at Gay Head in September, 1675. I am Mittark, sachem of Gay Head. The one named Omppauhinnik [sic] came there. He said, "I am older than you, and I should be sachem, for I was born first of our father Nohtouassuet; or else I should be given part of the land at Gay Head, and I would keep still, as the Indian sachems and chief men may find [right]."
>
> Accordingly, I Mittark, the sachem, and my chief men, and also the [common] people of Gay Head, accordingly we appointed a great court and we called the sachems of this island and the people as far as the mainland. We sought whatever would be right concerning us and Omppauhinnit, concerning his asking for land or the sachemship. And we did hold a court at that time, that year, in September 1675. And we found thus in our court. We formed or we sent out a jury. They were to be the ones to judge what [right] Omppauhinnit had at Gay Head, and we would do it. We gave them complete [?] power that whatever they did, we would confirm. And these are their names. (Goddard and Bragdon 85)

These recorded oral land transfers are early illustrations of how Wampanoag people used literacy and chronology in the service of their sovereignty and sustainability. The colonial authorities who recorded sachems' words were presumably after one thing: who "owned" a particular parcel or set of parcels (an ownership that, in any event, they would abrogate or ignore). But the sachems redirect these questions of boundary to emphasize the deep protocols attached to sachemship, the *collective* decisions and obligations that make it possible to understand Wampanoag land, and to even *be* on it. The documents also indicate that oral traditions supersede, and will outlast, the written iteration.

Western scholars have often imagined that literacy preserves or replaces orality. But the sachems participating in the recorded oral land transfers remind their transcribers of particular exchanges that are already decades old and that involve fellow leaders, the "common people" at Aquinnah, and their relations all the way to the mainland. These oral exchanges are thus bound to last for generations. In a separate study of these texts, Bragdon concludes, "Indian people saw themselves as participants in a plural society, in which newly acquired skills could be used to preserve an older way of life" (49). They saw alphabetic literacy not as a way to assimilate to European settler culture but as one of many available tools for asserting their sovereignty and sustainability. In this view, the written document is not quite irrelevant, but it registers as only one small part of the Wampanoags' much wider communication ecosystem.

Joan Tavares Avant: Mashpee Literary Curator

Media ecology is a field unto itself, one to which this book cannot do justice, but Ursula Heise offers a concise and useful summation of ecological approaches to communications. Reviewing media theorists' uses of ecological metaphors, she explains that they have tended to swing between describing media as totalizing and deterministic *systems* and as a way of imagining the interdependence and agency of human and other-than-human actors. Heise proposes that we might be better off considering how media constitute one environment among many: "If media do indeed function in some sense as environments for human thought, perception, and action, then a properly ecological approach to their study should include a consideration

41

of how they relate to other types of environments . . . noting that the metaphor of the 'environment' implies a spatial perception or experience" (165). In such a method, she says, we could ask, for instance, "How do encounters with different types of environments—natural, urban, virtual—alternate in the course of everyday routines? How do individuals and groups make the transition from one type of environment to another? Is the transition experienced as a connection or as a more or less abrupt disjuncture?" (166).

As hinted earlier, Wampanoag writers seem to treat written texts, oral traditions, (their) built environments, and natural geographies as much less disjunctive than many settlers do. This fluid movement from sacred space to heritage site to oral tradition to book continues among contemporary writers. One of the most prolific writers at Mashpee today is Joan Tavares Avant, who is intensely concerned with sharing and preserving tribal knowledge for future generations. She has done so in the full range of writing explored in this book: periodicals and newspapers, documents for cultural heritage institutions, academic theses, and a book of her own, *People of the First Light* (2010).

Avant has had a long and varied career. She has been a tribal chairperson, a director of Indian education for the Mashpee public school system, a chef, and a caterer. Later in life she sought formal credentialing, receiving a BA in 1993 and a master's degree in education in 1995. In 2004 she enrolled in the PhD program in education at the University of Massachusetts and is currently working on her doctoral thesis about Native American education under colonialism. Reflecting on what writing has meant to her, Avant says:

> I started writing when I was in the 8th grade during math class. I found math so boring. At that time I only wrote poetry and loved it. I daydreamed a lot about the trees, sun, moon and nature. Wondered how the moon and sun hung up in the sky. When I got to high school I wanted to learn how to write and told either a teacher or counselor. If you were a person of color, then the girls were

put in Home Economics, which I did not need; my mother taught me how to cook and sew. UMass Boston is where I began to learn writing skills. I always wanted to convey my concerns or interests by writing because I was very shy and afraid to speak when I was younger, although my grandmother inspired me because she was always writing or doodling. I wrote poetry for years, which was all lost when we lost our home in a fire while living in Boston.[11]

Like their Wampanoag forebears, the Avants embraced writing, enthusiastically, for their own purposes. (I will return to that writing and doodling grandmother in a moment.) This is a familiar story of Native writing persisting despite being actively discouraged in the first place, and being vulnerable to material loss in the second. It is shocking, but many prolific elders like Joan Avant do not have access to the corpus of their own writing. No one has (yet) taken responsibility for cataloguing and curating her countless newspaper columns, for instance. She believes that she published her first one in the 1990s but has not been able to locate that piece in several queries to the *Mashpee Enterprise* and *Cape Cod Times*, nor in searches of databases and her own packed filing cabinets. Avant also remembers that she published a piece in the first newsletter of the Native American Student Support Services at the University of Massachusetts, but again there has been no luck finding this.

Undoubtedly these items *are* findable, but it is not a straightforward or simple matter (or, in all cases, even desirable) to collect them and make them accessible, a conundrum to which I will return in chapter 5. In Avant's case, lack of publishing and archiving is not for lack of trying. In 1993 she produced *Wampanoag Cooking: A Prelude to the Soon-to-Be Published Wampanoag Foods and Legends*, with the help of Alicja Mann, a Mashpee resident whose small publishing venture has helped tribal member Earl Mills Sr. keep his memoir, *Son of Mashpee: Reflections of Chief Flying Eagle* (1996), in print, even issuing a second edition. *Wampanoag Cooking*, however, is now unavailable, and never did lead to a second book. Seventeen years later, Avant finally self-published *People of the First Light*.

1775-1776 Throughout the American Revolutionary War, Mashpee Wampanoag men sustained heavy casualties over the course of the conflict.

1822: Mashpee Indian Tribe listed as a Indian Tribe in U.S. War Department Records.

1833: Mashpee Wampanoag passed two resolutions:
(1) that they would rule themselves, having the right to do so according to the U.S. Constitution, and
(2) that they would not permit any white man 'to come on our Plantation, to cut, or to carry off wood, hay or any other article, without our permission after July next." This event is known as the "Woodlot Riot".

1834: Marshpee was incorporated for the second time as a district.

1852 Parsonage

1852: A parsonage was built which today sits on Route 130.

1859; A Commonwealth census discloses that the Mashpee Wampanoag to be the largest Native American tribe in the area.

1869: Mashpee Wampanoag's became citizens of the Commonwealth of Massachusetts. Court removes all restrictions to outsiders.

1870: Marshpee District abolished and Mashpee becomes a town. The letter 'r' was dropped.

1870-1954: All positions of the Town of Mashpee elected, non-elected, police and fire were held by Mashpee Wampanoag tribal members.
1877: Taxation was implemented in the Town of Mashpee. Ownership of land dwindled from the Natives because many were powerless and unable to pay.

2. Timeline in Joan Tavares Avant, *People of the First Light*, 18.
Used with permission.

The book conveys the urgency Avant feels about telling the Wampanoag story in Wampanoag terms. It includes a variety of forms: short essays, recipes, photographs, interviews, reprinted op-eds. This assemblage is not at all uncommon in twentieth-century Wampanoag books. Avant announces, "Everything I'm aware of has a blueprint. *People of the First Light: Wisdoms of a Mashpee Wampanoag Elder* celebrates what I envision as a 'soul' book, crammed with my writings and voices of our tribal people" (6). In this blueprint we can see the traces of a very long Wampanoag literary history, one that stretches back to those early recorded oral land transfers, taken by Wampanoag people who were writing down the words of their sachems, who in turn were recalling the words of their predecessors.

Like other Wampanoag books, this one features timelines prominently. Its first section comprises a historical essay and two separate timelines: one traces the history of Mashpees from 1621 (not the arrival of the Pilgrims, but the signing of the first treaty, by Massasoit) to federal recognition in 2007; another timeline is devoted entirely to colonial laws aimed at assimilating tribal people in Massachusetts. This is a direct challenge to Judge Skinner's vision of Wampanoag history as discontinuous and marked by disappearance. Avant emphasizes that, contrary to the master narrative that Indians somehow gave up their identities, settler colonists have assiduously tried to *legislate* Wampanoag people out of existence—and failed. See in figure 2, for instance, how she recounts some of those critical dates invoked in the 1978 land claims case.

On a single page Avant demonstrates that Wampanoag engagement with settlers is the *basis* for the community's survival, not its dilution or discontinuance. While the Skinner court declared, "1790: not a tribe," Avant lets readers know that, before and after that date, Wampanoag participation in "American" conflicts was enough to warrant at least one form of tribal recognition. And while Skinner "had instructed the jury that tribal status once abandoned could not be regained" (Campisi 61), Avant shows that the state could not detribalize the Wampanoags simply by declaring it so in 1869. This timeline shows that, whatever settlers wanted to call it, "tribe" or a "town," "Indian" or "assimilated," Mashpee remained, and remains, a Wampanoag community, led by Wampanoag people.

The placement of the parsonage in the middle of the page is crucial. Across New England, clapboard church structures are nostalgic signifiers of successful colonial settlement. Yet many are cherished by Native communities not as instruments of their assimilation under Christianity but as structures of sustainability, places where their ancestors and kin have gathered, celebrated, and resisted. Earl Mills Sr. explains that during the mid-twentieth century Mashpee people were organizing vigorously around preservation efforts for both the parish house, near the center of town, and the Old Indian Meeting House, located in the Indian cemetery. The latter building is the subject of a cherished poem by none other than Avant's writing and doodling grandmother, Mabel Avant (1892–1964).

"The Voice of Our Forsaken Church" is an important poem at Mashpee, as evidenced by its appearance in other Wampanoag books, including Russell Peters's. Another Avant poem, "Reveries of a Wampanoag Chief" ("They have taken our land but they cannot break / The proud spirit of our race") appeared in Mills's *Son of Mashpee*, as well as in Amelia Bingham's *Mashpee: Land of the Wampanoags* (1970). These poems are also recited or read aloud at Wampanoag community events. The persistent citation and recirculation of Avant's poem about the community church, within the community itself, fuses time and place, fuses tribal sustainability (their endurance over time) and sovereignty (their cultural distinctiveness and rights to self-determination and self-narration).

From the point of view of a literary historian who seeks to recover "forgotten" literature, usually by digging around in archives, the community curation of Mabel Avant's literary work is extraordinary, because she does not seem to have been published in her lifetime, outside small ad hoc pamphlets like the one in figure 3; and yet she remains one of Mashpee's most cherished writers. Her homestead is the site of the Mashpee Wampanoag Tribal Museum, which, despite its many struggles

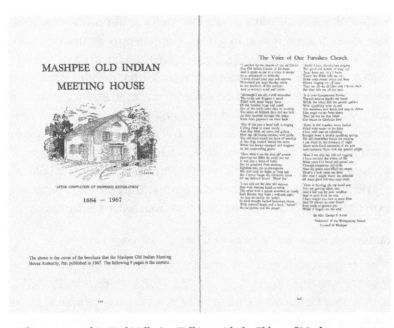

MASHPEE OLD INDIAN
MEETING HOUSE

"AFTER COMPLETION OF PROPOSED RESTORATION"

1684 — 1967

The above is the cover of the brochure that the Mashpee Old Indian Meeting House Authority, Inc. published in 1967. The following 9 pages is the content.

144

The Voice of Our Forsaken Church

145

3. Flyer reprinted in Earl Mills Sr., *Talking with the Elders of Mashpee*, 144–55.

to stay funded and open, preserves her memory in a physical setting. As a member of one of Mashpee's oldest families, the Pocknetts, Mabel Avant also embodied some of the oldest forms of female Wampanoag leadership. In 1935 she ran for tribal office with four other women on the "feminist ticket" (Campisi 126). She worked as a librarian and town clerk for Mashpee, in addition to conducting vigorous research in her capacity as tribal historian. Today she may not be widely known outside of Mashpee or much referenced in scholarly histories, but she is actively remembered and quoted by other Wampanoag writers.[12]

Wampanoag authors like Joan Avant, then, do not simply write histories of their people from a position of singular authority. They also steward their tribal literary history—culling, organizing, and annotating their ancestors' words, both written and oral, for future generations, always hanging this history on the basic framework of the timeline that illustrates that they *have* remained. In this way they hearken back to their seventeenth-century ancestors, who, Bragdon finds, used their new expertise with alphabetic literacy to work with their hereditary leaders, and thus "played a role in preserving certain records outside of the 'official' archives" (48). Such writers are always actively engaged with a much broader community that decides what shall be saved and how, even when colonial archives and mainstream publishers may be invested in erasing them, never mind preserving them. Their approach to preservation repeatedly deploys a particular genre, the timeline, within a diverse media ecosystem of written tradition, oral tradition, and physical place-marking to sustain their people against the colonial agenda of expropriating Native lands and denying Native cultures.

Cultural Heritage Institutions as Living Timelines

The "Forsaken Church" of Avant's cherished poem is the same Indian meetinghouse where, in 1833, the Pequot minister William Apess famously came to rally Wampanoag people against settler theft of timber from their land. His description draws on both romantic traditions of representing nature and on Indigenous ways of *seeing* the intimate relations among Indigenous heritage institutions and the land, trees, and water in which these institutions are embedded: "The sacred edifice stood in the middle of a noble forest and seemed to be about a hundred years old, circumstances which did not render its appearance less interesting. Hard by was an Indian burial ground, overgrown with pines, in which the graves were all ranged north and south. A delightful brook, fed by some of the sweetest springs in Massachusetts, murmured beside it" (170). This same meetinghouse is at stake when Peters says, "The Mashpees are [still] fighting for federal recognition as an Indian tribe, the rights to their museum and burial grounds, and for some land"; the same Indian meetinghouse where Earl Mills Sr., who has devoted years to the building's restoration, reflects, "So it is when people are born, reborn and born again . . . when I am in that House or wandering through its grounds, my thoughts turn to visions of the Spirit World and my connections to it and to the future." In all of these descriptions, the meetinghouse is inextricably connected to Mashpee water, trees, and ancestors, all of whom appear as animated participants in a partnership with the edifice and with the contemporary Mashpees who are working to maintain it.

The meetinghouse has had a long, intense preservation struggle. Its plaque announces that the building was erected in 1684, remodeled in 1717, and rededicated in 1923. Another timeline, another counter to Judge Skinner's attempt to read Mashpee history as one of discontinuity or dilution. A church—an instrument of intended colonization and assimilation—has become, at Mashpee, not only a symbol of Indian continuity but the very space where that community convenes and reaffirms its continuity. Even when the church was in some senses unusable, it was always actively remembered and sustained, and finally restored and reopened in 2009.[13]

This pattern of lapse and regeneration has been repeated throughout Wampanoag territory and indeed throughout Indigenous New England. Like small museums and heritage sites everywhere, most of New England's tribal historic sites have struggled with sustainability; unlike nontribal institutions, though, they have often been subjected to openly racist assaults from settlers trying to turn the myth of Indian disappearance into reality. The Avant House and Mashpee Museum has had an especially fraught history. Like the Indian meetinghouse, the structure dates back to early colonial days, having been built in 1793 by one of the Bournes, who were among Massachusetts's first settlers and colonial administrators. The tribe selected the house for a museum site in 1970 and spent three years renovating it and filling it with art, photographs, and other historical items. It was opened with great pride and ceremony in 1973. After the land claims suit opened, however, the town, which still owned the building, retaliated by closing the museum and firing its director, the tribal historian and author Amelia Bingham.

Today the Mashpee Wampanoag Museum is in tribal hands, open by appointment only, but the virulent response to its initial establishment shows what a threat Wampanoag historiography—and Wampanoag sovereignty and sustainability—are to colonial narratives of time. It is painful for any community to struggle with the preservation of a cherished building or site, but the Old Indian Meeting House was never really "forsaken," in the sense that, no matter the condition of the building, Wampanoag people continued to gather there, speak about it, and write about it. Tribal heritage sites, and tribal writing about those sites, are, to quote Earl Mills, where the Wampanoag people are "born, reborn and born again," as they are continually (re)connected both to "the Spirit World . . . and to the future." Wampanoag writings teach people who they are and where they belong; those identities and spaces, in turn, provide the occasions for community convening and further cultural production.

Still, given the violent histories and material challenges faced by Wampanoag heritage institutions, it is not entirely surprising that several Wampanoag authors, including Joan Avant and Linda Coombs, have also embraced work with non-Native museums, which are often better funded and more bureaucratically stable. Two Massachusetts heritage institutions—Boston Children's Museum (BCM) and the Wampanoag Indigenous Program (WIP) at Plimoth Plantation—became for a period between the 1970s and early 2000s unique producers of regional Native literature. Unlike the Wampanoags' own heritage sites, the BCM and Plimoth are colonial institutions, with vexed histories and relationships to the Native people they have employed. Their position is thus very different from the tribal museums': they are not owned or governed by Wampanoag people, and geographically they are a considerable drive or ferry ride away from the two largest Wampanoag reservations, though both Boston and Plimoth are well within traditional Wampanoag homeland. As Coombs has said, "Sometimes people ask us if we get tired of driving all the way to Plymouth every day. Actually we feel very fortunate to be on this part of our homeland, planning and working and (re)creating on the same ground as our ancestors. It gives comfort, satisfaction, inspiration and hope to know that they are with us" ("Hobbamock's Homesite" 3).

The BCM and WIP programs arose in a heady historical moment. In the 1970s, while Wampanoag activism was coalescing around land claims, larger national (and global) Indigenous rights movements were also gathering steam. For museums specifically, as the Cherokee historian Karen Coody Cooper has recounted, Indigenous people the world over started calling to task museums and other cultural institutions for their unethical displays of human remains and sacred items, their hoarding of Native material culture, and for their contributions to mythologies about "national heroes" like Columbus and the Pilgrims.[14] Both BCM and WIP were affected by these changes, and both made space for some extraordinary projects in Wampanoag authorship and cultural sovereignty.

Neither institution started out that way, however. Children's museums, in particular, have sorry histories with "Indian" displays.[15] Even during the 1960s and early 1970s, when the BCM was trumpeting its diversity and inclusiveness, it was, for instance, displaying Native human remains and using non-Native staff to reenact religious ceremonies using sacred objects like Kachina masks. One of those interpreters, Joan Lester, got the shock of her life when she enrolled in a graduate seminar at Harvard with fourteen Native American peers who directly challenged her for the way the BCM was handling American Indian history and material culture. Under Lester's guidance, the BCM made some immediate changes. It did several repatriations and reburials (well before the passage of the Native American Graves Protection and Repatriation Act), and it formed a Native American Advisory Board, possibly the first of its kind. It trained Native historians in museum business while empowering them as interpreters and co-curators, and it paid them to write copy for its exhibits and educational kits.[16]

These actions represented an important shift in Native content production. For example, one of the museum's educational kits put in the hands of teachers and children large cards with personalized accounts of contemporary Wampanoag life. Some of these are radical. One, by Cynthia Akins, invites children to consider the experience of modern land dispossession: "At all times of the year we did a lot of hiking around in the woods all over Gay Head. It really gives me a strange feeling now to see so many 'No Trespassing' signs up all over the town in places we used to explore." While this card is not an explicit timeline, it conveys a resolutely Wampanoag way of seeing time and space. Like the more complete timelines in both Peters and Avant, which show the long history of colonial expropriation and Native resistance, Akins's account tells young settlers that her people have always felt a close and embodied kinship with the Gay Head forests, despite the (at that time) recent expropriation of those lands in settler real estate transactions. Her "strange feeling" evokes grief for the interrupted ability to move freely on that land, coupled with an enduring sense of connection to that same territory. That sense of connection, in fact, is kept alive by this writing and its circulation.

Dramatically, then, the BCM stopped presenting Indians as artifacts of the past and started subtly introducing very young audiences to the concepts of sovereignty and sustainability, to the idea that Native people remain in New England and that they have the right to continue being and representing who they are, in whatever form they decide that will take. The BCM produced a permanent exhibit, "We're Still Here," showcasing *contemporary* regional Indigenous artists like Gladys Widdis, who made contemporary pottery out of the Gay Head Cliffs' multicolored clay—the very stuff of the Wampanoag homeland. Further, the BCM played an important role in encouraging and even directly publishing the writing of some prominent Native intellectuals from New England in the latter part of the twentieth century. Its "Multicultural Celebrations" book series published important children's books written by New England Native authors, including Paulla Dove Jennings's (Narragansett) *Strawberry Thanksgiving* (1992) and Linda Coombs's *Powwow* (1992).

Linda Coombs, Holistic Historian

Powwow describes a day in the life of a young girl dancing at her community's event. In New England, as in other parts of the United States, powwows are popular with tourists and other non-Native visitors hoping for opportunities to see Indians and learn about Indian culture. As relatively modern, pan-tribal events, they are also important opportunities for Native communities to reaffirm their ties to each other and to their land, as family who have moved away from home reconvene with those who have stayed.[17] The Mashpee powwow, held every July 4 since 1929, has become one of the largest and most culturally distinctive powwows in New England.[18] Coombs captures this heady mix of local specificity and intertribal exchange from the point of view of young Tina Howowswee and her friend, who excitedly wander the powwow grounds visiting vendor tents, which hold "ash and birch bark baskets from Maine and Canada, turquoise jewelry from the Southwest, and beautiful woven sashes and bags from Central and South American tribes" (6). Illustrations by the Seneca artist Carson Waterman emphasize the modernity of the girls' experience, for instance showing them eating their bacon and eggs next to their pickup truck. *Powwow* cuts off popular stereotypes of Native people in modernity being caught between two worlds, showing instead that learning from one's own community and elders, as well as from other communities, is precisely how Native people adapt and sustain their traditions.

Unlike the other Wampanoag authors discussed earlier, Coombs seldom uses explicit timelines or chronologies in her writing. Nevertheless she writes with a distinctly Wampanoag historiographic sensibility, one that makes her one of the most interesting theorists of tribal sovereignty and sustainability. As a member of the Aquinnah Wampanoag tribe, but someone who has lived in Mashpee for decades, she has intimate knowledge of both communities, as well as a larger view of Wampanoag territory. She works today as program coordinator for the Aquinnah Cultural Center, opened as a nonprofit in 2006 in another historic tribal homestead, that of Edwin DeVries Vanderhoop, a whaling captain and the first Wampanoag to serve in the Massachusetts state legislature.[19] Coombs began her career as an intern with the BCM, after which she spent over a decade with the WIP, eventually serving as its director. It was in this capacity that she produced some of her most powerful writing, publishing regularly in the museum's magazine, *Plimoth Life*.

Concurrent with the BCM's efforts to improve Native representation and engagement, Plimoth Plantation opened the Wampanoag Indigenous Program in 1973.[20] Long a popular tourist destination, Plimoth specializes in re-creating seventeenth-century colonial life in Massachusetts, with extreme attention to historic detail: reenactors take visitors through an English village, grist mill, barns, and a replica of the *Mayflower*. This is a fantasy of a very specific colonial moment, as the Plimoth website explains: "In the Village, the year is 1627, just seven years after the arrival of *Mayflower*. The Museum selected this year for re-creation because it is well-documented in the historical sources and shows the plantation (a word that was used interchangeably with the word 'colony' in the 1600s) just before the colonists began to disperse beyond the walled town and into other parts of what would become southeastern Massachusetts." Cultural heritage experts, including Barbara Kirshenblatt-Gimblett and David Lowenthal, have been nearly unanimous in their praise for Plimoth and almost equally united in their lack of interest in the Wampanoag presence in this history. Scott Magelssen, a theater professor who writes about living history museums, has only one complaint about the Wampanoag homesite: that the interpreters do not speak in the first person, as do the interpreters in the 1627 colonial village. The discrepancy, in his view, somehow prevents the best visitor experience (128).[21]

But the Wampanoag historians who created and interpret the Wampanoag homesite are adamant that "unlike the people you'll meet in the 17th-century English village, the staff in the Wampanoag Homesite are not role players. They are all Native People . . . and they will be dressed in historically accurate clothing, mostly made of deerskin. They speak from a modern perspective about Wampanoag history and culture" (www.plimoth.org/what-see-do/wampanoag-homesite). The stakes are high: this presentation has to interrupt visitors' expectations that Native people no longer exist, on the one hand; on the other, it is an opportunity for those Wampanoag interpreters to do much more than perform: they actively participate in ongoing cultural revitalization efforts that are part of their own modernization and sustainability. This living history acts like what Katrina-Ann R. Kapā'anaokalāokeola Nākoa Oliveira (Kanaka) calls "performance cartographies"—writings, songs, landscape features, historical markers, and sometimes actual performance that Indigenous people use "to reference their constructed places, legitimize their existence, and reinforce their legacies" (65). But more than simply mapping Wampanoag presence in Wampanoag territory, it also reinforces their sovereign, long-term sustainability, which has often been punctuated by periods of resurgence and relearning.

Coombs explains this dynamic and wip research methods: "Staff women study the documentary evidence, examine pictures and diagrams, gather the weaving materials and begin to construct a bag" ("Hobbamock's Homesite" 2). They also consult with other tribes with similar practices and materials. Through this process, Coombs asserts, Wampanoag people have "(re)acquired" a number of important skills, in addition to weaving baskets, making tools, burning dugout canoes, and building *wetu* (houses). The *reacquisition* of skills, so critical to long-term sovereignty and sustainability, is another rebuttal to a colonial view of history in which culture can move only unilaterally—forward, or out. Like the Wampanoag Language Reclamation Project, which uses those earliest colonial texts, including the Eliot Bible, to revive a language considered dead, the wip wanted to recover and relearn practices that formed the basis for Wampanoag community in place. With an understanding that reacquisition does not mean bowing to a static ideal of the past, the wip also implemented contemporary sustainability practices—negotiating, for instance, with a sawmill ready to process logs to use the bark for house construction rather than harvesting it from very old trees, as was done in the past. Throughout, Coombs insists on maintaining strong connections to Native communities: "wip cannot exist as an island, because tradition tells us our way is community. . . . It would not be a good thing to use our skills and our knowledge just for ourselves, or even just for the benefit of the general public. The Native community is integral to our work" (3).

In patiently describing Wampanoag purpose and Wampanoag insistence on self-determination, Coombs uses her position to articulate what the Osage scholar Robert Warrior has called *intellectual sovereignty*—a coinage intended to help Native and non-Native scholars alike understand that Native communities need not be merely the objects of study and need not only "write back" against colonialism, but can be considered active agents with their own unique contributions to make and their own specific tribal intellectual genealogies. In recent years this modest, seemingly irrefutable assertion has elicited all kinds of backlash from academics who have accused Native scholars of separatism or (that especially damning word) essentialism. These scholars have been eager to point out that there is no "pure" space outside of colonialism—as if Native people needed to be reminded of that.

But Coombs suggests that it is settlers who need constant reminding: "A new assumption is that when Native Americans speak of history, they are relating oral tradition; that is to say, oral tradition (myth/not real) history versus knowledge gained from scholarly research (the printed word/viable). There doesn't seem to be the understanding that Native Americans, in addition to having the benefit of oral tradition, can also read all the historical sources and analyze them as well as anyone else" (qtd. in Dresser 10). The very fact that, in 2013, a highly educated Native historian, one who hails from a tribe with one of the longest histories of alphabetic literacy in the continental United States, needs to make this simple assertion ("We can read, too") speaks volumes. It shows the sheer intractability of colonial historiography, which routinely disavows oral histories and Native literacy as a way of disavowing Indigenous sustainability. It also shows that, despite this intractability, Native people continue to write and speak back.

Thanks, but No Thanks

Unfortunately the vibrant Native programs of the Boston Children's Museum and Plimoth were among the predictable first victims of the early twenty-first century's new economic austerity measures. Today the BCM no longer employs Native staff, the internship program is over, its children's books are out of print, and a cutting-edge curriculum tracing Wampanoag persistence through the centuries was never finished. At Plimoth the WIP has been considerably reduced, and many of its original participants feel alienated and betrayed. And while Native presence in mainstream cultural heritage institutions diminishes, Massachusetts is currently—inexorably—gearing up for its four hundredth celebration of the Plymouth Rock landing.

The caprice of colonial institutions and colonial funding aside, Coombs and Avant have never stopped working—writing, speaking, and archiving documents and photographs, often in their own homes. With Joan Lester and another BCM colleague, Judy Battat, they have formed the Indigenous Resources Collaborative to independently preserve and share the materials they have collected over the decades of their shared work. Among other projects, the Collective is working on a response to the governor's revanchist proclamation establishing the four-hundredth-anniversary commission;[22] they are also strategizing counternarratives in the form of exhibits, talks, and writings.

As a historian and former Plimoth staff member, Coombs is well-acquainted with the colonial propensity for historic celebrations and knows how to counter them. Writing of Thanksgiving, for instance, she has posited that Wampanoags are "stuck with it," but she has never stopped speaking and writing about it.[23] In the program for a 2000 WIP conference, "Thanks, but No Thanks: Mirroring the Myth—Native Perspectives on Thanksgiving," she wrote:

> It will NOT be the story of the Pilgrims and their Indian friends sitting down together in peace and harmony at the First Thanksgiving and then living happily ever after. . . . Many people don't realize that thanksgiving was not a new concept to Native people. It was not brought here by Europeans. Native people have held Thanksgiving ceremonies since the time of Creation. . . . Presented today will be a history where the written word is analyzed for every nuance of meaning so that assumption, supposition, distortion and omission do not get perpetrated as fact. It will be a history where Native

perspective and oral tradition are acknowledged for the integrity and balance they bring to the written word.

Coombs's address to the mother of all "key dates" in regional Native history skillfully points to the need for both written and oral media. Like other Wampanoag timelines before it, this discussion of Thanksgiving gestures back before the arrival of alphabetic literacy and suggests a future beyond it. Indeed, if the timeline has become an enduring literary genre for Wampanoag people, one thing that might have contributed to its sustainability is that these writers have never relied solely on one form of media, be it print, oral, geographic, or material. The media scholar Ted Striphas has suggested that cultures can, in fact, "overinvest in a given communication technology, in part by conferring disproportionate amounts of credibility, prestige, and influence on the classes of people with whom it's most closely associated" (xii). He is talking, in particular, about the elevation of print culture over other forms of cultural preservation and transmission. The Wampanoags, conversely, have made exceedingly good use of alphabetic and print literacies, without ever allowing these to crowd out other forms of media and memory, including oral traditions, historic buildings, sacred sites, and natural sites. By maintaining these forms as part of a complex, mixed-media ecology, they achieve long-term "integrity and balance," as Coombs puts it.

This insistence on integrity and balance among multimedia forms appears as Wampanoags embrace new media as well. Russell Peters's daughter Paula, a well-known journalist, has drawn on a variety of social media and live events in the making of her documentary film *The Mashpee Nine* (2016), which tells the story of a group of Mashpee drummers arrested in a 1976 police raid. Her website for the film describes the Wampanoags' vibrant oral tradition and memory of the events as an important corrective to settler historiography—"court documents shredded, news accounts buried in microfilm" (P. Peters). Once again a Wampanoag writer zooms in on a date enshrined in colonial myth and celebration—1976, year of the U.S. Bicentennial—

and responds with a tribal take on that moment. And once again this is not simply a matter of self-representation, of creating a "better" timeline, but of sovereignty and sustainability. The year 1976 is important, Peters tells us, because the Mashpee Nine were engaged in a "revival of cultural and traditional values . . . at the same time tribal leaders and town government were clashing over land entitlement." The drummers convened and were violently arrested (riot police and tear gas) at Mashpee Pond, a place of central and *sustaining* importance for Wampanoag people, as it has been a fishing ground, gathering place, and site of the tribal museum; it was also the location of twentieth-century Wampanoag business enterprises, including the Hotel Attaquin and The Flume restaurant. As much as any place, Mashpee Pond represents Wampanoags' sustainability—their ability to endure and adapt as culturally distinct and self-governing people in their traditional territory. As she recovers and retells this story, Paula Peters—like her father and other Wampanoag writers before her—keeps a critical eye on the connections between tribal land and tribal culture and on the political exigencies that support or interrupt those connections.

This is a way of talking about sustainability that might be disquieting for settlers who are looking to Native cultural production to somehow reveal exotic traditional ecological knowledge, to say simply, "This is how we preserved our fishing areas." Rather, this vision of sustainability says, "This is how we stake our claim to this place; this is how we continue to be who we are." It is not solely about "natural resources"; it is a set of political questions, questions that require an understanding of history, questions about who gets to tell that history, and in what form. Using the form of the multigenre chronology, dispersed across multiple media and sites—written, oral, natural, and human-made—Wampanoag people are able to state powerful challenges to colonial ways of writing history. Just as important, though, they are able to steward their own relations to their land and to each other over the long haul. Wampanoag timelines do much more than depict tribal sovereignty and sustainability; they are a critical player in making them happen.

TWO

Tribal Periodicals

Stewards of Oral Tradition and Tribal Community

L ike the Wampanoag timelines and histories described in the previous chapter, tribal newsletters cost relatively little capital to produce and disseminate, though they do require significant community investment and support; people have to want to read them. In tribal communities worldwide, low-cost periodical publications have been a significant yet almost wholly unremarked source of tribal literary production. Shut out of mainstream publishing venues, Indigenous people in New England have relied on newsletters to produce a steady stream of poetry, essays, manifestoes, letters, language lessons, and recipes, all within the pages of their community circulars. Individually these publications can be ephemeral: a given newsletter might fold after as little as a year due to lack of money or labor. Still, we might say that periodicals have proved one of the most sustainable literary forms available to Indigenous people in the Northeast. They have helped tribes reach and gather far-flung members for purposes of political activism; they have disseminated materials (including language lessons and traditional stories) vital to cultural revitalization; and they have helped reconnect communities to each other and to their homelands. Tribal newsletters, in short, have helped steward tribal communities and tribal lands. In turn, they have been stewarded by those entities, depending on tribal people and tribal space to inform, produce, and even curate and preserve them.[1]

In New England, tribal newspapers, magazines, and newsletters have been a prime venue for a good many Native writers, but they have not been systematically catalogued or, in most cases, even systematically saved. In a preliminary search for regional Native periodicals, a graduate student and I found forty distinct publications.[2] We targeted only the six northeastern states. If we were to extend the search into Quebec and the Canadian Maritimes, we would find many more, as Canada has an even more robust Aboriginal press. Our search also covered only those periodicals that have already been catalogued in WorldCAT and that are therefore "discoverable," in library parlance.[3] It did not touch the countless newsletters and periodicals not held by any non-Native library, including newsletters produced by Native American student groups at colleges and universities and topical publications like *Skitemiq Nutacomit*, a quarterly from the Houlton Band of Maliseets' Department of Natural Resources.[4]

In some ways, it may seem counterintuitive to turn to such publications for evidence of cultural sustainability, precisely because so many of them are short-lived. The great majority of New England tribal newsletters emerged between the 1960s and the 1990s—not coincidentally, the heyday of federal recognition battles in this region. Like Wampanoag timelines, tribal periodicals write *against* the colonial erasure of Indigenous collectivities and long-standing land tenure. Like tribal historiography, they reassert tribal sovereignty, sustaining Indigenous communities in intimate partnership with tribal lands, waters, plants, and animals—sometimes by describing how their people have always maintained these relations, sometimes by bringing them together at specific Native locations. Like the histories, too, periodicals are multivocal and multiauthored. With their promise of future iterations, periodicals offer even more opportunities for community members to participate, make their own contributions, engage in debate, and plan future interactions. These tribal periodicals provide strong evidence of Indigenous traditions that have in fact endured. It's not just that they document the persistence of, say, particular ecological knowledge, recipes, and stories over time; that would be interesting enough. More compelling, tribal periodicals revitalize oral traditions and reconvene far-flung communities, both of which, in turn, steward and sustain the periodicals.

My argument in this chapter is in fact that tribal periodicals have helped steward, and have been stewarded by, oral traditions and face-to-face interactions. This is not generally the way that scholars, or even the general public, have understood print culture writ large, never mind print culture in Native communities. Print is often considered to be a stage to which cultures "progress" after orality. This idea was promoted most famously by Walter Ong, and though it has been subject to vigorous critique, it is stubborn.[5] Look, for instance, at the two most widely used college textbooks for teaching American literature, the Norton and Heath anthologies, both of which put Indigenous origin stories, trickster narratives, and poetry at the very front of the volumes, before Columbus or the Puritans. This tells students that "Native oratory" existed only in the remote past and was somehow replaced by writing.[6] It reinforces the idea that print and orality are somehow hierarchical and mutually exclusive. In this schema (promoted by other influential scholars, including Marshall McLuhan and Jack Goody), print is more permanent and enduring than orality; orality is more "primitive" than print. Literate "man" and "culture" are individualistic; "oral" entities are collective. Literate cultures are future-oriented, oral ones bound to their specific moment. However, a new generation of Native studies scholars has shown that orality and literacy are far from discontinuous for Native people and that tribal intellectuals have always conceptualized alphabetic writing as an extension of long-standing practices, including oratory, mapping, wampum, and basketmaking.[7]

When we look at tribal newsletters, we can see that the relationship between orality and literacy goes even further than one of continuance. Periodicals are also called "circulars," and indeed tribal periodicals establish a feedback loop between the oral and the literate. The very arrival of a periodical—at a community event, in a remote family member's mailbox (physical or electronic)—can offer occasions for remembering and *retelling* old stories; it can disseminate particular stories by offering print versions that can be read aloud or even memorized and performed anew. Tribal periodicals can also become the subjects of new oral traditions. Even in cases where few tribal members actually own copies of a historic newsletter, many still remember and talk about the publishers and writers. With tribal periodicals, then, print and orality work in close partnership, each stewarding the other.

This symbiotic and reciprocal relationship is another way that scholars have *not* generally thought about print media, as part of a larger communication ecosystem that includes face-to-face exchanges. The historian Benedict Anderson proposed, quite persuasively, that the massive rise of newspapers in the nineteenth century allowed for the creation of "imagined communities." In a time of rapid national expansion, industrialization, and urbanization, he said, newspapers gave new opportunities to citizens—many of whom did not have immediate personal contact—to feel they were part of a shared polity. Anderson's coinage has proved an appealing one for helping people understand how something as complicated as *Moby-Dick* or as simple as a Red Sox bumper sticker can construct a sense of shared identity. At the same time, this formulation also implies, like Ong's theories on print culture, a progression from small-scale, immediate communication to mass communication. It also tends to imagine reading as essentially silent and private. One critic has called Anderson's imagined communities "devocalized," countering that "newspapers are often read in public places in full view of passersby," even read aloud, with the events reported therein becoming the subject of vigorous, face-to-face debate (Fahmy 14).

In their very use and circulation, tribal newsletters likewise highlight the intricate paths crisscrossing printed texts, oral communications, and face-to-face exchanges. The act of publication itself can be an opportunity to physically reconvene, to bring families and relatives back into the fold, physically as well as virtually. In the cases I discuss in this chapter, these periodicals were started by communities in duress—as, for instance, when a community had been disenfranchised or even illegally detribalized—and saw an opportunity for rebuilding. In these cases, the production of the periodical itself generated considerable excitement and momentum, as community members gathered, physically, to collect, write, and edit materials—even to run the mimeograph machine; as they called for family and neighbors, sometimes living in diaspora, to submit and produce new writing; as they circulated these print texts, read them aloud, clipped them, shared them, and saved them.

In turn, tribal newsletters, overlooked by (or perhaps eluding) major catalogues like those of the Library of Congress and WorldCAT, are also the subjects of careful community curation and stewardship. Sometimes in tribal offices, sometimes in elders' filing cabinets, and sometimes online, tribal historic preservation officials and individual elders preserve these newsletters, talk about them, and share and recirculate them. They thus steward their oral traditions not in any static way, by capturing or preserving them in print, but by keeping them in circulation, by allowing them to reenter the community and gain new life, and by interacting with other cultural forms and institutions. This is a different way of thinking about sustainability than simply parsing texts for their representation of the ecological. While in this chapter I sometimes refer to tribal newsletters' reference to natural landscapes and other-than-humans, I am more concerned with the ways that tribal communities exercise literary stewardship as one facet of a much larger network of coupled human-natural systems. I illustrate these recirculations and interactions through a sampling of publications in three distinct historical moments: the time of federal Indian reorganization in the 1930s; the period of the initial New England tribal petitions for federal recognition, just before and after the 1970s and 1980s; and the early 2000s, as newsletters began to disperse and change under new media and economic realities for New England tribes.

Steward of Oral Tradition: The *Narragansett Dawn*

Published between 1935 and 1936, the *Narragansett Dawn* explicitly responded to the major piece of federal Indian legislation at that time, the 1934 Indian Reorganization Act (IRA). Hailed as "The Indian New Deal," the IRA aimed to undo some of the disastrous nineteenth-century policies designed to assimilate Indian identities and expropriate Indigenous lands; specifically the act sought to help tribes rebuild some of their land base and restore their own governments.[8] Its chief architect (and an admitted romanticist), Indian Affairs commissioner John Collier, saw Indigenous nations as espousing what we might now call "sustainability values": for example, "man and nature [are] intimately cooperant and mutually dependent," and "the individual and his society [are] wholly reciprocal" (qtd. in Taylor x). For the purposes of this discussion, the IRA arguably opened some room for new experiments in sovereignty and sustainability, even though its legacy has proved mixed.

Decades away from their own federal recognition fights, New England tribes were not at that time under formal federal jurisdiction, but many were nevertheless feeling the excitement of reorganization. In southern New England especially, fraternal pan-Indian organizations emerged and began researching Indigenous traditions and holding powwows. In Rhode Island, the Narragansett tribe formally incorporated in 1934.[9] For centuries leading up to that point, Narragansett people had been subjected to continual assaults on their land and collective identity. Many were living in diaspora: some had been sold into slavery in the West Indies after King Philip's War, and a large exodus had followed Mohegan minister Samson Occom and other Christian Indians to Brothertown, Wisconsin, in the eighteenth century. In the 1880s Rhode Island illegally detribalized the Narragansetts, divesting them of all but two acres.[10] Despite all this, the tribe held on to its historic church, annual harvest festivals, monthly political meetings, and other traditions. By the 1930s they were ready for new strategies of resurgence.

One notable strategist was Ella Glasko Peek (1896–1987),

who left her career as an artist in New York City during this period to return to her tribal homeland, where she built a long career as a cultural ambassador.[11] Under the name Princess Red Wing, she was a vigorous performer and storyteller, a favorite interviewee for newspapers and local history writers well into her eighties.[12] In 1958, with the anthropologist Eva Butler, she cofounded the Tomaquag Indian Memorial Museum, which has closed and reopened since its founding and where she spent much of her remaining life curating exhibits and giving tours. She also edited and published the *Narragansett Dawn.*

Printed on heavy stock, ten by seven inches, each issue ran about fifteen to twenty pages, offering political editorials, traditional stories, recipes, and language lessons. It had few images, though its back pages ran a small handful of advertisements from local businesses.[13]

The *Narragansett Dawn* appeared monthly, beginning in May 1935; by the end of that year, the publishers were expressing their hope of reaching one thousand subscriptions by Christmas ($1/year or 25 cents/issue). Red Wing contributed quite a bit of content, as did a few regular columnists (e.g., "Listen to the Medicine Man"). The title reflected the geographic and spiritual orientation of the community (subtitle: "We Face East"), but it also reflected the general optimism of the day about Indian reorganization. While it is not uncommon for periodicals to announce events and encourage people to attend, the *Narragansett Dawn* expresses special confidence about reconvening tribal members and reigniting old traditions. The very first issue includes a plea from "Eagle Eye" (also called "The Prophet"): "If you are a Narragansett, send in your name and join the tribe" (May 1935).

People did; they also sent their letters, stories, recipes, and announcements. Remember that for Indigenous people, especially for Indigenous people in New England, any claim to futurity is intrinsically radical. It is this futural quality of a periodical ("In the next issue you can expect this"), perhaps, that makes tribal newsletters so abundant and so abundantly powerful for sovereignty and sustainability, even though individual publications might be short-lived. The *Narragansett Dawn* itself ceased publication after just eighteen issues,[14] but it is remembered and discussed widely within the tribe, with selections quoted at public events. A cruel irony is that most Narragansett people today do not own even a single copy of the magazine; the Tomaquag Museum itself—still very much in existence and pursuing a new push to preserve its archives— does not own a full set. In chapter 5 I take up the question of what it would mean to repatriate such a text, to bring it back home. Meanwhile the magazine deserves much more study (and reprinting) because it has effectively stewarded oral traditions and *been stewarded by them*. Here I suggest just two ways it accomplishes those things. First, the *Narragansett Dawn* collected oral traditions for reprint and recirculation; second, it created and disseminated materials designed expressly for face-to-face exchange. These practices sometimes overlapped, and while they are not unique to this particular magazine, they do appear across many Indigenous print media, suggesting how Indigenous literature is, in effect, self-stewarding.

The *Narragansett Dawn* frequently appealed to readers to send materials for publication. A collection titled "Fireside Stories" in January 1936 includes one said to be more than two centuries old:[15]

> Ever hear the story of John Onion? It has been told for many years. Old John Onion lived in the Charlestown woods near the old Narragansett Indian school located about a mile back of the Indian church, on what is now called School House Pond. He came down to the pond to skate one bright cold night, feeling mighty frisky. He out-skated all the other lads, and vowed he could out-skate the devil. The other lads left him to his task. It wasn't long before he realized he wasn't skating alone. The faster and faster he skated, this figure followed. He shouted but no reply. Soon he recalled his vow of the early evening, and John asked no more questions. Breathlessly he skated to make the shore, but the dusky figure skated by him and disappeared. John did not stop to remove his skates but skated right up the banks of the pond through the woods, as fast

as his legs could carry him, and right on into the house. He never after tried out-skating the devil.[16]

This story has persisted to the present day, in a variety of literary forms and print and nonprint media. At Brothertown, a tribal genealogist says that it has "been told for many years," directly citing the *Narragansett Dawn* as the source for her own telling (Tigerman 345). A contemporary Narragansett poet, John Christian Hopkins, uses the story as the basis for a humorous ballad, "William O.":

Young William O.
Would never know
How he beat Old Scratch;
For the rest of his days
No hell did he raise—
Trying to avoid a rematch! (in Senier, *Dawnland Voices* 536)

In 2010 the Tomaquag Museum circulated the John Onion story as part of a curriculum it was offering to local schools. Tribal elder Paulla Dove Jennings tells the story on a DVD, attributing it to her father, Ferris Dove, who was well-acquainted with Red Wing and her contemporaries and whose own version of the story appears in a selection recorded by William Simmons.

It would be too simplistic to say that the *Narragansett Dawn* reprinted the John Onion story in the 1930s and thus somehow saved it for future retellings. The story clearly has a long and varied life of which the print iterations are only one part, albeit an important part. Just as important as the publication and recirculation of the story in the magazine is the presence of the *Narragansett Dawn* and the story of John Onion *on Narragansett land*. In the early 2000s Tomaquag issued a worksheet about the story, inviting students to reflect not only on general themes like "good v. evil," but also on what "John Onion" teaches about tribal history, particularly the location of the old school house pond.[17] Museum director Lorén Spears (Jennings's niece) says, "It's a story where someone goes a little too far but there is so much more behind it. . . . There is the history of the schoolhouse, the pond and the use of the land, which is what we are focused on in the curriculum" (Knight). Tomaquag thus connects this story—one that might not appear, on the face of it, to be either particularly political or particularly ecological—explicitly to tribal sovereignty and sustainability. The story is not overtly about these themes in the sense that many literary critics may be accustomed to looking for meaning within texts, but its circulation over time does help narrate Narragansett people's continuous presence in their traditional homeland. And it does so with a rather unconventional depiction of Indian land use. If we follow Spears's reading, this is no romantic tale claiming to reveal sacred knowledge of corn or beavers; it's a playful yarn about mischief and recreation—a kind of cosmopolitan, modern form of recreation, as you don't often hear ice skating associated with Indians. (This is not a story about snowshoeing, for instance.) The John Onion story has endured as a potent and long-lasting connector between people and their lands, as evidenced by its appearance, for instance, in the poetry of Hopkins, who has lived for many years in Arizona. His "William O.," then, is more than just an amusing remix of a quaint old story; it shows, quite directly, how Native people deploy literary traditions (oral and written) in the service of their long-term survival in—and in relation to—their lands. This is literary stewardship in the most capacious sense.

Much of the *Narragansett Dawn*'s content can be read this way: as stewarding and being stewarded by the Narragansett community and land relations. Matthew Ortoleva, one of the only scholars to have written about the magazine, persuasively argues that Narragansett people used it to articulate their own collective system of values in which humans are not the central actors but only some among many players in a large community (88). The *Narragansett Dawn* thus speaks to overlapping notions of sustainability. Its content does represent the kinds of coupled human-natural systems we find in sustainability science and other discourses, but its circulation and use speak to an even larger sense of sustainability, one in which tribal people demonstrate their long-standing endurance, as tribal people, in place, through a variety of human and natural, oral and print, and virtual and face-to-face practices.

In addition to soliciting and reprinting stories from the community at large, the *Narragansett Dawn* also created new materials designed expressly for reading, performance, and face-to-face exchange. Perhaps one of the most dramatic examples is the magazine's most regular, and apparently its most popular, feature, "Lesson in Our Native Tongue." The editors offered one lesson per issue—one on numbers, one on colors, another on bird and animal names. While it is often said that Narragansett had effectively ceased to be spoken around the time of detribalization, the *Narragansett Dawn* emphasizes and sustains what remains: "As many [Narragansett words, sounds, and phrases] as we can find we will endeavor to give to our public, because it is generally believed that nothing remains of the Narragansett tongue" (May 1935, 18).

Like the Wampanoag Language Resource Project, which repurposes colonial tomes for language revitalization (Mifflin), the *Narragansett Dawn* uses for its source Roger Williams's *Key into the Language of America*. The editors brush blithely by Williams's overtly religious and didactic passages, casting them not as instruments of colonial control but as words "the settlers learned first that they may find favor with the Narragansett" (88). They begin Lesson 1, for instance, with the first item in the *Key*, a salutation that is now ensconced in Rhode Island colonial tradition and tourism. "What Cheer, Netop" (All is well, friend) is how the hospitable Narragansetts were said to have greeted Williams at Slate Rock after he was banished by the Puritans. The story is rehearsed in nineteenth-century state histories, poetry, and plays; during the 1930s it became common in Rhode Island tourism and remains a staple. The phrase has obvious enduring appeal for settler colonialism, but for the editors of the *Narragansett Dawn*, it is a "delightful salutation" that can be reappropriated as the tribal community reconvenes and begins talking to each other again, in Narragansett.

As slight as these lessons may seem (only a page or less each), the editors do not present them as mere remnants. On the contrary, they express confidence that readers will actually start using them. At the end of only the fourth lesson's list of conversational questions, they announce, "Next month we will take favorable and negative answers to these questions, hoping by that time you have become a good questioner" (88). By Lesson 6 they are responding to a steady stream of questions and requests from readers (with a lesson on names for camps, for example). Lessons 7 and 8, combined in a single issue, include enough Narragansett phrases and words to make up a two-page play. Complete with stage directions and parenthetical line-by-line English translations, this script dramatizes a meal with ten guests—a short length and cast size that would have been very manageable for *groups* of readers, magazine in hand, to perform.

The *Narragansett Dawn* was therefore not memorializing oral traditions that were lost; it was actively remaking them, and remaking tribal community in the process. The common notion that print replaces orality, that print alone has the power to preserve oral traditions, is a static notion of orality and of sustainability. The anthropologist Julie Cruikshank, who has transcribed her share of oral narratives from Yukon women elders, has described an evident paradox in this thinking: everybody, scholars and elders alike, seems to agree that transcribing an oral text somehow freezes or limits it, robbing it of its power, and yet elder storytellers continually read, refer to, and cite those written versions when they are available. "Even stories narrated and recorded in English," she finds, "continue to be embodied . . . and to have an intense and complex social life in their communities" (xiv). The same thing happens in New England. Wampanoag people read aloud the poems of Mabel Avant, which were informed by oral traditions; Narragansett curators tell visitors to the Tomaquag Museum about Red Wing's editorial work and the stories contained within the magazine she edited. In Maine, the Passamaquoddy scholar Wayne Newell is known for using nineteenth-century ethnographies to retell Passamaquoddy stories; when he visited my class years ago, he used a book by the ethnographer Abby Alger to tell a story that he himself translated into Passamaquoddy. In moments like these, Native people steward their stories and their knowledge through constant relays from oral to print and back again.

There is no magic bullet here, of course.[18] Elders like Jennings continue to mourn the loss of their tribal language as one of the primary impediments to their ongoing sovereignty struggles. Still, periodicals like the *Narragansett Dawn* play an important role in keeping Indigenous language in play until such time as a community can garner the material resources necessary for an all-out revitalization movement, as has happened with the Wampanoag Language Reclamation Project. Jennings, like Linda Coombs (Wampanoag), worked with the Boston Children's Museum in the Native programs discussed in chapter 1, gaining curatorial training and publishing her own children's book, *Strawberry Thanksgiving*. Today, as a curator for Tomaquag, she continues to help produce occasional small newsletters, booklets, and curricula, which keep recirculating language lessons, individual Narragansett words, and other important cultural information. Like her Wampanoag colleagues, she and her Narragansett relatives pursue a multipronged sustainability agenda, holding oral tradition, print publications, new media, and archives in mutually reinforcing formations.

Stewards of Community: The *Narragansett Dawn* and the *Aroostook Indian*

Many, if not most, Native people live off-reservation. Jennings herself recently moved back to Rhode Island after years living with relatives in Mississippi; John Christian Hopkins is currently living and working in Arizona. Many other Narragansett people remain in Wisconsin, where their ancestors moved in the eighteenth century. These relatives are not forgotten, however, and in November 1935 the *Narragansett Dawn* printed a story of virtual reunion. The framing of this story is somewhat ironic; it appears embedded in an article published by Coe Hayne, a Baptist minister who also wrote novels romanticizing "lost tribes," the title of this very article. Like so many other settler historians, Hayne maintains the fiction of

Indian disappearance in direct contradiction of his own evidence. In the course of his eulogy for Indian "remnants" who have "eventually lost their identity as a people," he describes a July 1934 gathering at the Narragansett Indian Church, where "a large number of New England Indians" issued a greeting to their relatives in Brothertown. In Wisconsin a month later, he says, a "score of Indians" at the Baptist State Convention responded in kind: "We wish to acknowledge your kind and courteous greeting. . . . In the acknowledgement of your welcome greeting, we, the Brothertown Indians, regret that you could not have met with us upon this memorable occasion. As brothers and sisters to you, and to members of the Narragansett, Mohegan, Pequot, Montauk, Niantic and all tribes of the New England states, we take this opportunity to return to you our most hearty greeting. That this renewed friendship may be maintained and fostered throughout the future years is the wish of your sincere friends, the Brothertown Indians" (November 1935, 167).[19] When the *Narragansett Dawn* publishes Hayne's article, with its lengthy quotation of the Brothertown greeting nestled within some highly stereotypical history-writing, it cannily makes the Brothertown Indians' words available for much wider sharing and imagining. Those words pointedly reaffirm relations of family and friendship across state, reservation, and tribal borders. It is not that tribal periodicals construct these relations all by themselves; rather, they reaffirm and steward the values, kinship relations, and knowledge of place that are being maintained in a variety of ways: through oral tradition, family visits, and repeated moves.

Tribal newsletters have thus had the power to (re)build real, not just "imagined" communities. Fast-forward to the late 1960s and early 1970s, when New England tribes began reorganizing once again. For activists needing to reach tribal members living off-reservation or otherwise far from tribal centers, periodicals played a critical role. The anthropologist Renya Ramirez (Winnebago) writes that Native "fight[s] for rights to a collective sense of identity, sovereignty, and self-determination" very often take place "away from tribal land bases" (14). In northern Maine, two men whose tribes did not have formal reservations in 1969 took it upon themselves to claim a mimeograph machine at Ricker College in Houlton as Native space. Tom Battiste (Mi'kmaq) and Terry Polchies (Maliseet) started printing the *Aroostook Indian* on the eve of federal recognition research and petitioning. The Association of Aroostook Indians (AAI) had just been formed, with a declared aim to "improve the plight of the off-reservation Indian in Aroostook Co." (April 1970). Those conditions were severe: the depth of the poverty and discrimination that Aroostook Indians were facing is too well illustrated by the fact that Polchies and Battiste are said to have been the first two Native people to graduate from Houlton High School.[20] In this context, the *Aroostook Indian* sought to become a lively, movable center where people from different tribes could intermingle, produce new experiences and new knowledge, bring that new knowledge home, and bring "home" back to the newsletter again.

A mimeographed newsletter would have been more affordable to print and distribute than an individually authored book and would have permitted wider distribution of the writing, editing, and production labor than a more polished publication like the *Narragansett Dawn*. Unlike their colleagues at Mashpee and Charlestown, who lived in relatively tight-knit and geographically contained tribal communities (where they could conduct archival research, collect oral histories, and access printers that could issue their books and magazine), Polchies and Battiste needed to reach across much larger distances to much further-flung community members, all with very few resources.[21]

This need is palpable in the *Aroostook Indian*, an edgy, spotty, and sporadic publication printed on eight-and-a-half-by-eleven-inch paper. The editors occasionally apologize for missing an issue, and they call repeatedly for readers to write in with their recipes, traditional stories, and concerns. One of the most avid contributors, Tilly West (Micmac) of Ashland, implores, "To all our people in Aroostook County, You can write, just take pen or pencil in hand and write it your way. Say what you think, what you feel. How you want to live. Say it your way. It doesn't matter how it sounds. To me it sounds very beautiful. It's real, it's life that is very important to us. In order to have an Indian association, we need our people. Yes, we need you" (June 1970). With its insistent, second-person address to likely dispersed individual readers yielding finally to the group ("*we* need *our* people"), West shows how powerfully a newsletter can steward a community, even helping to revive it. Underlying this appeal are the editors' anxieties about having enough material to publish, likely compounded by readers' anxieties about writing; in addition to being excluded from education because of their race and poverty, some northern Maine Indians would have had enough experience and knowledge of Indian boarding schools to have ambivalent feelings about literacy. The capacious, inviting way West calls on her fellow Aroostook Indians to make their voices heard is a critical exercise in sovereignty and sustainability, calling for Native people to reconstitute themselves *as a community*, with appreciation for their own modes of expression.

Similarly the newsletter provided a forum for and connection to relatives living elsewhere: expressions of thanks from Nova Scotia friends passing through for the hospitality they received; dispatches from Boston (long a center for many Mi'kmaq people); invitations to send letters to a community member serving in Vietnam. One issue even tried to broker a physical reunion: a tribal member visiting Houlton from the Eel Ground Mi'kmaq reserve in New Brunswick picked up a copy of the newsletter and found a reference to the name of a missing grandfather, who had left home in 1948, "after the confusion between him and another man" (October 1971). Editors republished a letter from this reader with a plea to readers to get in touch with information about the missing grandfather. The importance of letters from readers in this context cannot be overstated. One scholar has compared Native periodical readers to embedded reporters, providing accounts from their own families and localities.[22] Collectively (and at times anonymously) authored, the *Aroostook Indian* represented the physical movements of Mi'kmaqs and Maliseets across their traditional homelands and beyond and sought to strengthen the affiliations among them in motion, in diaspora, and at home.

Another vital mechanism for strengthening and stewarding such affiliations was the newsletter's inclusion of recipes. There is an established scholarly literature on the connections among food, cookbooks, and nation-building. Recipes can call imagined communities into being, but they are also readily available for clipping, modification, and further face-to-face exchange as people prepare the food and enjoy the results.[23] The *Aroostook Indian* published recipes that seem to pull in multiple and contradictory directions. Some mark themselves as specifically local or Indian, like elderberry stew, to be served with fry bread (September 1973). Others represent locally available foods prepared in ways meant to be attractive to children, like fried "pigtail" potato (September 1973). Still others feel like they were pulled right out of *Good Housekeeping*: Spanish rice, peanut butter chews, and a banana milkshake made with evaporated milk (July–August 1976). To contemporary readers who know even a little about the history of diabetes and food degradation in Indigenous communities, these recipes might give pause.[24]

"Food sovereignty" has become another commonly invoked phrase in sustainability circles and even in the popular press, but, as with the term "sustainability" itself, it is worth remembering its history within Indigenous and grassroots antipoverty movements.[25] We can see the roots of this sensibility—calling for culturally and geographically appropriate foods, equitably distributed and locally stewarded—in much earlier Indigenous writings and oral traditions. It did not take the rise of Monsanto for Native people to intuit the dangers posed to the food systems that had kept their communities alive for centuries. In New England, moreover, Native people have been writing their food sovereignty in a way *not* necessarily focused on agriculture at all, but on hunting, gathering, and fishing, on adaptation to seasonal changes as well as to historic and colonial ones. Tellingly, when the Mohegan archivist Faith Davison chose her submission to *Dawnland Voices*, she offered recipes: johnny cakes (a regional specialty made of corn meal), cranberry-stuffed squash, steamed mussels. For Davison, food *is* history and archive. As we have seen, Wampanoag writers have also been ardent food historians: Joan Avant has published numerous recipes in local newspapers and in her own books and in newspapers; Linda Coombs writes about some of the oldest food gathering and preparation methods. This writing crosses gender lines as well, as Earl Mills, who ran a Mashpee restaurant called The Flume, has published his own cookbook.

In a sense, the Wampanoag and Mohegan recipes represent a kind of maturation of food-sovereignty discourse over what we see in the *Aroostook Indian*, insofar as they explicitly position themselves as reclamations of Indigenous heritage, even as they *indigenize* ingredients and methods that are more recent arrivals. As Dian Million (Tanana Athabaskan) puts it, "Food profoundly organizes a sense of Indigenous polity. . . . The knowledges that are involved in growing, procuring, and understanding [traditional foods] . . . inform and generate spiritual practices, sense of family, communal roles, responsibility and order" (171). And yet if food is irreducibly political, we can also see an attempt to reinforce and revitalize the Maine Indian community and sustainability even in the *Aroostook Indian*'s recipe for a common fruit whip (mashed fruit with sugar). On the one hand, such recipes are clearly driven in part by poverty; on the other, they involve clear *play* and pleasure. At the bottom of the first page of the newsletter's first issue, for instance, we find this helpful hint from activist Shirley Levasseur: "If your kids won't use the clear colored Karo syrup from surplus foods, heat the bottle and put in a few drops of Maple extract and shake it up and PRESTO!!! Maple Syrup!!" (October 1969).

It is tempting to greet this mournfully. ("How sad, that the Indians weren't tapping their trees!") But the very position of this helpful hint suggests something more complicated. Squeezed in between the announcement of the AAI's formation and a report on an education conference (where the topics included "Burn false history books and tell truth about Indians" and "Learn about the treaty rights"), Levasseur's plucky advice shows that sovereignty and sustainability are always *processes*. To this day Maine Indians are fighting for their sovereign rights to gather some of their traditional foods, including elvers and fiddlehead ferns.[26] In the meantime, like most other Americans who are trying to eat more sustainably, they make a variety of choices that are variously economic, playful, strategic, or casual; like most other Americans, too, they are constrained in the kinds of choices they can make. We may choose to see cultural loss in the recipe for a no-knead, refrigerator dough to be braided into a sweet "legendary Indian basket" (June 1970), but we can also see convenience and enjoyment. Along these lines, Paulla Dove Jennings likes to regale her audiences with a recipe for "Indian strawberry bread." She begins, "You take a packet of Jiffy Muffin Mix," then waits for people to chuckle as they get caught out in their assumptions about what is "traditional." Given that sustainability involves an understanding of coupled human natural systems, an understanding of food sovereignty—and of the way New England's Indigenous people write and exercise that food sovereignty—needs to take these multivalent meanings and deployments of "Indian recipes" into account.

The *Aroostook Indian* is only one of many Indigenous periodicals that have come and gone in Maine, where the concept of a Wabanaki Alliance (based on the historic confederation among Micmac, Maliseet, Penobscot, Passamaquoddy, and Abenaki people) has enjoyed a resurgence in recent decades. The historical trajectory of the *Aroostook Indian* highlights both the possibilities and the limitations of federal recognition for sovereignty and sustainability. While its writers did call for recognition, they hardly ever did so in the language widely used since the IRA: the language of tribal specificity, clearly demarcated land bases, and "government-to-government" nation status as (in some iterations) conferred by the United States. Instead the *Aroostook Indian* emphasized indigeneity writ larger and more regionally, as in this acrostic by the irrepressible Tilly West in March 1970:

R ecognize Aroostook Indians
E nvalope [*sic*] all my people.
C hildren, all Indian children.
O pen your hearts to my people.
G ive my people your help.
N one shall be forgotten.
I ndians are people.
T ime has come to change.
I ncome for my people.
O nly change will bring results.
N ations will be recognized.

The material conditions of living in Aroostook County ("Income for my people") and a desire for border-crossing tribal nations and alliances—"*all* [my] people" and "*all* Indian children"—were the governing themes of the *Aroostook Indian*. Unfortunately, while the rise of recognition battles in that period surely prompted many Maine Indians to write and publish, the outcome of their federal recognition cases, at least in the short term, also seemed to stymie these intertribal imaginings. In 1980 the Maine Indian Claims Settlement Act conferred recognition on the Houlton Band of Maliseets but not on the Aroostook Band of Micmacs, divesting the latter of aboriginal title as well as benefits and services they had managed to accrue by that time (Prins 64). Within two years the *Aroostook Indian* had ceased publication, and the AAI itself had disbanded. The periodical impulse and intertribal alliances, as I illustrate below, can resurface in later times and other media, but in the case of the *Aroostook Indian*, federal (non)recognition played an outsize role in the sustainability and stewardship of the newsletter itself.

Stewards of the Future: Contemporary and Digital Newsletters

The historian Brian Klopotek (Choctaw) has cautioned that "the impact of petitioning for recognition on tribal culture is difficult to unravel from what might be called the 'long' Indian renaissance of the last half century, since the pursuit of federal recognition is a product of the Indian renaissance and at the same time a catalyst for revitalization in its own right" (245). Scholars in Native American literature are well acquainted with the idea of a Native American Renaissance, beginning with N. Scott Momaday's publication of the Pulitzer Prize–winning novel *House Made of Dawn* in 1968 and followed by an explosion of literary production by authors who have achieved canonical status, including Louise Erdrich, Leslie Marmon Silko, James Welch, and Simon Ortiz.[27] But Klopotek is right to suggest that we need to expand the idea of a Native renaissance to still other arenas, including political activism and other forms of cultural production, and that we need to remember that the "renaissance" didn't come out of nowhere but has long and deep roots in tribal histories. While it's impossible to deny that, in New England, federal recognition cases and other colonial interventions (such as the Indian Reorganization Act and new Bureau of Indian Affairs guidelines for recognition) helped spur new tribal literary production, these settler actions are far from the only factor driving the writing of histories, newsletters, and other texts.

Many interesting periodicals have been produced by tribal groups throughout New England that have either not won federal recognition or not sought it in the first place.[28] These include a variety of Indian associations, such as the Boston Indian Council, which published at least three different bulletins during the 1970s and 1980s and for which a young Louise Erdrich was once an editor. They also include several off-reservation publications that, like the *Aroostook Indian*, were essentially one- or two-person shows. From the late 1960s to the early 1970s, the indefatigable Penobscot poet and activist ssipsis published the *Maine Indian Newsletter* out of her own home. From a stack of local and national newspapers and magazines, as well as a handful of tribal correspondents, she selected (and retyped) items of interest to Wabanaki people during the years of the Red Power movement, sometimes twenty pages' worth or more per month. Between 1994 and 2001 Cheryl Watching Crow Stedtler did something similar. She wrote and published *Nipmucspohke* from her own computer at her home in New Jersey, mailing it to her fellow tribal members in Massachusetts as they fought (unsuccessfully) for federal recognition.[29] Like the *Narragansett Dawn* and the *Aroostook Indian*, these and more recent newsletters document the struggles of dispersed and unrecognized tribal people to (re)build their communities, (re)claim their cultural heritage, and (re)place themselves on their tribal territories.

One of the longer-lasting newsletters was *Aln8bak News*, published by the Cowasuck Pennacook Band of the Abenaki from 1993 to 2010. The Abenaki comprise numerous bands located across New Hampshire, Vermont, and Quebec and are not federally recognized in the United States. For a period in the 1990s, however, the Cowasuck Pennacook Band did consider a bid for recognition. *Aln8bak News* was one mechanism for reaching out to tribal members who had moved as far away as California.

The lion's share of the labor (and cost) in writing, printing, and distributing *Aln8bak News* was assumed by Paul Pouliot, who has served as sagamo and speaker for the band since the 1990s. Pouliot wanted more than a list of social events; he wanted a vehicle for communicating Abenaki history and concerns, "in our own words, to verify our continuing existence."[30] *Aln8bak News* covered band council actions and policies; editorials; educational items (Abenaki language lessons, history, and features on traditional foods and plant uses); and entertainment (book reviews, poetry, crossword puzzles). Like the other newsletters discussed in this chapter, it encouraged tribal members to come back to the fold, reaching out across sometimes vast geographic distances. Also like many others, *Aln8bak News* was often in financial and logistical trouble and probably overly dependent on the labors of one person, though it lasted a good deal longer than some others—long enough to undergo some dramatic formatting changes. Pouliot started publishing it on his own dot matrix printer, transitioning eventually to (costly) offset printing and a digital color laser printer in 2008, which allowed him to add color images. The newsletter finally migrated to a digital version, and many issues are archived on the band's website, cowasuck.org. In 2010 Pouliot made the decision to stop producing the newsletter altogether, though he maintains a Facebook page, mainly for sharing quotations from famous Native American leaders, with occasional links to news events.

The transition to digital platforms, for Indigenous people as for all people, raises interesting questions about the sustainability of specific media. This is a subject to which I return in greater depth in chapter 5, which looks at regional Indigenous digital publications and projects, including born-digital texts as well as the emergence of digital archiving. But to conclude the chapter at hand I would like to ponder why so many regional tribal periodicals seem so short-lived, and whether that is actually a problem. The preceding pages have been mainly concerned with how and why Indigenous writers in New England seem to have migrated toward the community periodical as a genre, and how this genre has helped them steward their communities and land bases, while also being the subject of community and territorial stewardship. I have argued that these periodicals reprint and recirculate oral traditions and help reconvene face-to-face as well as imagined tribal communities. In turn, those oral traditions and communities help steward and curate the newsletters. Tribal people remember their publications, even when they are decades old; they tell stories about them, quote them in new writing, and read from them at community events. In partnership with these newsletters, they steward their relations to their homelands—sometimes using the newsletters to broker physical gatherings in important or sacred places, sometimes reading and sharing stories that help them picture themselves and their ancestors in those places.[31]

This is a different way of thinking about literature and sustainability than simply asking whether a particular text represents or advocates for ecologically sound practices. When most people hear the words "sustainability" and "stewardship," they tend to think immediately of land *use*, of human beings' (usually negative) impact on the natural environment. Certainly New England tribal newsletters do often refer to traditional ecological knowledge (to older methods of food preparation, or stories about animals), and they often decry destructive settler practices and mobilize activism against those. Just as often, however, they promote a much more capacious understanding of "land," one in which humans and more-than-humans are active co-stewards and kin. Robin Wall Kimmerer, the Potawatomi biologist, says, "If land is just real estate, then restoration looks very different than if land is the source of a subsistence economy and a spiritual home. Restoring land for production of natural resources is not the same as renewal of land as cultural identity" (328). As we have seen in international Indigenous sustainability discourse, the land-culture matrix means that every act of Indigenous resurgence—whether it is a mini-language lesson, a retold story about ice skating on a pond, or a recipe drawing on traditional or commercial foods—is also a sustainability intervention.

This is also a different way of thinking about literature and sustainability than that implied by discourses around cultural preservation, including literary preservation. In a good deal of institutional literary criticism, we tend to assume that Literature with a capital L is that which has "stood the test of time." We call for the recovery of forgotten works; we bemoan the late age of print and the apparent demise of reading and publishing. Literary endurance (sustainability) seems utterly beholden to mechanisms like staying in print, reaching a wide audience geographically as well as temporally, appearing on college syllabi, garnering awards. Assumptions about cultural value and authenticity inhere in these enduring biases, despite decades of critique of literary canonicity.

I find interesting purchase on these debates in the work of Jeff Todd Titon, an ethnomusicologist who writes thoughtfully about cultural sustainability and heritage preservation—about what happens when cultural professionals identify "folk masterpieces," and highly resource-intensive institutions evolve to protect these. For instance, he says, when UNESCO designated the Royal Ballet of Cambodia a "masterpiece of intangible cultural heritage," it unwittingly prompted the creation of a specific display repertoire deigned for tourists. Meanwhile the more dynamic, local, and continually evolving modern Cambodian dance forms came to be seen as less "authentic" and languished. To Titon, cultural sustainability interventions, like ecological interventions, can have unintended consequences, especially when they target a specific cultural form without regard for the long-term health of the system overall (126–29). Another way of putting this might be to say that storytelling and verbal art (like dance, music, and other forms of so-called intangible heritage) are endeavors that human beings have pursued across time, under a variety of material conditions; but that the sustainability and stewardship of these forms is ultimately a matter of the institutions and collective practices that people evolve to preserve, adapt, and transmit them.

Tribal newsletters work, perhaps, despite their ephemeral nature, or even because of it—because the people who write, share, and cherish them understand "the long-term health of the system overall." They have been undeniably ephemeral, vulnerable to economic and political shifts. Still, they seem predicated on an understanding that Indigenous storytelling and verbal art are practices that will continue, though their particular incarnations may come and go. During a talk at the University of New Hampshire about his work, including the publication of *Aln8bak News*, Paul Pouliot said, "From a traditional perspective, words have the power to maintain peace and last seven generations." At the same time, he added (provocatively for this listener) that he "didn't really think about print being permanent." A newsletter can be thrown away or shredded; books (especially Native-authored books) routinely go out of print. But spoken words, including words once printed, can be remembered and reconveyed. In this view, print is not elevated over other forms of communication media but is only one of many vehicles for expressing and achieving Indigenous resurgence. In the end, the tribal periodicals seem to help get the job done, with or without the kinds of institutional support, outside community recognition, or mechanisms of literary prestige that professional literary scholars might associate with "enduring" Literature.

THREE

Novels of the Anthropocene

Stewards of Past, Present, and Future Relations

The anthology *Dawnland Voices* showed that authors Indigenous to New England have written much more than people outside their communities have realized, in a much wider variety of forms. They have written continuously, despite a lack of material support for publishing, and they have remembered and preserved their tribal literary histories, even when their writings have been ephemeral or gone out of print. They have been able to do this, I have argued, because they see literature as a form of stewardship—as a "fiduciary duty of care or the duty of loyalty" (Carpenter et al. 1069) to human and other-than-human kin and to traditional territories. These writings take that duty of care to tribal sovereignty and sustainability, and to all of the stories and writings that have gone before.

Admittedly, however, regional Indigenous writers have not produced quite so many *novels*. The first was likely *The Road to Black Mountain*, a 1976 novella by Joseph Bruchac (Abenaki). Identifying the first of any genre is always a bit of a game: the genre can be defined differently to include earlier works, and sometimes earlier works are discovered. During the 1930s, Molly Spotted Elk (Penobscot) was reportedly working on a novel, which she never published (McBride 189); during that same time, Henry Red Eagle (Maliseet) was publishing short stories in boys' magazines. But for now, Bruchac appears to be the first and by far the most prolific Dawnland novelist, having published well over one hundred books, including dozens of children's books and young adult novels. No other author in this area approaches his output, and only a small handful have even attempted publishing novels. John Christian Hopkins (Narragansett) published his first, *Carlomagno*, in 2003, and has since published two more. Melissa Tantaquidgeon Zobel (Mohegan) began publishing speculative fiction just one year after that, and now has a total of four novels published. More recently, Larry Spotted Crow Mann (Nipmuc) published a novel called *The Mourning Road to Thanksgiving* (2015); Scott Francis (Passamaquoddy) self-published *'Qotuhkayiw Kahkukuhs Wosossemok: Alone in the Crow's Nest* (2017).

In some ways it is curious that Indigenous New England, with its long history of alphabetic literacy, has not produced more novels, given that novels can be (a) excellent hosts of the kinds of long-form narrative already well established in oral traditions; (b) popular forms for retelling history, representing contemporary life, and exploring issues of multiculturalism; and (c) powerful conferrers of literary prestige. In the previous two chapters I suggested that timelines and newsletters might operate as extensions of oral traditions—not just because they often reprint or re-cite those narratives but also because they do much of the stewardship work that oral traditions have historically done, including strengthening community ties and helping Indigenous people maintain their relationships to their lands, waters, and other-than-human kin. Arguably, novels can do this work too, but it takes serious resources to *be* a novelist (labor, time, money) and serious privilege to be able to access increasingly competitive publishing structures (agents, fellowships, and MFA degrees).[1] Further, for a community to be able to boast a novelist from within its ranks, it needs critical mass. While we could name any number of prestigious novelists from among the Anishinaabe, for instance (Louise Erdrich, Gordon Henry, Marcie Rendon, Gerald Vizenor), New England tribes are generally much smaller. For these communities, historical pamphlets and newsletters are, in all likelihood, simply quicker and more affordable to produce.

Some Indigenous writers might also intuit that novels could be approaching the end of their usefulness—perhaps not during our lifetime but in the not too distant future. One day, partly for fun, I posted on Facebook this deliberately provocative question: "Is the novel a sustainable art form?"[2] The ensuing discussion brought out the social-media-fatigued ("God, I hope so, it's the only thing that keeps me sane"), the charmingly cantankerous ("The only threat to the novel I see is the application of commercial terms like 'sustainable'"), and a couple of ebullient medievalist friends. One said, "Wow. I guess it takes a medievalist to recognize the historicity of the novel as a literary form. . . . It isn't going to last; further than that, there will come a point where it no longer fits the culture or expresses things in the zeitgeist anymore. Indeed it may not now. In those terms— the terms of popular/mass culture in which the novel rose to popularity—it may have already been supplanted. By the feature film."[3] The other responded, "It is important to separate the novel's mode of production and consumption from the kind of narrative it hosts. Its modes of production and consumption are decidedly modern. But the kind of story—the series of adventures, characters undergoing profound changes, consumers feeling changed—all of that is present in the medieval romance. Indeed, thus the French shared named for the medieval romance and the modern novel: le roman."[4]

Literary historians understand that no cultural form is inherently prepared to stand the test of time. Rather, a variety of factors (social, economic, political, and environmental) conspire to facilitate historic phenomena like the rise of the novel—and, for that matter, to facilitate arguments *about* phenomena like the (apparent) rise or (putative) fall of the novel.[5] What interests me, in the case of regional Indigenous writers, is why they have chosen, collectively, to invest in some forms rather than others. Medievalist Friend #2 reminds me that Native communities have always produced long-form narrative—in ongoing oral traditions as well as in newsletter pieces and poems that allude to and recirculate those traditions—and that these narratives do have many of the features we have come to associate with The Novel, including intricate plots and structures of feeling. But Medievalist Friend #1's words also hint that perhaps, as they have sustained their own long-lasting literary traditions, regional Native writers have often preferred to present that narrative experience in other forms.

Sustainable or not, the novel is becoming a subject of new debate among literary historians, who have noticed that the form coincides a little too neatly with the Anthropocene, that "powerful if paradoxical ascendant concept for defining the geologic contemporary, its forms of art in the present tense, and its geologically inscribed histories of the future" (K. Marshall 524). The rise of the novel has been famously dated to the late eighteenth century, the same moment as this newly defined epoch of human-generated planetary change and destruction.[6] Some readers feel, now, that the loose baggy monster so beloved by followers of Henry James simply can't tackle the realities of geological time and global catastrophe, not even in its surrealist and magical realist forms (Ghosh 27). Another Facebook friend portended that day: "As we truly enter the horrors of the runaway Trumpian Anthropocene, with ever-increasing and ever more awful natural disasters, open warfare over ever-decreasing resources, and permanent dictatorships of the brutal and stupid, the novel's usual focus on individual sensibility will simply begin to seem irrelevant. It will stagger on, of course, as an accoutrement of the shrinking class of the hyper-wealthy, but the breadth and depth of the carbon-age novel will be lost forever."[7]

The jury is still out: for every person proclaiming the death of the novel, there is another who argues that it is in fact the quintessential literary form for working through large-scale problems of climate change, species depletion, and contemporary human disaster.[8] In her riposte to Amitav Ghosh, Ursula Heise contends that science fiction has already demonstrated that it is more than up to the challenge: in its "dual focus on nature and culture," its "embrace [of] nonhuman agents," its penchant for "extraordinary events," and its refusal to "limit itself in temporal or spatial scale" (*boundary 2*). We might add that Indigenous oral traditions, still very much alive (often in the form of novels), do all of these things as well. Telling the story of large-scale disaster is nothing new for Indigenous people, because they have already witnessed and experienced it. Grace Dillon (Anishinaabe) has an often-quoted line in her introduction to *Walking the Clouds: An Anthology of Indigenous Science Fiction*: she says that among Indigenous people, "it is almost commonplace to think that the Native Apocalypse, if contemplated seriously, has already taken place" (8). Daniel Heath Justice (Cherokee) echoes this sentiment:

> [Apocalypse] is more than speculation—it's experiential, even in its most fantastical, because in a very real way it hasn't ended. Our nations are still subjected to the terrible traumas of colonialism. . . . Our apocalypse isn't a singular event, it's an ongoing and relentless process, not unlike settler colonialism itself. Our nations' resistance continues, as does our hope that there's a better world beyond the apocalypse. Our stories affirm this hope, most often by exploring kinship and its powerful capacity to strengthen us, our commitments, and our resolve. . . . Indigenous writers confront the racial logics of the state and their effects, not just on the human world but the other-than-human as well. (168)

This emphasis on *story* as the linchpin of Indigenous sovereignty and sustainability—often figured in such terms as "resistance," "resurgence," "survivance"—has become a common theme in a good deal of Native American and Indigenous studies scholarship. This scholarship now accepts that Indigenous literature functions in these ways: resisting settler colonialism, reasserting tribal connections to traditional land bases, reinforcing their kinship ties, and stewarding millennia-old forms of knowledge. In this chapter, I consider why Hopkins, Bruchac, and Tantaquidgeon Zobel, all of whom have written in a wide variety of genres, turn specifically to novels, when novels seem not to have been the genre of choice among their own communities. In *Carlomagno*, Hopkins stewards one of the oldest and most apocalyptic stories in Native New England, that of King Philip's War (1675–76) and the subsequent removal and enslavement of Indigenous people in the West Indies. Bruchac's *Hidden Roots* likewise stewards a story well-known among Indigenous people but kept more or less secret among settler historians—that of the 1930s Vermont eugenics program. Both Hopkins and Bruchac use character-driven plots and generic conventions to communicate how regional tribal communities have sustained their relationships to their kin and to their homelands against the most catastrophic settler violence. Tantaquidgeon Zobel updates old tribal stories about extreme weather and seasonal change for the climate-change era. These novels are all acts of literary stewardship, (re)imagining tribal sovereignty and sustainability through recirculations of some of the oldest stories that have done this cultural work.

Hopkins's *Carlomagno*: Remembering Relations and Homeland in Diaspora

Carlomagno is an unabashedly, exuberantly cheesy pirate novel. Set in the seventeenth-century Spanish West Indies, it gathers a huge cast of stock characters: Blackbeard-like cutthroats, dashing corsairs, comedic buffoons, renegade slaves, and busty wenches. It trots out historical figures like Thomas Modyford, governor of Jamaica from 1664 to 1670, and the privateer Sir Henry Morgan, who became the inspiration for *Captain Blood* and many other popular pirate stories and films. When the novel opens in 1678, its titular hero is fleeing a Spanish plantation owner. He is none other than the son of the Wampanoag leader Metacomet, and he has been sold into slavery.[9] After his escape from the plantation, Carlomagno assembles a motley transnational crew, becomes master of his own ship, and falls in love with the beautiful and mysterious Lady Pickford. Ever a reluctant pirate, Carlomagno builds an interracial, self-sustaining utopia for his friends and family on Hispaniola. In the very last pages of this sprawling book, he decides to set sail back to the land of his birth.

This may seem like a strange place to begin a discussion of

New England Indigenous novelists' address to tribal sovereignty and sustainability. But Hopkins is no stranger to these issues. He got his degree in journalism from the University of Rhode Island in 1987 and wrote for southern New England newspapers, including the *New London (CT) Day*, *Fall River (MA) Herald News*, *Norwich (CT) Bulletin*, and *Westerly (RI) Sun*, as well as the *Gallup (NM) Independent*. He had a syndicated column with Gannett News Service from 1992 and 1995, and he also wrote for the Native publications *News from Indian Country*, *Indian Country Today*, *Pequot Times*, and *Navajo Times*. His journalism covered a number of serious environmental and political issues, including the infamous 2003 police raid on a Narragansett shop that was selling tax-free cigarettes—a bid for tribal economic sustainability (Senier, *Dawnland Voices* 530–33).[10] Hopkins served on the Narragansett Tribal Council from 1994 to 1996 and now lives in Tuba City, Arizona. He writes about home, and he writes about diaspora.[11] As we saw in the tribal newsletters, attentiveness to relations living far from their homeland is a critical component of Indigenous literary stewardship: these writings remember these people, speak to them, include their words, and sometimes even reconvene them. Hopkins's own role in recirculating the story of John Onion, as discussed in the previous chapter, suggests that he sees creative writing as a tool for reaching broad audiences while stewarding tribal stories and relations.

Carlomagno stewards the story of a most painful and critical moment in Indigenous regional history: the removal and enslavement of Wampanoag and Pequot people after King Philip's (Metacomet's) War. As the historian Jill Lepore has shown, settler colonial historiography has narrated King Philip's War, over and over, as the effective *end* of Native presence in New England, as the moment when virtuous Mary Rowlandson rises to replace her bloodthirsty captors as the first American. So for Hopkins to imagine what happens afterward—to the Indigenous people who survived this holocaust—is a radical act, one that Indigenous people have practiced locally for centuries. Indeed his hero, Metacomet's son, looms large in regional memory. The Pequot minister William Apess declared, in his 1836 *Eulogy on King Philip*, "The most horrid act [of the war] was in taking Philip's son, about ten years of age, and selling him to be a slave away from his father and mother. While I am writing, I can hardly restrain my feelings, to think a people calling themselves Christians, should conduct so scandalous, so outrageous, making themselves appear despicable in the eyes of the Indians" (301).

As Apess's words show, the wholesale removal of tribal members in the aftermath of that conflict left a wound that was still deeply felt a century and a half later, and that indeed is still deeply felt today. In her important new book *Our Beloved Kin*, Lisa Brooks exhorts us to consider the *afterlives* of King Philip's War, including "the heavy recruitment of Native scouts, who . . . negotiated for their kin," and the colonies' "campaign of extermination and enslavement, alongside the concrete political and environmental factors that left families exposed" (302). Wampanoag, Narragansett, and Pequot people have in fact continued to exercise their fiduciary duty of loyalty to these kin in a number of ways; since at least the early 2000s, they have convened physical reunions, in New England and in Bermuda, with their long-lost relatives.[12]

To this long-standing regional remembering Hopkins contributes a novel that imagines the survival and *return* of King Philip's son, in a playful but extremely compelling way to think about tribal sovereignty and sustainability. Transforming Philip's son into a swashbuckling hero is a lighthearted way to communicate serious themes of colonialism, including slavery, genocide, and settlement. How do you get to fantasize about being Errol Flynn while also critiquing empire? In part, by indigenizing the pirate. (I defy anyone to find me another.) "A pirate," Hopkins writes, "was the enemy of all nations, safe from none. A privateer acted with the unofficial blessing of some government, which in turn received a percentage of any plunder taken from enemy nations" (137). Carlomagno himself is neither wholly pirate nor privateer: he "didn't see himself as a pirate; and maybe that was the problem. He didn't ask to come to the Caribbean, he was brought here against his will, in chains" (111). He does, however, cut a dashing figure while fighting villains and reconstructing tribal ideals and relations in a new place. Like his father, Carlomagno is mockingly named for a European king, as a way of devaluing his authority.[13] His embrace of his new name and new identity comes only reluctantly, after he learns that colonists killed his father in the war back home.

Throughout his adventures Carlomagno remains acutely sensitive to his earlier losses, including his sense of place: "If he were home, he could draw in the dirt and mark the place of his village. From there it would be no trick to mark where other villages—such as Agawam or Montauk—were located. But in this strange, new land drawing in the dirt was useless for he did not know exactly where he was" (2). Without such an earth-based, kinetic writing system to reinscribe his relationship to his homeland and his neighbors, however, he does maintain his memories. He remembers that his own people have "societal laws, maybe not written in great tomes or carved in stone, but laws and customs known through practice" (76); he also remembers "his father's dream of saving his people from the encroachment of the English" (39)—highlighting that there is no uncoupling an understanding of Indigenous sustainability and survival from a recognition of Indigenous sovereignty.

The reluctant-pirate figure lets Hopkins write something entertaining and new while also commenting on colonialism and plunder. *Carlomagno* plays out against the backdrop of a brutal empire on its last legs. The Spanish King Philip's control over the region is crumbling with the arrival of English, French, and Dutch smugglers, explorers, and settlers (93–94). Exiled, Carlomagno is unwilling to join the European regimes, and he cannot rebuild ecological relations with his home territory. But he *can* rebuild relationality out of these ruins. One of the more interesting scenes in the book is his establishment of the community he calls Sequanakeeswush, named after the corn-planting season in Wampanoag. His friend Diego (half-Spanish, half–west African) tells another member of their merry band that Carlomagno wants "to create his own little world here on Hispaniola, something like what he left behind when he was sold here as a child" (135). As a leader, he is anti-authoritarian: "Nobody ever gave me no paper saying I was a captain. I guess I am just because the other men follow me. Where I came from, leaders held their positions just that way" (85). He buys slaves from abusive owners and frees them, a practice that "roared like wildfire through the slave community," such that "hearty runaways were making their way to him—in hopes of gaining freedom" (204). Carlomagno treats these former slaves seriously as "builders, craftsmen and thinkers" (135), fully integrating them into his community along with his Spanish and French comrades.

The place they build together is a mishmash of international styles and literary tropes. Carlomagno and Lady Pickford's main house is a stone manor evidencing romantic standards of taste, having "colonnades . . . like Greek columns, with intricate designs etched in them." The community rapidly builds a thriving agricultural export trade based on sugarcane and tobacco, and its members enjoy regionally sustainable foods, including turtle soup and *salmagundi*. Sequanakeeswush is a picturesque island paradise, rounded out by beautiful beaches and protected by Carlomagno's own ships and cannons. It is a surreal, amusing space, but it is also an indigenized space, one that recalls Jeff Corntassel's descriptions of Cherokee storytelling and fire-keeping as "everyday acts of resurgence" that "reclaim, restore, and regenerate homeland relationships" (89). As such, even though Sequanakeeswush is itself a settlement (and an unashamedly capitalist one at that), it poses a distinct threat to colonial settlers. To borrow from Kyle Powys White (Potawatomi), it "delegitimizes settlers' claims to have honorable and credible 'missions,' universal property rights, and exclusive political sovereignty" (10). Indeed Carlomagno rightly intuits that European governments "would not take kindly to an upstart 'state' growing in their midst. And Sequanakeeswush was becoming its own self-sustaining state" (Hopkins 204). In the final pages of the novel, Carlomagno's gang is attacked by a British warship. They rebuff this attack with the help of their friend, the French corsair Persifal Kerbourchard, and decide to sail for America. The book's last paragraphs capture the novel's playful combination of Indigenous survivance and generic convention:

> As they bobbed across the friendly sea, Carlomagno stood by the rail and watched the Caribbean sunset. He had grown up there; he had founded and lost an empire. . . . "Perhaps, there is a paradise awaiting us in America?"
>
> America.
>
> It had a ring to it, Carlomagno admitted to himself. He was going to find a new life in America. Carlomagno, the son of King Philip, was bound for America.
>
> He was coming home to a place he'd never been before. (255)

Carlomagno is a bit long and shares some of the same features of other masculinist pirate novels, including a good deal of male gaze and stereotyping. Hopkins had been working on stories about King Philip's War for over a decade prior to the publication of this book. These projects seemed to elicit interest and the occasional prize but never a publishing contract. He told me:

> I was finding strong encouragement for a novel called "Shadow across the Sun," which took place during King Philip's War.
>
> Originally I sent sample chapters to now-defunct Clarion Press, out of Atlanta in 1993. They asked to see the full manuscript. Later, they rejected it—citing names that sounded "like something from a John Wayne movie." I wrote back to tell them the names they objected to—Ninigret, Canonicus and Canonchet—were real names of my Narragansett ancestors. They did not reply.[14]

Finally, to get this story into circulation, Hopkins self-published it in 2003 with iUniverse, one of many predatory companies that charges authors hundreds and even thousands of dollars for services like book design, ISBN generation, and copyediting. He paid a $100 fee and got about that much help with editing and marketing. He republished it in 2011 as *The Pirate Prince Carlomagno* with wampumbooks, a Native publishing outfit run by Stephanie Duckworth-Elliott (Aquinnah Wampanoag), which unfortunately did not last more than a year or two.[15] Blue Hand Books, an Indigenous e-publishing company founded by Trace DeMeyer (Shawnee/Cherokee descent), Hopkins's former colleague at the *Pequot Times*, picked it up in 2013 as *Carlomagno: Adventures of the Pirate Prince of the Wampanoag*.[16] So Hopkins has managed to keep the book in print with help from his friends and his own determination, but it has not received the rigorous editing it deserves and has not attracted any major reviews or notice.

Nevertheless *Carlomagno* is a vital contribution to regional Indigenous literary history. It participates in the stewardship of a story that settlers have willfully suppressed but that Indigenous people have long remembered—that of the exile and survival of Native people after King Philip's War. It gives Philip's son not a tragedy but a spirited adventure and romance. Imagining any future for Native people in New England beyond King Philip's War—beyond the event that is supposed to have signaled their demise—is a radical act. Imagining it as hopeful, joyful, and even campy is equally radical. Most compelling, *Carlomagno* insists on the kinds of reciprocal relations we have seen in earlier Indigenous writing from New England. It imagines a beloved son rebuilding reciprocal kinship relationships abroad. And it suggests that despite displacement and settler violence, Indigenous people have held on to what has served them well, saving this knowledge and these practices for such times when they can become useful again—for when they can return home.

Bruchac's *Hidden Roots*: Sustaining Land and Kin against Ecological and Bodily Violence

Joseph Bruchac has been serious about the stewardship of Native literature itself for his entire career. As I detail in the next chapter, he has been almost single-mindedly devoted to publishing and promoting regional Native authors. He has also been specially dedicated to publishing books for children and young adults, actively cultivating a new generation of readers for Native literature—a sustainability intervention if ever there was one.

Marketed for grades 5 through 9, *Hidden Roots* is a coming-of-age novel. Awkward young Howard Camp grows into a popular basketball player and reconciles with his angry father and distant uncle. But under this cloak the book does something daring for young readers, introducing them to the dark history of the Vermont eugenics project. Like the story of Indigenous people sold into slavery after King Philip's War, this is a story remembered and retold for generations among Native people, though actively suppressed by settlers. As documented in Nancy Gallagher's book *Breeding Better Vermonters*, the state Eugenics Survey was formally organized out of the University of Vermont between 1925 and 1936 and resulted in the 1931 Law for Human Betterment by Voluntary Sterilization. Abenaki people were a primary target of this law, along (or conflated) with the poor and "feeble-minded." They were targeted precisely because their history tied them to desirable lands. The Abenaki historian and artist Judy Dow, whose own family was identified by the survey, explains, "Most of the people recorded in the survey lived along the Intervale and Lake Champlain in Burlington. Burlington's wealthy wanted more from this beautiful location than a home for the city's poor; they wanted their scenic view. Time and again, they went back to the same addresses, institutionalizing families and breaking them up." To Dow, Bruchac, and other Indigenous writers, the relationship between settler destruction of the land and of Indigenous bodies and cultures is palpable, a recent apocalypse whose effects are still being lived and felt.

The family at the center of *Hidden Roots* is a product of this destructive history. They have fled Vermont for the Adirondacks, near where Bruchac's own family has lived for generations, and they are living there without openly acknowledging their Abenaki heritage, "hiding in plain sight," in the words of one character and indeed of many Abenaki people.[17] Howard Camp is eleven years old, an only child living with his mother, Martha Henry, who has had two unexplained miscarriages, and his father, Jake, a self-loathing domestic abuser. Howard's Abenaki grandfather is mysteriously called Uncle Louis and said to be French Canadian. The plot is structured less by conflict and resolution than by seasons, calling on traditional planetary references to time. It begins by explicating the protagonists' back stories in August ("Moon of Ripening") and September ("Moon of Leaves Changing Wood"). In October ("Moon of Leaves Falling") Jake Camp is injured in an industrial accident, whereupon he undergoes something of a character change and becomes much gentler; in the novel's final chapter, December ("Moon of Long Nights"), Howard's grandfather tells him their family's secret, showing him the 1932 certificate ordering the sterilization of his grandmother. The story crystallized in this tiny family and this tiny timeline is thus a much bigger story, one belonging to Indigenous people throughout the world. It contains the destruction and expropriation of tribal lands and the destruction and appropriation of Indigenous bodies and cultures—a full-frontal assault on Indigenous sovereignty and sustainability.[18]

Some scholars have described the Anthropocene as "a primarily sensorial phenomenon: the experience of living in an increasingly diminished and toxic world" (Davis and Turpin 3). But Indigenous people (and indeed other dispossessed people) have been experiencing this "sensorial phenomenon" well before the era of climate change and in fact centuries before the era of industrialization. Howard Camp experiences it both locally and globally. His story opens in 1954, the year of the hydrogen bomb test in the Pacific, of duck-and-cover drills, and of neighbors who fled the Jewish Holocaust.[19] That is also the year the Cleveland Indians are defeated in the World Series—for settlers, a defeat of the savage Other, but for the novel, a subtle defeat of vicious stereotyping. Indeed if this novel conveys a sense of "living in an increasingly toxic world," a big part of that toxicity is representational. This Abenaki family, which cannot speak openly of their own Native identity or access much of their Native community, land base, and traditions, is awash in inauthentic signifiers of Indianness. Jake suffers a traumatic brain injury on an Indian motorcycle (23–24). His uncle uses Red Man tobacco to give ceremonial thanks for fire (65). Asking for books about Indians at the local library, Howard gets only *The Last of the Mohicans* (84). These representations mask the ongoing violence of settler colonialism by relegating Indians to the remote past.

The Camps live on a moribund farm in upstate New York near the Hudson River. It "used to be a real farm once, but those days were gone. The only planting we did was Mom's little vegetable garden out back. . . . The fields where past generations had done haying and raised corn had grown up with sumacs and fire cherry, except for two acres that had been planted with Scotch Pine for Christmas trees that still had to grow another three years before any of them could be harvested" (9–10). Similarly the family has ceased to hunt; young Howard learns about hunting only from a trip into the woods with Uncle Louis. Howard believes his parents would be happier farming and fishing, but "there was no real money in it" (10).

These cultural changes are not some unmotivated form of assimilation but stem directly from the town's paper mill. In the twenty-first century Indigenous people in New England are still fighting the environmental destruction caused by paper mills on their lands and in their waterways; the Penobscot Nation's protracted fight to protect their river in Maine is perhaps the most visible example. The mill in *Hidden Roots* is based on the Hudson River Mill in Corinth, New York, built by International Paper in 1869. It closed in 2002, leaving behind paper sludge and asbestos and having done considerable damage to workers' bodies and livelihoods, pulling them into unsustainable, dangerous employment with substandard wages (Scarce 22–25). Thus Jake comes home each night tired and angry from working in the mill, and he eventually loses a finger to the much-feared Machine No. 3. He is angry about more than the damage to his own body; when his young son comments that the river looks pretty and "full of rainbows," Jake tells him, "They hurt our river, son. They poison it and they kill the fish. Someday we're all going to have to pay for what they're doing now" (*Hidden Roots* 52).

The effects of this extractive industry, then, are far-reaching; moreover, Bruchac shows, Abenaki people understood and lived these effects in ways that anticipated more au courant ecocritical theories of entanglement. Uncle Louis himself, we learn, was conscripted into cutting down trees to build the Sacandaga Reservoir in the 1930s. This had predictable effects in driving away game and thus disrupting Indigenous sustenance practices. Those people who weren't starved out were forcibly removed: "More than trees were cut out of the valley. Whole towns were moved, even their churches and cemeteries. Most didn't talk about it, but Uncle Louis said some of those in the valley who were forced out were men and women who had no paper title to their land, people living in the simplest way in log cabins and little houses with shingles made of bark" (56). This passage poignantly highlights two registers of apocalyptic violence: this twentieth-century New England removal not only destroyed particular Abenaki communities and ecosystems; it also targeted the very systems that helped Abenaki people endure in their traditional territories.

In particular, the extractive logging and milling industries targeted Abenaki relationships with trees. The Camps' relations lived *in* the woods, in homes made *of* the woods ("little houses with shingles made of bark"); more profoundly, the Camps continue to identify *with* the woods. This shows up in the book's evocative language. For instance, Jake refers to his lineage as "white trash Indian" (122), which obviously reflects internalized ethnic and class hatred but also resonates with Uncle Louis's "trash wood" (55), the subject of an earlier chapter about Louis's practice of continuing his old livelihood by collecting firewood for impoverished neighbors. "Trash wood" was in fact "the best burning wood you could imagine" (55), dry and well-seasoned. In other subtle expressions of the affinity between people and trees, young Howard rejects the idea of ever working in the paper mill, thinking, "I won't be one of those turning what's wild and free into napkins and toilet paper" (14). These references are subtle, but they evoke traditional Abenaki understandings of trees as ancestors. In other writings, Bruchac has recounted an Abenaki creation story, in which the first people stepped out of trees after the creator shot arrows into them (Caduto and Bruchac 238; Carlson 3). "Abenakis say that trees are, quite literally, our relatives," he writes. "Trees that were mere commodities to Europeans, a means of gaining wealth, were ancestors, deeply felt symbols, life itself to Native people. Trees were acknowledged as living, sentient beings" (*Our Stories Remember* 28).

On social media, Indigenous people registered quite a bit of hilarity when Peter Wohlleben's 2016 book, *The Hidden Life of Trees*, was being hailed as groundbreaking. Its argument? That trees are "sentient beings" that "live in families, support their sick neighbors, and have the capacity to make decisions and fight off predators" (Schiffman). Zoe Todd, the Métis scholar who has so trenchantly criticized settler scholars for imagining they have "discovered" the entanglements of "nature" and "culture," would likely laugh as well. Contemporary ecocriticism has issued many calls for literature that can help us think to *scale*, to see the planet as "a moving, shifting character, full of its own vitality in a longer storyline that precedes and exceeds us" (D. Harris 180). But Todd takes issue with the very concept of the Anthropocene, insofar as it is "*intensely preoccupied with the human, the anthropos*" ("Indigenizing the Anthropocene" 246). In place of this preoccupation, she offers the idea of the "ecological imagination," which she attributes to the Papaschase Cree scholar Dwayne Donald. In Donald's formulation, the ecological imagination is "an ethical imperative to see that despite our varied place-based cultures and knowledge systems, we live in the world together and must constantly think and act with reference to those relationships" (qtd. in Todd, "Indigenizing the Anthropocene" 249). Todd responds,

> Rather than engage with the Anthropocene as a teleological fact implicating all humans as equally culpable for the current socioeconomic, ecological, and political state of the world, I argue that we should turn to examining how other peoples are describing our "ecological imagination." To tackle the intertwined and complex environmental crises in which the world finds itself, a turn toward the reciprocity and relationships that Donald addresses . . . must be seriously considered, as locally informed responses to *in situ*

challenges around the globe cannot be constructed using one phil-osophical, epistemological, or ontological lens. Art, as one mode of thought and practice, can play a role in dismantling the condos of the art and academic world and help us build something different in their stead. ("Indigenizing the Anthropocene" 252)

Todd insists that any discussion of sustainability must account for colonialism (not "all humans" are "equally culpable") and for the reality that Indigenous people have a wide range of time-honored values and practices that cannot be ignored as humans reckon with their implication in planetary disaster. She declares, too, that sovereignty and sustainability are end-lessly dialogic, things to be worked through collectively, rene-gotiated over very long periods of time, with shifting human and natural formations.

Bruchac's characters in *Hidden Roots* (and living Abenaki people as well) respond to economic, ecological, and cultural violence with stewardship in the form of everyday acts of resur-gence. Jake and his mother walk in the woods with Uncle Louis, who teaches them to track animals and listen for their sounds. The Camps are "putting their bodies on the land," as Leanne Simpson would say ("Can Fracking Showdown" 21), one of the most radical acts that Indigenous people can undertake, when they are supposed to have vanished. Whereas Carlomagno con-tinues to be Indigenous in diaspora, the Camps continue to be Abenaki in their traditional territories, but as quietly as possi-ble. "Sometimes the only way to survive is to hide," Uncle Louis says. "The deer do it and we can do it, too. Even if we have to do it in plain sight" (*Hidden Roots* 39).

The publication history of *Hidden Roots* points to some of the factors that allow literature to do its sustainability work—and to how Native communities will continue to recirculate and steward their stories with or without the benefits of well-resourced or prestigious publishing mechanisms. The novel was first published in 2004 by Scholastic, but, like so many other regional Native books, it went out of print fairly quickly.[20] In 2011 Bruchac chose to republish it himself, with his imprint,

Bowman Books, the subject of my next chapter. In his postscript to the new edition, he explains that this story was "forgotten by everyone except the Abenakis. Almost every Vermont Abenaki family has a story about the period when the sterilization law was in effect" (134). Stewardship is not an individualistic matter, not something that can be carried out by one author or one text. And for better or for worse—since we are talking about trees and paper mills—Indigenous authors' exclusion from mainstream novel publishing and/or their preference for other forms has allowed them to avoid some of the damage done by mass publishing. "How many pundits have seen the book as a destructive technology?" ask Richard Maxwell and Toby Miller in their monumental study, *Greening the Media* (45). Large publishing houses like Scholastic destroy or recycle a full 40 percent of the books they publish every year, about 1.5 billion volumes; "if that overproduction were cut in recognition of the reality that most books are now purchased and read online, 60,000 acres of trees would be saved and carbon output diminished to the equivalent of two million medium-sized automobiles" (45). The fact that Native people in New England have not published many novels has allowed them to avoid complicity in some of this damage, while also perhaps making the portended demise of a single literary form, the novel, seem a bit less catastrophic.

Tantaquidgeon Zobel's Climate Fictions: Mohegan "Weather Lore" as Indigenous Stewardship

Contemporary Indigenous novels are "Anthropocene fictions" insofar as they obviously appear during this epoch but, more substantively, decolonize the very idea of the Anthropocene.[21] When most people hear the term "Anthropocene" nowadays, they think not first of Indian enslavement or destructive paper mills and eugenics but of climate change. To Indigenous people, however, climate change's attendant miseries (forced migration, large-scale disease, destruction of traditional habitats and subsistence foods) are not new. As Kyle Powys White puts it, climate change is "an intensification of colonialism" (156); it represents only the latest in a long series of geographic, cultural, and political removals to which Indigenous people have lost a good deal and to which they have been forced to adapt. *Carlomagno* and *Hidden Roots* describe some of these earlier experiences with colonialism's violent relocations and destruction. They also suggest that Indigenous people have "ecological imaginations" that long preceded and will outlast our present moment of industrial-fueled planetary disaster.

Now Indigenous people are writing about climate change too, and, all kidding aside about whether or not we are witnessing the last gasp of the novel as a sustainable literary form, we can expect to see climate change appear in more and more Native fiction. Cherie Dimaline's *The Marrow Thieves* (2017) and Rebecca Roanhorse's *Trail of Lightning* (2018) are two recent novels that show Indigenous people surviving long after the electricity goes out, familiar coastlines are washed away, and energy wars break out in earnest. In New England there is at least one writer of Indigenous cli-fi working today: Melissa Tantaquidgeon Zobel, Mohegan historian, medicine woman, and writer of speculative fiction. Climate change informs most of her novels, even if they do not explicitly announce themselves as cli-fi. It is the backdrop to her first novel, the futuristic *Oracles* (2004), which explores how the Yantuck Tribe (modeled on the Mohegans) is surviving a world in which "the weather had simply gone berserk" (15).

Tantaquidgeon Zobel's fiction represents tribal sovereignty and sustainability as it imagines climate *futures*. Like Hopkins's and Bruchac's novels, hers exercise a fiduciary duty of care to tribal stories, which in turn steward tribal ecologies and tribal relations. Mohegan people have a long and remarkable history of telling—and *writing*—stories about extreme weather and seasonal change, two features of intense interest to climate historians. Scientists and ecological historians have been working to reconstruct past climates through a variety of tools: meteorological instruments, proxy data like ice cores and tree rings, and, increasingly, historic documents like newspapers, diaries, weather station records, and ships' logs.[22] They have not generally looked to Indigenous writing, but if they looked to Mohegans alone, they might find some illuminating information. The eighteenth-century minister Samson Occom's journals often noted extreme cold, rain, and snow that impeded his travels, sometimes reckoning the weather's severity by his neighbors' perceptions: for instance, the winter and spring of 1785 in Connecticut were "judged by the oldest men we have, to be the Hardest in their memory, the most spending" (Occom and Brooks 291). His contemporary Joseph Johnson kept similar journals, noting repeatedly when a day "look[ed] very likely for Storm" (Johnson and Murray 105, 111). More than a century later another Mohegan diary, by the medicine woman Fidelia Fielding, recorded diurnal patterns (sunrise, sunset), the clarity of the skies, the cold and the heat with a nearly ritualistic regularity that eclipsed much in the way of personal information.[23] Fielding's protégée (and great-aunt of Tantaquidgeon Zobel), Gladys Tantaquidgeon, documented "Mohegan weather lore," partly as a result of her training in anthropology at the University of Pennsylvania, including such local knowledge as "A display of northern lights, aurora borealis, is an indication of colder weather to follow" and "To hear talking or wood chopping from a greater distance than usual indicates that a storm is brewing" (90).

Does Mohegan literary history provide compelling quantitative data for climate history? From a positivistic standpoint, scientists and historians obviously want enough documented information that they can make persuasive claims about, among other things, what kinds of climatic variation different populations have experienced in the past and how they have adapted, or failed to adapt. But what if we considered Indigenous weather narratives not as so much data to be harvested but as exercises in the sustainability of narrative itself—of the power of stories to connect people to their local environments, to teach them how to exercise their stewardship toward those places and each other?[24] Weather narratives (oral or written, Native or non-Native) are one way that humans register or try to predict what is going to happen, for instance, to food sources. That much seems obvious. They are also, however, a matter of *culture* and therefore of cultural sustainability and stewardship.[25]

In some societies, historians have found, climatic variation has been viewed as evidence of sin, leading to collective behaviors like witch hunts (Mackay). Mohegan weather lore, conversely, seems more invested in sustaining kinship ties among humans and other-than-humans. New England weather is famously unpredictable, the subject of much joking among northerners; weather aphorisms, among Native and non-Native people, provide some sense of a larger design behind the relentless cold, the sudden storms, the summers that seem cruelly delayed. Mohegan weather stories, moreover, seem to have been transmitted and adapted with incredible efficiency in written as well as oral narrative.

For instance, Tantaquidgeon Zobel's second novel extends the work of her literary forebears by recording and remembering extreme weather events while exploring how people made meaning of them. *Fire Hollow* (2010) is a Victorian Gothic set on her fictional Yantuck reservation in 1899. It follows a young medicine man, based on Tantaquidgeon Zobel's own great-grandfather, who is orphaned and sent to live with an Irish schoolmaster and his mysterious housekeeper, who turns out to be another medicine person. Fire Hollow itself is a crossroads, a haunted place based on a spot on the Mohegan reservation known as H's (or Hobbomock's) Hollow. In the very middle of the novel, a tornado tears through the neighboring town of Garden City "like a wild eggbeater, whipping through trees, wagons and homes like warm butter" (132–33). Connecticut did in fact experience a tornado in 1899, one that began in the coastal city of Norwalk and raged through several towns, though "a peculiar feature of this storm [was] that people living a quarter of a mile out of its path knew nothing about it" ("Tornado in Connecticut"). In *Fire Hollow*, there is a contrast between Garden City, which is ravaged by the tornado, and Fire Hollow itself, which is untouched. There is also a contrast between the reaction of the Irish neighbor Tara, who reads the storm moralistically, remembering that a tornado "whisked mother away from Ireland for a year and a day—until she came to her senses and returned to the greatest husband in the world" (132), and that of the medicine woman

Nettie, who treats it matter-of-factly, as though Nature has its own agency. Amusingly, Nettie does remark that another elder, Mequin, is "one Indian who would surely appreciate seeing the white man's world turned upside down" (136).

Extreme weather and the places it hits or saves, Tantaquidgeon Zobel shows, are ripe for interpretation, for contested interpretation. Telling stories of these events and places is one way that Indigenous and non-Indigenous people anchor themselves to their homelands; for the Yantuck in the novel, however, this is not a romantic or superstitious enterprise but a way of remembering some dark colonial histories as well. Indeed, far from painting a static picture of old rural New England, *Fire Hollow* depicts a land that is undergoing considerable loss from settlement and industrialization, including reductions in sturgeon and alewife populations (23), the disappearance of heath hens and black bears (28), and phosphorous sickness among match-factory workers (102). The novel itself may be playfully Gothic, but in her afterword Tantaquidgeon Zobel emphasizes that "the Victorian era was a dire time for Mohegan family solidarity," that her people at that time "held out little hope that the tribe would survive" (317). The importance of putting such stories in novelistic form cannot be understated. Like the stories of King Philip's kidnapped son and of the Vermont eugenics project, the story of Mohegan survival during a time when things seemed so very bleak is actively remembered and recirculated among Mohegan people themselves. What happens when the people who remember such stories die or, for whatever reason, stop sharing them? Putting such stories into novels allows them to continue to do their work in new ways, in new settings. This is not the same as saying that oral traditions need to be written down in order to be saved or preserved. Rather, it is understanding that stories have their best chances at longevity when they are recirculated by multiple people, in multiple forms.[26]

In addition to stewarding stories of the tribal past, including past extreme weather events, Tantaquidgeon Zobel writes about climate *futures*. Kyle Powys White, who parses contemporary tribal climate mitigation plans, explains that "Indigenous peoples often imagine climate change futures from their perspectives (a) as societies with deep collective histories of having to be well-organized to adapt to environmental change *and* (b) as societies who must reckon with the disruptions of historic and ongoing practices of colonialism, capitalism, and industrialization" (164). His framework, taken alongside the history of Mohegan writing about weather, can help us read three of Tantaquidgeon Zobel's climate-change fictions: in addition to *Oracles*, the novel *Wabanaki Blues* (2015, the first in a planned trilogy), and the short story "Butterfly" (2017, published online by the *Charles River Journal*). All three of these most recent stories feature young Indigenous women as visionaries; in each, the protagonist undertakes some kind of sacrifice or transformation in the interest of resetting relations between humans and their other-than-human kin.

In "Butterfly," New England (now "New Island") is in the final stages of complete flooding. Ket (short for "Nantucket," a name given to her by parents nostalgic for old islands and coastal places) and her friends are being evacuated to the Northwest Territories of Canada. Ket stays behind to unite with a mythical, bearlike creature called Elder Brother. Telling her peers not to be afraid, she says, "He is our Watcher. Our ancient stories say he was the one who brought us into this world. Now he's come to lead us into a new one." A year later these friends receive a message from Ket, one of profound hope: "I have seen the future. I know that Mother Earth will recover. We, humans, will be replaced by a higher version of ourselves, a loftier species, covered with thick glistening crimson hair. In this future, these Elder Brothers and Elder Sisters will occasionally claim to spot one of us mythical human beasts. A few crazies among them will allege that a handful of us survived in a remote northern cave. But their leaders will quell those rumors with their elegant oratory. For this species will be known for its great poetry."

It is intriguing, and significant, I think, that Tantaquidgeon Zobel envisions a future not only in which humans and their other-than-human kin can recover their relations of reciprocity and mutual care but in which *verbal art* survives as a critical cultural form. In "marrying" Ket to Elder Brother, she dramatizes what she has described elsewhere as a radically relational world where "Indians can be sexy as/with other-than-human beings and in/with noncolonized gender roles" ("Algonquian Naming, Power, and Relationality in a Rare Native Love Poem" 215).[27] She also points to the power of story as a form of stewardship: stories, collectively retold, can out-survive individual generations, but they also connect those generations to each other, prompting reflection on the kinds of circumstances that people (and their nonhuman relations) have survived in the past, as well as aspirations for how to do better in the future. "Butterfly" merges the fantastical with the practical: Ket may seem larger than life, even "crazy," but the world she is leaving is a miserably realistic product of colonialism and capitalism. Her friends are reading this missive from the Wendigo Mines, where they are being forced to work on building a survival habitat in an old mining site in the Mackenzie Mountains. Though Tantaquidgeon Zobel doesn't spell out these references specifically for her online readers, the Mackenzie Mountains have been the site of conflict between First Nations and settler governments over tungsten mining (tungsten being among the infamous "conflict minerals" that power our electronic devices), and Wendigo is a monster in Algonquian oral traditions known for his voracious, cannibalistic behaviors. (More recently, many Native authors have deployed this figure as a metaphor for colonialism.) Embedding colonial histories and Indigenous tropes in a climate-change narrative, "Butterfly" is an otherworldly but powerfully emotional story. It conveys deep grief for worlds lost and pain inflicted, but it also asks us to think bigger, to consider that other-than-humans and humans can *see* each other and care for each other.

Similarly, *Oracles* portrays Indigenous survival in the context of climate change, with people directly reckoning, as White puts it, with the "disruptions of colonialism and capitalism" (164). Like "Butterfly," this novel asks what happens *after* the weather has "simply gone berserk." If one function of old Mohegan weather lore was to give communities a sense of comfort in the existence of some cosmic pattern, the weather of the future stymies with its complete irrationality: "Too little rain was followed by too much flooding. Searing heat waves were halted by blizzards" (*Oracles* 15).[28] *Oracles* goes even further than a short story like "Butterfly" is able to go in exploring not only climatic disruptions but also the many ecological, political, and cultural consequences of climate change. For instance, deforestation in *Oracles* has been so thorough that traditional medicinal plants are losing their efficacy (15). The stand of remaining trees that the Yantucks have been carefully stewarding has become a bit of a tourist destination, with busloads of "young cyberbrats" coming to see them (52). Ocean pollution and acidification are implied in a tribal oyster farm, based on a modern Mohegan aquaculture project (17). And internally, tribal members are arguing about the best ways to sustain their cohesion and traditional practices for the future: market their spirituality to hungry outsiders? Reject modernity and retreat into their oldest ways?

Perhaps one of the most interesting possibilities explored in *Oracles* is the collapse of the tribe's major foray into capitalism. As the novel opens, the lights have dimmed once and for all on the tribal casino, allowing the young medicine woman Ashneon Quay to finally see the stars. Visitors to Connecticut will know that the Mohegan tribe operates one of the largest casinos in the United States, the Mohegan Sun. Readers will also remember J. Kehaulani Kau003nui's argument about "the Connecticut effect"—the legacy of racism against Indigenous people in New England precisely because they have availed themselves of their sovereign right to operate such enterprises under the 1988 Indian Gaming Regulatory Act. This racism includes environmental racism: settlers, including environmental activists, have been far too eager to claim that, in operating such enterprises, Indigenous people have somehow relinquished any claims to environmental stewardship.[29] It is as though such activists have never entertained the possibility that Indigenous people might debate and deliberate—in informed ways—among themselves about the strategic benefits and long-term costs of such enterprises, or that they may be structurally shut out of other economic development opportunities and in some senses essentially cornered into operating gaming enterprises. Around New England, at least, you will hear some schadenfreude among non-Native people that Mohegan Sun and the neighboring Foxwoods resort, operated by the Mashantucket Pequots, are now in debt, but you will also hear Native people say that no one expected these casinos to last forever. Rather, they saw them as strategic opportunities to generate capital that they could invest in their communities.[30] The Mohegans have made some rather extraordinary investments, for example, in education and elder housing. Tantaquidgeon Zobel has described some of these internal debates and calculations in an essay, "The Accomac Business Model," "Accomac" meaning "the long view from across the water." In this long view, she writes:

> As someone who truly lives and works in the middle of a tribal world, I often see hostility between the proponents of cultural and business interests. That situation exists not because both sides necessarily have different goals, but because many Natives equate good business with the values of the Non-Indian world. That means that many traditionally-minded folks feel compelled to oppose tribal business development, because they sense that it is eroding tribal culture. I work in my tribe's cultural department, so I sometimes hear culture-advocates saying that they wish our business would go under, so tribal people can focus wholly on culture. This sort of attitude makes business-minded Natives defensive. They do not see how they can successfully promote tribal economic enterprises and participate in cultural activities, without exposing themselves to ridicule. Their discomfort often triggers a knee-jerk reaction, in which they defend non-Native business practices and values, rather than separating good economics from tag-along values which are anathema to their own.

One value of writing a novel like *Oracles* is that Tantaquidgeon Zobel can *dramatize* such dialogues, giving them affective weight. For example, when the conservative medicine man Tomuck in *Oracles* gives a tree tour, he gets into a debate with one of the young cyberbrats, asking her what she thinks she knows. She tells him, "Over time, we have had to change our ways to survive. . . . We can learn how to destroy the natural world or, I believe, how to save it. The choice is ours." When he reminds her that "not all change for our people has been good," she tells him that she has also learned "about how our people nearly destroyed this reservation, and that all we were able to save was the mountain. . . . You saved the people and the mountain, Chief" (59). There is a place for practices construed as traditional *and* those construed as modern in the world of this novel. Ashneon understands that modernity comes with costs and benefits: she is happy to see the casino burn down, but she is simultaneously horrified at the tribal museum's "proliferation of organic matter as a preservation nightmare" (60). For her, the museum and the woods are part and parcel of the same stewardship project—the same way that oral traditions, newsletters, novels, and rock art are part of the same stewardship work. She says, "I always knew that the museum and the woods were the same and that these woods hold all that we are as Yantuck people. I also knew that when they go, we go. But what I didn't know was that these woods and these artifacts give a window into other worlds and beings" (71). This moment recalls Dwayne Donald's formulation of the ecological imagination: it suggests the need to be embedded in specific place-based knowledge systems while also remaining open and alert to interdependencies with other knowledge systems, both human and other-than-human.

Why is it important that the casino blinks out to let Ashneon see the stars? Without going so far as to envision a new race of crimson-haired beings, *Oracles* envisions a similar kind of sacrifice for Ashneon as "Butterfly" did for Ket. With apologies for the spoiler, Ashneon dies at the end of the novel, joining her ancestors and relations in the form of stars. According to an "Ancient Yantuck Indian Story" at the very opening of the book, the original prophets were transformed into stars "that they might shine safely from afar" (3). The problem with such oracles being too close to people—according to the story, they were first transformed into rocks, and then trees—is that when people discover sacred knowledge, they "flock" to it, potentially destroying it and overrunning it. So when Ashneon becomes a star, she is told, "We may not pass on all our knowledge to the living, only the way to that knowledge—which takes longer than any single human life time" (157). The problem of sustainability, these stories suggest, cannot not be solved quickly or simply. They require intergenerational, collective deliberation.

Ashneon and Ket have a sister in seventeen-year-old Mona Lisa LaPierre, the protagonist of *Wabanaki Blues*, who is sent by her estranged parents to spend the summer with her Mohegan grandfather in the northern woods. There she comes into her own as a blues guitarist, meets an attractive young man, and—along the way—discovers who killed a former student from her high school. With her north woods setting, Tantaquidgeon Zobel honors her Abenaki neighbors; Mona Lisa's grandmother was Abenaki, and her grandfather tells her, "These woods are Abenaki country, your territory. They'll always keep you safe" (43). The setting also lets her illustrate some effects of climate change. In late summer Mona Lisa finds, "Everyone in New England is depressed right now. A true catastrophe has hit our region. Our autumn leaves have failed to produce their usual radiant color" (272). This is a real phenomenon: as Tantaquidgeon Zobel and other New Englanders were starting to notice changes in fall colors, so too were climate scientists, who find that warmer temperatures, sometimes accompanied by drought, are delaying or diminishing the vibrant fall foliage that is such a critical factor in New England's regional tourism, among other things.[31] Mona Lisa's love interest, adorably named Del Pyne, is a student at the Yale forestry school who is studying this issue; the novel recognizes that climate change needs all hands on deck.

Jake Camp has to learn who he is over the course of *Hidden Roots*; Mona Lisa knows she is Native American, but over the course of *Wabanaki Blues* she grows into a greater understanding of her family's and her own deep relationship with and responsibilities to the forest. She makes the acquaintance of an eccentric (and hilarious) Abenaki great-aunt, Black Racer

Woman, whom she visits late in the novel, in a deeper part of the woods. Black Racer Woman tells Mona Lisa that she lives there alone expressly to fend off logging interests and because "living this way helps me see things the old way. Every tree is precious to me. That old mindset helps me stand in the way of what some people call progress" (287). This is stewardship not as paternalistic protection but as a mutually beneficial duty of care. Most extraordinarily, Black Racer Woman also tells Mona Lisa that the younger woman must kill a bear to save these woods. With more spoiler apologies, at the end of the book Mona Lisa has a car accident in which she does in fact kill an old bear—a mysterious creature that few but she and her grandfather had seen.

Tantaquidgeon Zobel is using *Wabanaki Blues* to update a traditional story of the Hunter and the Bear. In a time, she explains, when "the leaves weren't so colorful as they are now" (287), humans and animals found themselves depressed at the approach of each winter. To combat this melancholy, the Great Spirit instructed the hunter to kill a bear—a sacrifice for the bear, of course, but also for the hunter, who did not want to destroy an animal so great. The bear's blood and fat dripped over the leaves, creating beautiful colors and, presumably, sustaining humans and animals in balance. For the record, *Wabanaki Blues* presents this story as only one way to make meaning: Mona Lisa's grandfather thinks the story is baloney or just a general allegory for sacrifice, whereas Black Racer Woman seems to insist on it literally. Either way, as in *Oracles*, traditional story seems to have the ultimate agency. Like Ashneon before her, Mona Lisa lives out a traditional narrative without necessarily intending or wanting to, to participate in a ritual orchestrated by tradition itself, by her ancestors and their narratives, to reconnect her to her land and her people. If none of these stories feels like much of a practical climate-change mitigation plan, they *are* potent reminders that sustainability calls for renewed "senses of place and planet," as Ursula Heise might say. Sustainability requires political will and policy decisions around carbon emissions, certainly; perhaps more profoundly, however, it requires *cultural* and collective negotiations of reciprocal relationships with skies, trees, plants, and waters. When Mona Lisa attends a local powwow, she hears her grandmother's voice saying, "The point of powwows is to dance on somebody else's territory and realize it's all part of the same dusty earth. We humans are huddled together on a tiny blue bead, spinning through the star-studded universe" (134). Like Ket and Ashneon, Mona Lisa has a sense of the local, of the celestial, and of time—of the long history (and the long future) of Indigenous relationships with the land, with the water, with the forests, and with spirit and each other.

Oracles, and arguably all of the fictions discussed in this chapter, are what Jodi Byrd (Chickasaw) would call "transgeneric": they "experiment, refuse categorization, and . . . genre-bend" ("Red Dead Conventions" 346). Genre, Byrd argues, exercises a colonizing force of its own: "It collects, categorizes and arrays textual productions into shelved units for instant marketability and digestability, and, in the process, produces its own others" (345). So *Fire Hollow* is part Victorian Gothic, but it is also part bildungsroman and part folk tale. *Oracles* is part sci-fi, but also part romance. *Wabanaki Blues* is part angsty bildungsroman, part romance, part murder mystery. All of these books are part environmental cautionary tale; all of them resonate with Heise's definition of science fiction, with their "dual focus on nature and culture," their "embrace [of] nonhuman agents," their penchant for "extraordinary events," and their refusal to "limit [themselves] in temporal or spatial scale." If we follow Byrd's lead, considering them as transgeneric fiction, then we might say that transgeneric fiction gives Hopkins, Bruchac, and Tantaquidgeon Zobel a way to join a larger literary field, on the one hand, by trafficking in readily *recognizable* tropes, while on the other hand doing the same things we saw tribal histories and community newsletters do: folding in oral traditions and tribal historical memories in the service of stewarding these for future generations. Novels aspire to reach larger audiences than community newsletters or even tribal histories. They offer long-form, *imaginative* representations of the remote past and distant future—of the ways that Indigenous people have survived from time immemorial and the ways they might survive for generations to come.

Like a number of Indigenous writers around New England, Tantaquidgeon Zobel came to literature by way of tribal history writing.[32] She took a semester off from her undergraduate studies in history to help with research and writing as the Mohegans were putting together their federal recognition case, won in 1994. At first, she says, "they needed something short and easy to give to the government guys."[33] But the tribe also invested in a large print run of the winningly titled booklet *The Lasting of the Mohegans* (1995), a sixty-eight-page collection of text and images that is easily the most authoritative published Mohegan history to date.[34] Later she parlayed some of this initial work into a book about Gladys Tantaquidgeon, called *Medicine Trail* (2000). She also published numerous poems and essays in anthologies. Her novels have followed the same kinds of exigent publishing histories as Hopkins's and many of Bruchac's. *Oracles*, like *Medicine Trail* before it, was published by the University of Arizona Press.[35] *Fire Hollow* was published by Raven's Wing Books, a small mystery publisher in Massachusetts that has since folded. *Wabanaki Blues* was published by Poisoned Pencil, a small publisher based in Arizona and specializing in young-adult murder mysteries; they too have folded, or at least closed to new submissions since 2016. This is the situation facing all too many talented Indigenous writers. In the early decades of the so-called Native American Renaissance (especially during the 1980s and 1990s), university presses and small independent publishers were doing most of the heavy lifting in supporting cutting-edge work by Native authors.[36] Many have since had to scale back their commitments to fiction, if they haven't shut down operations altogether, leaving Indigenous literature (and multicultural literature more generally) without reliable publishing and distribution channels. I discuss this phenomenon in greater length in chapter 4 but presage my argument here by noting that publishing returns us to questions of sovereignty and sustainability and that Indigenous authors clearly know this. Settler institutions have generally failed to produce, circulate, and validate Indigenous literature—particularly Indigenous literature of New England—leaving Indigenous communities to supply and adapt their own creative strategies of stewarding the words and stories that are most meaningful to them and that have helped them and their ecologies survive colonial violence.

Alexis Wright (Waanyi), an Aboriginal writer from Australia who has penned a climate-change novel of her own (*The Swan Book*, 2016), has said that stories are how "Indigenous people have retained knowledge through a cultural sense of what the great ancestors in the environment are telling us," that they "tie us to the land as guardians and caretakers, and the land to us as the most powerful source of law" ("Deep Weather" 73). She describes a Category 5 cyclone that tore across northern Queensland in 2011, leaving the largely Indigenous community of Palm Island unscathed. Provocatively, Wright attributes this survival (and the islanders' choice not to evacuate) to "other ways of knowing, of understanding, of feeling the land and sea, environment and its climate" (78), but she never says exactly what that particular traditional knowledge *is*. She *alludes* to ancient stories, including rock art, but she emphasizes that these "cannot be 'read' piecemeal." Rather they are "a gift from the ancestral spirits, to care for and learn from" (79). Instead of sharing this traditional ecological knowledge about extreme weather, Wright turns to an insistence on treaty. She excoriates settlers for failing to understand and communicate with Aboriginal people and for refusing to recognize and work with traditional forms of Indigenous governance. Only decolonization, she finally insists, in the form of treaties and acknowledging each other's laws, will "help create the confidence and trust required to start talking about the ancient stories of this country—that knowledge that goes back thousands of years. This is where you will find the weather charts, the records about the climate, and how the Indigenous peoples learnt how to survive on this continent" (81).

I summarize Wright's essay at a little length because I think it says something important about Native literature's approach to sovereignty and sustainability generally and is instructive for the three writers under discussion in this chapter specifically. All of these writers represent sovereignty exercised outside the parameters of formal tribal governance, in the sense of formally elected governance that is acknowledged by colonial settler rule. This is true even though two of them, Hopkins and Tantaquidgeon Zobel, have themselves been quite politically active in their federally recognized tribes. Years ago the Dakota scholar Elizabeth Cook-Lynn famously decried mainstream publishing's favoring of what she called "cosmopolitan" American Indian novels like *Love Medicine* over more tribal-centric novels like, well, her own, which explicitly depict tribal officials going about the daily business of governance and decolonization.[37] She has a point, insofar as the world is still waiting to read a novel in which, say, Narragansett activists confront state police over their right to operate a tax-free cigarette shop. Still, the novels I discuss in this chapter are deeply concerned with sovereignty, even if they do not represent it in such overt, nation-to-nation ways. Thinking of sovereignty itself as something that must be sustained and stewarded, these writers join ongoing, difficult deliberations about what constitutes sovereignty in the first place (discussions I referenced in chapter 1). Their novels illustrate how models of tribal self-governance and survival both precede and expect to outlast the vagaries of colonial state recognition.[38]

They also represent traditional ecological knowledge (or knowledge about sustainability) outside the modes of straightforward representation. These are not ethnographic accounts of sacred knowledge for settlers to ransack in hopes of saving themselves from their own destruction; they are closer to what Audra Simpson (Mohawk) calls "ethnographic refusal" (104–5). Perhaps it is undesirable to share such knowledge with outsiders; perhaps, as *Oracles* suggests, it is not even possible to share such knowledge simply and straightforwardly within one's own community. And even if it were possible to convey these things simply, what would it avail Indigenous people to do so? The narrator of "Butterfly," a young man infatuated with Ket, remarks, "At first, we hung on every word she said about how the planet was changing and we needed to change with it, in order to achieve our higher nature. Then she started rambling about honoring Mother Earth and the Sacred Waters, like her folks always do." Carpenter and her colleagues have observed this settler obtuseness as well: "Indian leaders have long tried to explain their own land use traditions to the majority society. Unfortunately their statements have been reduced, and sometimes mistranslated, into stereotypical rhetoric . . . as quaint anachronisms at best and as justifications for denying Indian property rights at worst" (1048). At some point, when Indigenous people try to explain, settlers tune out or appropriate that knowledge for their own ends. Perhaps it is *only* in literature—in long-form narrative and verbal artistry that requires people to wrestle with meaning—that sovereignty and sustainability can truly be stewarded. Perhaps, to paraphrase a well-known practitioner of the form, reports of the novel's decline are greatly exaggerated.

FOUR

Sovereign Poetics and Sustainable Publishing

Cheryl Savageau and Bowman Books Acting in Stewardship

U nbeknownst to most outsiders, Indigenous people in New England have been writing since before contact, voluminously, in a wide range of alphabetic and non-alphabetic, English- and Native-language forms. Historically a good deal of their English-language writing has been more or less instrumental: alphabetic literacy has worked to challenge colonial power, disseminate urgent calls to action, and pass on local histories and knowledge to immediate communities and future generations. As we saw in the previous chapter, however, tribal communities in New England do also contain writers who want to devote their lives to writing as a craft, who consider writing their main vocation and profession. Novelists like John Christian Hopkins have a particularly tough time of this, because novels—and *being* a novelist—are so labor- and capital-intensive, and because the support for regional Indigenous novelists is so scant.

Poetry, on the other hand, has often presented itself as more accessible to Indigenous writers in this region, including amateur writers. Poems appear in all of the tribal newsletters discussed in chapter 2; they appear in powwow flyers, in booklets Xeroxed in and disseminated from tribal offices, and (increasingly) on social-media platforms like Facebook. Poems can be easily reprinted, even retyped or rewritten by hand; they can be memorized and recited, as in the case of Mabel Avant's poems (discussed in chapter 1). Poetry presents itself as a short(er)-form, lower-capital way of exploring aesthetic concerns and values alongside the political.[1]

In the 1840s, for instance, Thomas Commuck (Narragansett) wrote to a Rhode Island judge and state legislator asking for help securing the rights to his family farm in Charlestown. His entire letter was in rhymed quatrains:

> I sougt your aid, you promis'd to,
> That you would try, what you could do,
> That you my case, would take in hand.
> And help me thus to gain my land.
> (in Senier, *Dawnland Voices* 503–5)

Despite the conventional disclaimer ("Pray don't offended be / For writing in this style to thee"), versification gives Commuck a way to illustrate the worthiness of his claim—indeed to illustrate the worthiness of his words and his very self.[2]

Many more tribal members across New England have tried their hands at verse, especially during the heyday of tribal newsletters beginning in the 1980s. One frequent contributor to the *Aroostook Indian*, Tilly West, often used poems as strategies for making literacy and the literary more inclusive. In "Aroostook Ship of Indian Future," she used a fairly common extended metaphor for the state, that of a ship:

> Ship's crew—All Indians of Aroostook County, Maine.
> Ship's items—Relics, Basketry, Crafts.
> Rough seas—Housing problems, discrimination, unemployment.
> Anchor ship with—Indian hope.
> Aroostook Ship shall sail on a wave of prayer.
> Aroostook Ship shall not sink.
> You are encrusted with Culture, weighed down with Indian heritage.
> Ship ahoy!!! Aroostook Indians.[3]

Using a quite old and self-consciously literary device and loading it with features that would be readily recognizable to her readers (racism, joblessness), West means to encourage her Native readers to give it a try. She often chooses literary devices that seem relatively easy to replicate; another of her poems, for instance, is in the form of an acrostic. Where Commuck's letter is a bid for cultural capital with a more privileged reader, West's poems try to extend that cultural capital to people who she believes deserve it.

In both of these cases, while the aesthetic remains an irreducible feature of these texts, it still takes a backseat to more overt and immediate political goals. There is, however, a new generation of Indigenous New England writers that has emerged in force since the era of the federal recognition battles. These writers seek the same kinds of wider audiences, marketability, and prestige that poets, novelists, and playwrights everywhere do. Raised in their traditional territories and attending college and graduate school (sometimes far away, sometimes closer to home), these writers have received diverse intellectual training and helped drive this period of Indigenous revitalization and resurgence. Besides Hopkins, they include the novelists Joseph Bruchac and Melissa Tantaquidgeon Zobel.

They also include numerous poets. Like the novelists, these writers have been precariously dependent on small presses and self-publishing. They include ssipsis (Penobscot), who produced two wonderful collections, *molly molasses and me* (1988) and *Prayers, Poems and Pathways* (2007), both with a small outfit in Maine that cannot keep them in print or disseminate them widely.[4] Alice Azure (Mi'kmaq/Métis descent) has published individual poems in well-respected literary magazines like *Yellow Medicine Review* and published several books of her own, largely through a relationship with Chicago-based Albatross Press. And Carol Bachofner (Abenaki) has published with a series of small presses and built a hyperlocal reputation as the poet laureate of Rockland, Maine (2012–16), where she teaches frequent workshops.[5]

This chapter looks at regional Indigenous poetry production and publishing as exercises in literary stewardship. In the first part, I discuss the career of one poet who has considerable literary prestige, Cheryl Savageau (Abenaki), who has published three books of poetry, all with highly regarded poetry presses. Savageau has received awards from entities like the National Endowment for the Arts; she was nominated for a Pulitzer Prize; she has taught at the Bread Loaf School of English. These accolades are enormous, especially since such prizes and appointments have tended to ignore Indigenous writers altogether, never mind Indigenous writers from New England. And yet winning them is no guarantee of a livable career as a writer. Like Hopkins and Tantaquidgeon Zobel, Savageau has faced distinct challenges getting her work into print and keeping it there. While writers of all races and genders obviously struggle to make a living, this is a story about how close to the edge professional Indigenous writers in New England are living, even as their work is highly valued within and beyond tribally based networks of value and respect.

The answer, for many, has been to take matters into their own hands, not just by self-publishing but also by connecting to regional Indigenous publishing networks. In the second part of this chapter, I discuss the long-running publishing enterprise sustained by Joseph Bruchac and his family. Emerging from a long tradition of Abenaki tribal publishing and printing, Bowman Books is clearly an exercise in Indigenous sovereignty; it is also a bid for cultural sustainability. Bruchac himself has used that very word to refer to Native publishing, as in his 1980 guide, *How to Start and Sustain a Literary Magazine*. There he describes sustainability as much more than mere financial viability or pragmatics: "A sustained literary magazine creates, through the years, a meeting place for our culture" (2).

Used in concert, the terms "sovereignty," "sustainability," and "stewardship" help elucidate a phenomenon not quite captured by any one of them alone: namely, the ways that some of the most marginalized yet most resilient Indigenous groups in North America have used and cherished their literature to care for their human and other-than-human relations, their home-lands, and their literary traditions themselves—the words of those who have come before and those who will come after. When Wampanoag historians write their own timelines of colonial history or Narragansett people collect and publish oral stories in a magazine, they are not just preserving these traditions in print. They are promoting their active recirculation, creating the conditions wherein these texts will be exchanged, shared, recited, and re-cited; they are helping these stories to continue stewarding tribal relations and ecologies. When a Mohegan novelist updates traditional stories about extreme weather for a broader audience concerned about climate change, she is likewise exercising her fiduciary duty of care for her people, her other-than-human kin, her traditional territory, the plan-et(s), as well as for those stories that have historically helped to steward relations among all these entities. Indigenous writ-ing calls for—and provides the occasion for—*continual recon-nection* to Indigenous community and Indigenous land. Native writing in New England has thus been centrally concerned with Native sovereignty and Native sustainability, not just because it depicts or argues for these things but because it practices and protects them.

Cheryl Savageau: Poet, Visual Artist, Memoirist

Federal recognition, as we have seen, is no guarantee of liter-ary productivity, success, or support; it's not even a guaran-tee of tribal economic support. For Hopkins, a Narragansett, recognition seems to have brought very few material rewards, though he did find a measure of employment, at least, on the *Pequot Times*, funded by the neighboring Mashantucket Pequots after their own recognition. For Mohegan writers like Tanta-quidgeon Zobel, tribal recognition does seem to have yielded a degree of economic stability and even access to intracommunity publishing.[6] No New England tribe has done what the Chick-asaw Nation has done: found a tribally operated press, which publishes dictionaries, children's books, biographies, and fic-tion. The Chickasaw model, "created in response to the basic need of the Chickasaws to own their own history," shows that tribal publishing is a matter of "cultural and intellectual sovereignty" (Chickasaw Press).

Interestingly, one of the continuous traditions of Indigenous print publishing in the Northeast comes from the unrecognized Abenaki, people whose homeland covers New Hampshire, Vermont, and large areas of eastern Maine and Quebec.[7] "Unrecognized" does not mean "unorganized" or "vanishing," of course. As the ethnohistorian John Moody explains, Abenaki governance structures were historically less centralized than those of some other tribal nations. In the view of some Abenaki people today, it is precisely this continuing decentralization that has enabled their cultural persistence and long-term survival. To be sure, as economically and politically dispossessed as they may seem compared to some of their neighbors who have won federal recognition, the Abenaki have an awful lot of published writers. There are Abenaki journalists, like Donna Laurent Caruso, who has written for the national newspaper *Indian Country Today*; historians and university-based scholars like Lisa Brooks, whose studies *The Common Pot* and *Our Beloved Kin* have been much-hailed contributions to the study of Indigenous literature; anthropologists like Margaret Bruchac, who recently published *Savage Kin: Indigenous Informants and American Anthropologists*; and many, many poets, including Carol Bachofner and Suzanne Rancourt, who has published widely in literary journals and anthologies, as well as her own book, *Billboard in the Clouds* (2004) with Curbstone Press.

Among all these Abenaki poets, and perhaps among regional Indigenous writers in toto, Cheryl Savageau has probably garnered the most literary prestige. In addition to her Pulitzer nomination, she was a finalist for the Paterson Poetry Prize and a recipient of awards from the Massachusetts Art Foundation, the McDowell Colony, and many more. Savageau grew up on Lake Quinsigamond, near Worcester, Massachusetts. Her father was French Abenaki, her mother French Canadian. She graduated from Clark University with a degree in biology and English and pursued a master's degree in American studies at the University of Massachusetts. Economically Savageau has followed the pattern of contingency that is all too familiar for writers (particularly women writers, writers of color, and people with disabilities): she has moved from job to job teaching creative writing and Native and ethnic women's literature in schools and universities, once moving across the country for a short-lived position at the University of New Mexico, as well as teaching (gallingly uncompensated) at the University of Massachusetts's Osher Lifelong Learning Institute. As a poet, however, Savageau has been quite successful. She published her first book, *Home Country*, with Alice James Books in Maine (1992); *Dirt Road Home* with Curbstone Press (2005); and *Mother/Land* (2006) with Salt Publishing. All of these presses are esteemed publishers of poetry.[8] Savageau has also written a well-received children's book, *Muskrat Will Be Swimming* (1996), which received the Smithsonian's Notable Book for Children Award as well as the Skipping Stones Book Award for Exceptional Multicultural and Ecology and Nature Books. Most recently she has completed a memoir, *Out of the Crazywoods*, about living with bipolar disorder.

For Savageau, as for the other writers I have been discussing in this book, sovereignty and sustainability are not simply themes represented in her work; they are the way she does business. Like those other writers, Savageau continually cites tribal oral traditions and other tribal people, creating poems that curate those words for future generations. It is now an accepted argument within Native American and Indigenous studies that Indigenous writing forms, be they alphabetic or nonalphabetic, are not discontinuous: the written has not replaced the oral, nor does it mark the assimilation or attrition of Indigenous cultures. Rather, Indigenous oral traditions, written traditions, and material traditions participate in mutually sustaining relations of stewardship. In this vein, Savageau works in a variety of media that are mutually sustaining, that extend the long history of Abenaki literary production and publishing. For instance, two quilts serve as companions to her poem "Red":

4. Cheryl Savageau, "Jazz Autumn." Courtesy of Cheryl Savageau;
photo © Dana Marshall Photography.

> A hundred years ago these hills were bare of trees
> the stone walls that wind through them
> the illusion of ownership Now the hills are red with maples

The "Illusion of Ownership" is all soft green and birch; "Jazz
Autumn" (fig. 4) is a fugue (her term) in vibrant reds.[9] Like the
now famous African American quilts of Gees Bend, these pieces
are signs of improvisation and resistance. They take a purport-
edly European, domestic practice and indigenize it, infusing it
with tribal concerns and aesthetics. And they take a decidedly
long view of the New England landscape. That landscape is currently marketed as a forest recreation land, but northeastern
forests are recently revived from old forests that were cleared

away for farming during the seventeenth and eighteenth centuries. Today those brilliant red maples are enjoying a resurgence as dramatic as that of Indigenous people—and (as we saw in chapter 3, in the discussion of Tantaquidgeon Zobel's fiction) as vulnerable, given the realities of climate change. In Savageau's vision, stone walls, usually considered picturesque and enduring features of the settled landscape, turn out to have a surprising impermanence.[10] She represents them by attaching strips of stony-patterned fabric to the quilt with safety pins, thus highlighting their essential remove-ability (something violently attributed to Native people).

These quilts and this poem engage in what Tom Wessels, a forester at Antioch College, calls "read[ing] the forested landscape." But where Wessels's popular handbooks show people how to read old traces of human activity (agriculture, logging), animal activity (beaver ponds), and ecological processes (blowdowns, fungus), Savageau's poems and quilts teach us to read the fragility of settler colonialism and the vibrancy of Indigenous survival. They do not do so from a position external to nature; instead Savageau emphasizes that writing, trees, and Indigenous bodies are absolutely inextricable, part of the same sustainable system. "Birch trees," she says, "are particularly important to Abenaki people because their bark provided everything from containers, to canoes, to awikhigan, our first pictographic books, which we had long before contact with Europeans" (Center for New England Culture, "The Illusion of Ownership"); recalling an idea from chapter 3 in relation to Joseph Bruchac, Savageau writes, "In Abenaki creation stories we are told that we were made from the trees, that the trees are quite literally our relatives, and their survival and ours are intimately connected" (Center for New England Culture, "Jazz Autumn").

Sustainability scientists call these kinds of interrelations "coupled human/natural systems," but Niigaanwewidam James Sinclair (Anishinaabe) goes further and calls them Indigenous poetics, insisting on the mutuality and genuine partnership of the human and other-than-human. For example, he considers the Cree/Anishinaabe word "Winnipeg" to be a form of Indig enous poetics, one that "not only embodies a place, but also its makeup and how it interacts with the world":

> Stopping to consider the power within words like Winnipeg, one quickly gets a sense with many sentient, subjective, and even competitive parts. It illustrates how we are surrounded by entities offering us chances to form independent and interdependent ties with them—and a living network. It also gestures to a world made up of balances and powers that throw this balance out of sync. In other words, we don't need cellphones, the Internet, or Facebook to show us how we are all connected, earth wind, and "dirty water" demonstrate this to us already (and do it far better). Understanding this is not easy: it's difficult, intellectual work—like trying to form a relationship with knowledge itself. This is a process requiring time, care, and consideration about geography, philosophy and science all at the same time. Winnipeg offers these kinds of gifts; it is a word that gestures to processes on how we can forge a collective and sustainable home. (207)

"Difficult, intellectual work"—work that, as Kristen Carpenter and her colleagues have argued about Indigenous models of stewardship, settlers have not been particularly inclined to do, preferring to reduce Indigenous understandings of human-ecological interrelationality to quaint anachronisms and stereotypes. Indigenous poets are one group who seek to convey these notions in forms that require us to do that intellectual work, to draw us into these ongoing "processes" to "forge a collective and sustainable future." In her powerful new memoir, Savageau poetically describes her experience with a late-life diagnosis of bipolar disorder. Mental illness is widely discussed among Indigenous people as a side effect of colonialism, and yet it is relatively underexplored in Native literature and literary criticism.[11] *Out of the Crazywoods* situates mental illness in broken colonial systems such as heteropatriarchy and lateral racism, and it looks for responses, if not "healing," in Indigenous kinship systems and ecologies.

"Stories and Storms," an excerpt published on dawnlandvoices .org, reminds one of the differing settler and Native responses to storms that Tantaquidgeon Zobel described in *Fire Hollow*. There is the superstitious response of Savageau's French Canadian grandmother, who blesses the doorways with holy water and huddles with the children, "talking about the angels washing the floors upstairs, about bowling alleys in heaven." Then there is her Abenaki father, who likes to open the windows. He explains, "If you see the lightning, it's already missed you. Thunder is just reminding you that you're safe." With this understanding, the family can experience storms on their porch and experience their part in these larger systems: "Surrounded by the wet air, the rain splashing around us, we were part of the storm, the wind, the invigorating smell." Most important, storms become the occasion for *story*: stories of other storms, stories about family, stories about local waterways, their grasses and stones. These stories, Savageau makes clear, are not just for human benefit: "The storms gave us rain and wind and the good deep breaths we took of charged air. We gave back our attention, our applause, our stories."

Here are sovereignty and sustainability exercised (stewarded) outside of the parameters of state recognition and capitalist green rhetoric. Savageau shows us a form of stewardship, pursued intergenerationally by Indigenous people in their traditional territories, as Indigenous people tell each other stories that help them make sense of the world and their place in it, that help them exercise their fiduciary duty of care toward that world. In this capacity, Indigenous poetry bears a striking resemblance to what Glen Coulthard describes as the historical Indigenous pursuit of "political and economic relations that would foster the reciprocal well-being of people, communities and land over time" (86). In their poetry, writers like Savageau seek to do this same work.

Despite winning major awards, Savageau has been shut out of some of the other kinds of recognition and support granted to other, equally talented poets (not least of these being a university job). Within Indigenous literary communities, however, she is revered. In a recent study of literary prizes and prestige, James English calls for more attention to the "neglected agents and instruments of cultural exchange" (14). He means arts prize administrators, arts endowment managers, directors of authors' historic homesteads, and other cultural heritage professionals. But if we expand that attention with specific consideration of race and colonialism in mind, we find a vast array of tribal elders, Native nonprofit directors, volunteer archivists, and others who have taken care of Indigenous writers. These include literary networks like the Wordcraft Circle of Native Writers and Storytellers, through which Savageau has mentored other writers, including Lisa Brooks and Alice Azure (Mi'kmaq). They include anthologies like Joseph Bruchac's seminal *Returning the Gift: Poetry and Prose from the First North American Native Writers Festival* (1994) and MariJo Moore's *Genocide of the Mind* (2003), which have considered New England's Indigenous writers on an equal footing with writers from more recognizably Native regions. Other Indigenous "agents of cultural exchange" include nonprofits like Gedakina, a regional organization that has been sending Savageau to Native communities around New England to run writing workshops for young women.

This is what is so compelling about regional Indigenous literary canons: that Indigenous communities—sometimes tribal, sometimes intertribal—have taken care of their writers, and been taken care of by them, when the mainstream mechanisms of literary curation and prestige have failed them. None of this is to say that Native writers do not want or deserve recognition from the likes of Knopf and the National Endowment for the Arts. It is, however, to say that as mainstream publishing and prestige-granting organizations become more vertically integrated, more commercial, and arguably more conservative, everyone interested in Indigenous writing and sustainability can learn something from the tribally based publication and dissemination strategies pursued by writers like Savageau.

Bowman Books: The Search for Sustainable Native Publishing

It's not that *nobody* is supporting Indigenous writing in New England. But those who do have been economically vulnerable, like the Mashantucket Pequot Museum. Others have been overly dependent on the vision of one person, like former Maine state senator Neil Rolde, who encouraged Tilbury House to publish books by Native authors. These include *Muskrat Will Be Swimming*, Savageau's children's book; children's books by Donald Soctomah (Passamaquoddy), Allen Sockabasin (Passamaquoddy), and Lee DeCora Francis (Penobscot); and *In the Shadow of the Eagle* (2008), Donna Loring's (Penobscot) memoir about her time in the Maine state legislature.

In addition to self-publishing platforms and small presses, New England's Indigenous authors have access to one of the longest-running Indigenous publishing enterprises in North America: Greenfield Review Press, operated by the enormously prolific Abenaki writer Joseph Bruchac. Beginning in 1971 with his wife, Carol, Bruchac was supporting Native American literature at the very moment of its emergence in the academy and in trade and scholarly publishing.[12] Greenfield has supplied steady small-press support for multicultural poetry, fiction, and nonfiction that might otherwise never have seen print. In so doing, it is continuing a tradition of Indigenous publishing that stretches back more than a century. In the late 1800s Pial Pol Wzokhilain (also known as Reverend Peter Paul Wzokhilain, or Osunkherhine) ran his own letterpress at Odanak, Quebec (Wzôkhilain and Bruchac). Two other Abenaki chiefs from the Odanak community also published books: Joseph Laurent wrote *New Familiar Abenakis and English Dialogues* (1884), and Henry Lorne Masta wrote *Abenaki Indian Grammar, Legends and Place Names* (1932). Documenting and promoting the Abenaki language and conceptions of place, these books are clearly pointed at tribal sovereignty and sustainability. In the twentieth century the Bruchac family has continued this tradition.

In a most welcome assessment of Joseph Bruchac's career, Christine DeLucia described it as moving from "rather generalized" (i.e., pan-Indian and indeed more broadly "ethnic," as Greenfield initially published a good deal of literature by African and Caribbean authors, as well as incarcerated writers) to a more "assertive defense of keeping cultural heritage materials firmly linked to their tribal-national points of origin" (88).

Today Greenfield has a new imprint, Bowman Books, devoted to Indigenous writing and oral tradition primarily from the Northeast. Raised by an Abenaki grandfather (Jesse Bowman, for whom the imprint is named and in whose house and store the press operates), Bruchac has been especially plugged in to the vibrant, enduring Native literary traditions of this region. Everyone in Native American and Indigenous studies knows Samson Occom and William Apess, but to ignore the many talented writers who are still writing here, still carrying on their legacy, is to perpetuate the myth of New England: birthplace of the new colonial nation, purged of Indians early on.

By registering the continuous presence of northeastern Native writers, Bowman Books literalizes the commonly heard refrain "We're still here." The imprint's first publication was *The Wind Eagle and Other Abenaki Stories* (1985) a collection of Gluskabe narratives told by Joseph Bruchac and illustrated by John Kahionhes Fadden (Mohawk). This partnership was a harbinger of the imprint's approach to region: sensitive to both the erasure of Indigenous people from New England yet also to the highly constructed nature of that region, Bowman Books has pulled in other Haudenosaunee writers from around its home base of upstate New York, as well as Abenaki authors located in Canada, across the artificial international border that divides them from their southern kin.

Bowman Books is a physical and metaphorical gathering place, enlisting Bruchac family members and friends across the full range of textual production, from writing and editing to printing and distribution. Bruchac's son Jesse is a key force here. He came to the project with a desire to publish more bilingual texts in the service of language revitalization as well as the technical know-how to harness the power of new print-on-demand platforms. Jesse has arrived at an eminently more affordable, and hopefully more sustainable, means of publishing by formatting authors' texts in PDF and selling them, one copy at a time, through lulu.com. His first project was the bilingual children's book *Mosbas and the Magic Flute* (2010), which he wrote and translated (loosely based on a traditional story) and illustrated with his young daughter Carolyn in an advisory role. In just four short years he has published sixteen books using this method.[13] You can feel the urgency of this project: at a 2010 conference at the University of New Hampshire (a gathering including many people named in this chapter), Joseph and Jesse discussed their print-on-demand work with reference to a problem that is all too common for Native authors and for those of us who teach this literature: "No Native writer who wants to be published should be denied the opportunity, and no Native writer who wants to remain in print should ever have to go out of print" ("Indigenous Publishing").

For the Bruchacs and other Indigenous publishers, to be sure, Indigenous publishing means more than just employing Native people to write, edit, typeset, and distribute books. It means respecting Native protocols for what should and should not be published, consulting with elders and community members, remaining mindful of traditional values. DeLucia says that Bruchac has brought together "diverse webs of thinkers for reasons inflected by more than personal standing or profit"; she conceptualizes his work as based on "reciprocal relations" (72). This phrase tellingly shares a great affinity with the phrase "network of relations," employed by Brooks throughout *The Common Pot*. These two scholars—one discussing contemporary writing, the other excavating earlier regional literary histories—provide a useful framework for understanding the work of Bowman Books as a networking project and for reading many of the individual texts it has published.

Some of Bowman Books' first publications have been devoted to language revitalization, documentation, and translation—a fitting enterprise, given Jesse Bruchac's own position as the preeminent scholar and teacher of the Abenaki language in the United States. Abenaki is an Algonquian language, and seriously endangered, but as a young man in the 1990s Jesse studied with Cecile Wawanolette (1908–2006), an elder who was teaching at the Odanak reserve in Quebec as well as in the Abenaki community at Missisquoi, Vermont. Since then he has built a significant repository of language resources at westernabenaki.com, including online lessons, YouTube videos, and recordings of the language with Wawanolette's son, Joseph Elie Joubert, with whom he works closely.

Bowman Books has already published half a dozen bilingual texts, including Joubert's *Nitami Podawazwiskweda: The First Council Fire* (2011). In his preface, Joubert expresses some of the urgency he feels in publishing: "I was fortunate to have lived in a time when the Abenaki language was still paramount. . . . Today, I can count on my fingers those who are fluent Abenaki speakers." He also expresses the urgency of maintaining the gathering place: far from romanticizing so-called precontact times, Joubert's book describes the early days of Alnôbak ("the people"), fighting over land and resources with "no laws to explain how to live in harmony with the other tribes" (5–6). After Kchi Niwaskw, the Great Spirit, vanquishes Madohodo, an evil spirit, he asks the elders "to return to that place when the leaves turned red and to bring their families to receive the gifts that will last forever" (19), in an annual ritual of feasting, hunting, fishing, and remembering "the laws that were made [that] eventually unified all the tribes" (30).

In renarrating some of the first gatherings of the people, this slim volume hearkens back to some of the earliest Abenaki-language texts. In the late nineteenth and early twentieth centuries, as now, tribal intellectuals pursued a robust publishing agenda, particularly in Quebec, where they produced a number of language books that remained in use among Abenaki people on both sides of the border throughout the twentieth century. Bowman Books has begun reprinting and retranslating some of these older books, thus rematerializing the network of relations between past and present Abenaki authors. Brooks argues that these early writers did much more than document grammar: they also conveyed tribal cosmologies, "demonstrating the continuance of names and stories associated with particular places in communal memory, even for those families who lived . . . outside the original home territory" (*Common Pot* 249). The first such book that Jesse Bruchac retranslated and republished was an 1830 Abenaki-language rendering of the

Gospel of Mark by Pial Pol Wzokhilainare, who attended Dartmouth College and returned to his home in Odanak (Wzôkhilain and Bruchac). This republication was closely followed by another, Laurent's *New Familiar Abenakis and English Dialogues*, and a reissue of Masta's *Abenaki Indian Grammar, Legends and Place Names*.

Jesse Bruchac is not just reprinting these works; he is also retranslating and recontextualizing them.[14] In his hands, these texts, and the Abenaki language, are living and dynamic. He published what he calls "the first attempt at creating a 'how-to' manual within the Abenaki language," *L8dwaw8gan Wji Abaznodakaw8gan / The Language of Basketmaking* (2010; Jesse Bruchac et al. x). This book is itself a gathering place, as Jesse wrote it with Elie Joubert and Jeanne Brink, a renowned Abenaki basket maker from Vermont. Brink has hosted language camps at her home with Jesse and Elie, so that the book helps stimulate new gatherings. Literary scholars have tended to talk about written texts as somehow preserving or freezing language, but the publication and circulation of Bowman Books' volumes shows that communities see much more complex, mutually sustaining interactions between the literary and the oral, the virtual and the face to face.

Like his father, Jesse writes and publishes for all ages. In addition to *Mosbas*, he published his brother James Bruchac's monster story, *Be Good* (2010), as well as his own retelling and retranslation of *The Woman and the Kiwakw* (cannibal giant), gorgeously illustrated with computerized renderings of birchbark art by the Passamaquoddy artist Tomah Joseph (1837–1914). There are additional bilingual texts for adult readers, including *Nisnol Siboal / Two Rivers* (2011), poems in English and Abenaki by Joseph and Jesse together. Like other Bruchac enterprises, this chapbook is deeply rooted in Abenaki but gestures to other cultures: the concept of "two rivers," the Bruchacs write in the preface, "reflects not only our two generations of father and son, but also the flow of language from two different yet deeply connected cultures." The poems are centered on each page "rather than flush left to mirror the balance we continue to seek and the flow of a stream." "N'Mahom / My Grand-father" is designed to be read aloud:

N'mahom
w'gigm8dwa
lintow8gan wji nia

lintow8gan
nd
elintoji
Mina ta mina

Grandfather
Whispers
a song to me

It's a song
I will sing
again and again. (18)

These poems seem written to be heard, and happily some of them, including "My Grandfather," can be heard on Jesse's Western Abenaki radio show (Episode 8) at westernabenaki .com, discussed in chapter 5. Bernard Perley, a Maliseet anthropologist who generally takes a pessimistic view of contemporary language revitalization efforts, argues that, despite the commonly heard criticisms of new media—that the internet and TV are to blame for the cessation of the language because they disembody communication—"we are faced with the irony that [these media forms] may actually provide the community with viable options for promoting language revitalization and cultural identity" (191), precisely because they are disembodied and available to anyone who wants to access them. The Bruchacs, and the vast network of relations involved in Bowman Books, seem to take the longer view. They have the benefit of history—a long history of a language in trouble, which has nevertheless been stewarded in a variety of forms, including YouTube and, for that matter, books.

While working steadily to steward northeastern Indigenous

language and community, Bowman Books is also making a major contribution to Native American literature with its new Native New England Authors series. Contemporary Native New England authors continue to be marginalized within both big-house and small-press publishing, a situation that contributes to something Greg Young-Ing describes in Aboriginal publishing in Canada: "It has had the effect of silencing the Aboriginal Voice paving the way for a rash of non-Aboriginal writers to profit from the creation of a body of literature focusing on Aboriginal peoples that is based on ethnocentric, racist and largely incorrect presumptions" (165).

Bowman Books' Native New England Authors series is wide-ranging, including some of the bilingual books named above (*The First Council Fire* and *Two Rivers*), some fiction, and one memoir to date. It gives pride of place, however, to regional poetry. The very first book in the series was a reprint of *When No One Is Looking* by Carol Dana (Penobscot, aka Red Hawk/pipikwass). This beautiful chapbook was first published in 1989 by Little Letterpress in Knox, Maine, which the year before had published ssipsis's *molly molasses and me*. Both books, sadly, went quickly out of print.

When No One Is Looking includes poems about broken homes and loving ones, about past traumas and present successes (e.g., the tribe's hundred-mile spiritual run up Mount Katahdin in Maine; 6), about depression ("a stillness / and loneliness / I haven't been able to shake"; 34) and gratitude ("I must say we have been fortunate / To have reached out, loved and shared / in a way uncompared"; 41). It includes many poems about women—women raising children, struggling with deserting partners, women who "stand strong, stand together" (28), and at least one enigmatic grandmother who inspired Dana's own work in Penobscot-language revitalization—a figure that fans of writers like Louise Erdrich will appreciate: "Little did I know the ladies joked about having fun, teasing, and sex / They talked about human qualities, / What the neighbors said or done" (35).

If the Abenaki-language texts demonstrate, as Brooks puts

it, "the continuance of names and stories associated with particular places in communal memory," Bowman Books' contemporary publications do the same. Dana, for instance, slides effortlessly from naming a sacred place in the first line to naming Penobscot ancestors and families:

> Kthadin, Pamola, Atahando
> Attean, Susep, Nicola
> Were people on the move
> Who laughed, loved, cried and died
> Over eons of time
> We're forever grateful to be
> from Molasses Molly, Swasson, Susep
> Francis, Neptune and Dani. (*When No One Is Looking* 9)

The Bruchacs have encouraged Dana, thankfully, to publish more of her poetry, now available in a second book, *Return to Spirit and Other Musings* (2014, No. 15 in the series). This book continues to map Penobscot homeland, history, and language, with some fully bilingual poems as well.

The Native New England Authors series also brought an established Abenaki poet, Carol Bachofner, into the fold. Bachofner has been steadily publishing her own themed chapbooks through small presses, but *Native Moons, Native Days* (2012, No. 7 in the series), her most overtly Abenaki collection, is a specific tribute to her Indigenous homeland and language. "It is important," she says in her prologue, "for the reader to be able to see [Abenaki] words as they are in the old language. A visitor may notice that New England, Ndakinna, is full of strange-looking place names, and wonder where they originate. These are words from the original language of the place. . . . For tribal people of the northeast, coming upon a place name in some version of the old language is like finding a long-lost relative in the pages of the phone book of a visited town" (6). In "We Speak the White Man's Language" she writes:

> Our words are a clearing, a place for fire.
> Where did the language go when the black robes

threw holy water on it? Did it disappear
when the switch was on our backs? Into the trees,
into the streams, into our wombs to wait. (28)

Blurring the distinction between land, fire, and Indigenous
words, Bachofner charts the violence of colonialism and of
Abenaki resilience. This is a collective project, reconstructing
Indigenous language and space in the Northeast, and a reader
can map the continuities across Bachofner's and other books
in this series. Like Jesse Bruchac, Bachofner writes about baskets ("Abazenoda, an Abenaki Basket Tale"); like Laurent and
Masta, she revels in the words for the waterways that connect
her people. This book is full of poems about water, with the
names of rivers, like the place names in Dana's poems, exercising an incantatory power:

Sebastivcook, Seninebik,
    Skowhegan, Baskahegan,
Our stories flow
Through little channels. ("Naming Water" 12)

Given the watery geography of the Northeast, and given Native
people's historic and current use of rivers and lakes as gathering places, it is not surprising that water figures so heavily
throughout the Native New England Authors series.[15] It is an
organizing motif for another series book that has received high
praise, the Maliseet poet Mihku Paul's *20th Century PowWow
Playland* (2012, No. 9 in the series). With roots that traverse
colonial borders (she is an enrolled member of the Kingsclear
First Nation in New Brunswick, though she grew up in Maine, in
Penobscot territory, and lives now in Portland), Paul celebrates
the Wolastoq (St. John River) watershed that connects Maliseet
lands and kin: "Picture this. Great rivers snake through a forest; water road, traversed in season, straining and / swollen at
ice out, moving endlessly to the sea" (1). This motif, Paul has
said, "reflects the importance of these waterways to my people, and is symbolic of time-flow, history and memory as they
function to both create and maintain identity."[16]

Paul loves to experiment with form; she has written trio-
lets, villanelles, and other older forms. "Return" is a sestina
that has the poet "travers[ing] Katahdin's rocky spine" (55),
referring again to the mountain that is sacred for all Wabanaki
groups and the location of many creation histories. Many of these
poems came out of an exhibition Paul put together in 2009 at
the Abbe Museum in Bar Harbor, Maine, a gallery focused on
Wabanaki culture. "Look Twice: The Waponahki in Image and
Verse" included Paul's poems and drawings alongside historic
photographs of Wabanaki people, including her relatives. The
poems and the photographs speak to each other, reinforcing
networks of relations between present and past Wabanaki. In
the title poem of the book, for instance, we see "two faces stare
out, children, sepia-toned, museum / quality, pressed to pages"
from a photo of Maine's hundredth-anniversary celebration:

> In 1920, a centennial celebration, time measured,
> Commemorating that moment
> When everything changed.
> A separation, renaming territory, viciously tamed,
> Carved and claimed, settled, the state of Maine. (58)

"Time-flow, history, and memory," creating and maintaining identity and community, are themes in a more recent series
publication, *Dreaming Again: Algonkian Poetry* (2012, No. 10 in
the series), by Joseph Bruchac's sister Margaret. Now an assis-
tant professor of anthropology at the University of Pennsylvania), Marge Bruchac parlays her historic research into poems
that speak to a variety of homeplaces, including Santa Fe as well
as the Adirondacks and Deerfield, Massachusetts. There are
poems devoted to historical personages like the Mohawk saint
Kateri Tekakwitha and the Wabanaki medicine woman Molly
Ockett, and poems dedicated to contemporary northeastern
Native friends (including Brooks and Tantaquidgeon Zobel).

As a scholar and performer, Marge Bruchac has been brilliant at indigenizing space, at revealing Indigenous presence
where it is has been considered invisible or a thing of the past.
A particularly beautiful instance of this is her telling of the Old

Man in the Mountain, a beloved rock formation in New Hampshire's White Mountains, which collapsed in 2003. Long known
to Abenaki people, the Old Man was "discovered" by settlers in
1805 and became a state emblem, appearing on license plates,
coins, mugs, and other kitsch. Precarious for decades, it had
been held together with chains, steel rods, and concrete gutters;
the state's famously antitax citizens also demanded a memorial or replacement for a time after it fell. In Bruchac's rendering, however, the Old Man was ready to go home:

> Ah, kadosmida,
> He is saying,
> Wligonebi, the water feels good
> The people need me. (40)

These writers take the long view. Brooks explains that the
Abenaki word for "birchbark map," *awikhigan*, came to "encom-
pass a wide array of texts, and its scope is still expanding" (*Common Pot* 249). Margaret Bruchac likewise

> look[s] to those ancestors,
> who knew how to make do, to shape whatever
> came into their hands
> whether ochre, shell, bone, paint, wool or metal.

She invites readers

> if you think you can keep your feet on a good path
> your head and your heart connected
> and your spirit intact
> no matter what language
> no matter what tools
> then send me an email
> and I'll meet you at the trailhead. (41)

This is literary stewardship that moves continually from
electronic text to "putting our bodies on the land," as Leanne
Simpson would say ("Can Fracking Showdown"). Bruchac's
lines describe what Andrea Riley Mukavetz and Malea Powell
call "Indigenous rhetorical practices": *continuous* systems of

communication, both alphabetic and nonalphabetic, that "maintain 'right' relations" with "land, animals, people, and spirits who persist here" (140–41). Moreover, with her second-person address, Bruchac engages in a very old Wabanaki practice of drawing guests and interlocutors into these right relations. In a study of eighteenth-century Wabanaki protests against the damming of the Presumpscot River in Maine, Lisa and Cassandra Brooks explain that Native survival on that river was based on a long-standing and complex web of social and ecological relationships and that "Wabanaki people strove to incorporate [colonists] into these reciprocal networks" (15). Settlers resisted, and continue to resist, but Wabanaki scholars like Brooks and poets like Bruchac continue to insist that our mutual survival will be achieved only if we are able to keep adapting and keep communicating.

The early decades of the twenty-first century are shaping into a tremendously exciting time for Indigenous poetry in the United States and Canada. As I write this, Heid E. Erdrich's just released *New Poets of Native Nations* is the No. 1 New Release in poetry anthologies on Amazon. The poets represented therein have an impressive roster of their own publications, awards, and distinctions. Layli Long Soldier (Oglala Lakota) won a 2016 Whiting Award and the 2018 National Book Critics Circle Award for poetry. Tommy Pico (Kumeyaay) won a 2018 Whiting Award and numerous prestigious fellowships. Natalie Diaz (Mojave) has won Lannan and Ford fellowships. She also reviewed Long Soldier's *Whereas* for the *New York Times Book Review*, a welcome change from its historic neglect of Indigenous reviewers.[17]

More and more Indigenous writers, then, seem to be gaining access to what James English called those "agents and instruments of cultural exchange": prizes, awards, fellowships, teaching appointments, reviews in influential newspapers. Regrettably, Indigenous writers from New England are not yet quite gaining this access. The disappointment, locally, that not one poet from New England was included in *New Poets of Native Nations* has been palpable. The frustration of writers like Savageau and Hopkins, who could be even more prolific with a modicum of material support, is painful. The difficulty these writers have had just in finding agents calls to mind something especially dispiriting that Elizabeth Cook-Lynn has observed: that "Native American writers, as a result of editorial and agented assistance in getting their manuscripts accepted, assume that under such strict circumstances their own efforts toward the recovery of memory through writing seem thwarted" (80). The continuing occlusion of Indigenous New England, as the tides seem to be rising for Indigenous writers elsewhere across North America, demonstrates that we remain, as Joyce Rain Anderson puts it, "thoroughly soaked in . . . a single story of how [America] began" (162).

Regionally, however, Indigenous writers *do* have their own established mechanisms of circulating cultural value. To borrow a truism often heard among scholars and heritage professionals concerned with *cultural sustainability*, storytelling and verbal art are practices in which humans have engaged, and will continue to engage, transculturally and transhistorically—no matter where they live, or when. The question, then, is really what kinds of *institutions* we create to value, archive, and continue these practices. We might say that Euro-American literary history, and the most prestigious literary awards and institutions, have been rather single-minded about preserving and canonizing individual authors and individual works. We might ask how sustainable that practice really is. It takes a vast amount of economic and human capital to keep even a single book in print, in classrooms, and in libraries in its infinite iterations.[18] This is not to be glib about the fact that too many Native-authored books go out of print almost the minute they are published; it's not to say, of course, that writers don't need to eat.

But what is remarkable about the intervention of the Bruchacs—the Bowman Books imprint and the accompanying array of digital media and face-to-face classes and events—is that it sustains very old mechanisms for stewarding tribal literary histories. Print-on-demand is a far from perfect technology, but it comes closer to ecological responsibility than the mainstream book publishing industry and its practice of over-printing and pulping books. Moreover it is only one of many interlocking strategies. The Bruchacs have firsthand experience with the fragility and waste of both print and electronic media. Joseph Bruchac's second novel, *The Dreams of Jesse Brown*, is nearly unavailable today since the publisher, Cold Mountain Press, went out of business and the warehouse where all copies of the book were being stored had a fire.[19] Greenfield Review Press lost its entire electronic catalogue in a computer crash. The Bruchacs thus use their book publishing and websites to draw people into face-to-face exchanges like Jesse's language classes and events at their Ndakinna Education Center, again "putting their bodies on the land" while also sharing stories and the books themselves. There is no overinvestment here in any one medium, no hypercanonization of any one text or author. Like Wampanoag timelines and tribal newsletters, these are lower-capital, interlocking methods of making literature steward human and ecological relationships and of allowing those human and ecological relationships in turn to steward the literature.

Publishers like the Bruchacs, along with writers like Savageau, Hopkins, and Tantaquidgeon Zobel, are finding ways of bypassing the usual capitalist and nation-state mechanisms for getting their work disseminated and recognized. Even though, individually, many of these writers have experienced significant personal strife and economic hardship, this is in fact an exciting time for Indigenous literature in New England. We are seeing a profusion of new writing, new publishing, mentoring initiatives, and community readings—all firmly grounded in the reconstruction of tribal community and the reassertion of responsibility to tribal lands, histories, and futures. This is perhaps another paradox of Indigenous resurgence (to borrow Waziyatawin's phrasing once more) and another story of sovereignty and sustainability: that just as the death of the book is being widely declared, New England's Native people seem to be experiencing their own literary renaissance.

FIVE

Indigenous New England Online

Network Sovereignty and Digital Stewardship

As the previous two chapters illustrate, Indigenous authors, like authors everywhere, are increasingly turning to digital methods of creating, sharing, and archiving their work. Print publishing is not getting any cheaper or easier for them, despite the existence of print-on-demand platforms like lulu.com and Amazon's CreateSpace. Most regional Native writers who self-publish still do so at considerable financial risk to themselves; certainly none of the writers discussed in this book, or represented in *Dawnland Voices*, is making a robust living from writing alone.

Still, books like Joan Avant's *People of the First Light* and John Christian Hopkins's *Carlomagno* represent significant achievements for these writers and their communities. Digital platforms have given these authors new opportunities not only for publication of their own work but also for the exercise of literary stewardship, as their communities disseminate, curate, remix, and protect their long literary histories. For these authors, electronic publishing is seldom a matter of simple self-expression; it helps them exercise what the multimedia artist Cheryl L'Hirondelle (Métis/Cree) would call the imperative to "publish, distribute, and disseminate . . . in order to sustain life and ensure our world views continue to be accessible and viable survival tools for future generations." On this matter of digital cultural sovereignty, L'Hirondelle quotes fellow Métis/ Cree artist Ahasiw Maskegon-Iskwew: "To govern ourselves means to govern our stories and our ways of telling stories. It means that the rhythm of the drumbeat, the language of smoke signals and our moccasin telegraph can be transformed to the airwaves and modems of our times. We can determine our use of the new technologies to support, strengthen and enrich our cultural communities" (qtd. in L'Hirondelle 147).

Like the Wampanoag historians, tribal newsletter writers, and others I have been discussing throughout this book, L'Hirondelle and Maskegon-Iskwew see newer media iterations as continuations of their oldest communicative practices— practices that have for millennia helped their communities survive and that are embedded in much larger ecosystems. Digitization touches on both sovereignty and sustainability. To be sure it is often framed—in environmental studies, media studies, archives, and libraries—as a sustainability issue, as people worry about the sustainability *of* our many electronic gadgets, tools, and platforms. Computers and smartphones, we know, exact terrible environmental and human costs, from conflict-mineral extraction and labor abuse to mounting electronic waste. Social media and electronic publishing platforms, meanwhile, often seem incredibly fly-by-night, and large-scale digital projects like web archives are often dispiritingly labor- and resource-intensive. Digital activity also always begs the question of how much energy it uses and of what ultimately happens when the power goes out.[1]

Thus when Indigenous people in New England use digital tools, they do so not out of any technophilic hope that e-books and web archives are the answer or the future but as one means among many of stewarding a wide variety of reading and writing artifacts and practices. It is no coincidence that, as the pressures of globalization have so many people concerned about preserving biodiversity and ecological stability, many are also concerned about cultural diversity and preservation. Digitization is seen as one new way to preserve writing and make it accessible and available for the future; it is one place where the field of cultural heritage management (or historic preservation) meets *cultural sustainability*. We are thus seeing an explosion of new works about and new terms for sustainability in the cultural arena. Heritage management. Heritage preservation. Curation. In this chapter I continue preferring the term "stewardship" as a way of eliciting that sense of fiduciary responsibility to objects and to the landscapes and human and other-than-human communities in which those objects are reciprocally embedded.

For Indigenous people, cultural and ecological sustainability efforts are not merely analogous or parallel; they are utterly interdependent. Just as they used timelines, newsletters, poetry, and other forms of alphabetic literacy in concert with oral traditions, heritage sites, and sacred sites, so too do they deploy digital expression only as part of much larger media ecosystems—as part of larger human-natural ecosystems, period. A Penobscot activist group uses Facebook to recirculate a traditional narrative about water monsters and thus galvanize activism around the Penobscot River; a young Passamaquoddy poet converses with ancestors and other-than-humans at a sacred petroglyph site and publishes verse in a digital magazine that can draw her community protectively around that site; tribal museums scan and share their treasured print documents and reconvene tribal members for ceremonies and other face-to-face exchanges. It is not my claim that Native communities are exceptional in using digital media to broker activism or other gatherings; rather, it is that they are exceptionally intentional about the interrelations among their communication media, their larger communities, and their land bases. Even if land is not the direct subject of their writing and media productions, it is never far behind. This is not just media ecology, but what Steven Loft (Mohawk) proposes we call media *cosmology*, or

an Indigenous view of media and its attendant processes that incorporates language, culture, technology, land, spirituality and histories. . . . The phrase "all my relations" is often used to express the interaction of all things within an evolving, ever-changing social,

cultural, technological, aesthetic, political, and environmental intellectual framework . . . and can certainly be applied to the landscape
of media. Cosmological intellectual ecosystems exist as media, as
message, and as a form of knowledge transferal. They are epistemological environments wherein notions of nationhood are inter-
spersed with, connected to, and integrated with a larger sense of
the plurality of life. (Loft and Swanson xvi)

This formulation explicitly repoliticizes the notion of inter-
connectedness, an idea often invoked in sustainability discourse
and in talk *about* Indigenous people but less often understood
in the context of extractive settler colonialism. Indigenous writers online are seeking nothing less than a total transformation of the ways that digital media represent them and their
intellectual property, nothing less than a reassertion of their
collective rights to self-determination over their cultural *and*
natural resources. The explosion of new web-based platforms
has arisen alongside a global Indigenous resurgence movement, marked by rising protests around incursions against
tribal governance, violence against Native women, and disastrous development proposals like the Keystone XL pipeline.
Twitter campaigns such as #IdleNoMore and #MMIW (Missing
and Murdered Indigenous Women) have brought global attention to contemporary sovereignty and sustainability struggles.[2]
Across the globe Indigenous writers are taking to the blogosphere, speakers and performers are taking to YouTube, and
musicians are taking to SoundCloud.[3] In New England, tribes
are running their own websites to narrate their own histories,
using electronic tools to aid in language revitalization and heritage preservation, and turning to Facebook to mobilize activism and share their cultural heritage materials.

The visibility and empowerment of Indigenous people are
no more guaranteed in cyberspace, however, than they are in
real space. Many observers find, as does Angela Haas (Eastern Cherokee descent), that in digital space too "global colonial
rhetorics work to reduce the plurality of ongoing, contemporary, complex, and diverse American Indian cultures to one

uniform, flat, static, prehistoric, and ancient culture" (192). For every #NotYourMascot there is a #SavetheChief; for every Ryan McMahon there is a *Revenant*. Haas and other Indigenous scholars therefore call for decolonizing digital space. In this chapter I trace some of the successes and struggles that New England's Indigenous communities have experienced as they try to indigenize or decolonize digital space. I am not prom- ising any kind of comprehensive survey, only offering a small number of representative projects that illuminate the relations between sovereignty and sustainability. In Haas's formula- tion (riffing on Scott Lyons's idea of "rhetorical sovereignty"), "American Indians want *digital and visual rhetorical sover- eignty*, too, or 'the inherent right and ability . . . to determine their own communicative needs and desires, to decide for them- selves the goals, modes, styles, and languages of public dis- course' in digital spaces and visual media" (197). Marisa Elena Duarte goes even further and calls this *network sovereignty*, or the ways that "Native and Indigenous peoples leverage infor- mation and technology to subvert the legacies and processes of colonization as it manifests over time across communities in many forms" (14–15).

The phrase "network sovereignty" has a richness and reso- nance for thinking about the interplays among sovereignty, sus- tainability, and stewardship. The ability of Indigenous people to exercise their sovereignty can never be separated from the question of resources, whether they are confronting the impe- rial extraction of their lands and minerals or the extraction of their languages and history in cyberspace. In this horri- ble neoliberal era, with relentless cuts to public funding and assaults on cultural heritage, we find communities the world over, from the national to the local, now asking pointed ques- tions about what is being sustained and saved—for whom, by whom, and why. In this chapter's final section I discuss some of the politics of digital archiving and ponder why such archiving might be happening more traditionally or even sustainably on social media platforms like Facebook and independently hosted projects than in some of the better-resourced, university- and museum-based digital projects. These questions bring us full circle to issues of sovereignty and sustainability.

Timelines on Tribal Websites

A critical exercise in digital rhetorical sovereignty is the tribal website, sanctioned by tribal leaders, carefully vetted for accuracy of information. There is much to be said about tribal websites, but I focus here specifically on how some New England tribal websites redeploy a form I discussed in chapter 1: the timeline as a genre that helps reconnect Indigenous communities to each other and their land. Beginning with that 1620 master narrative, in chapter 1 I argued that Wampanoag people have used chronologies—oral, print, and electronic—to challenge colonial historiography, which has buttressed the expropriation of Indigenous lands and resources, ecological as well as cultural. Wampanoag timelines are ways of reasserting the continuous presence of Wampanoag people as distinct cultural communities in their distinct territories. They provide a way of representing the Indigenous longue durée (Clifford, "Varieties of Indigenous Experience" 199), or, if you like, the sustainability of this particular community, in this particular place.

The Penobscot Nation Cultural & Historic Preservation Department achieves something similar on its own substantive website, which includes a page labeled "Tribal Timeline." Among other things, this website realizes the mandate of Maine's LD-291, An Act to Require Teaching of Maine Native American History and Culture in Maine's Schools, authored by Donna Loring (Penobscot) while she was a tribal representative to the state legislature. Pedagogy and sustainability are therefore deliberately intertwined in this chronology. It begins in 12,000 BP, situating Penobscot people in their territory thousands of years before the arrival of European settlers. It puts European exploration in Indigenous perspective by noting the first *documented* contact in 1524. The timeline leads up to 2004, with the establishment of the Penobscot River Restoration Trust.

We might say, in fact, that this entire timeline underscores Penobscot survivance—construing "Penobscot" as the people *and* their river—amid ongoing global resource wars. It enumerates early arrivals of various explorers from Spain, France, and England; the escalation of wars over fur and land; and the codification of treaties. It charts the vicissitudes of colonial control, as the Penobscots make treaties with the Massachusetts colony and are then subject to the laws and interference of Maine after it becomes a separate state in 1820. It also charts Penobscot people's cultural survival and adaptability, noting, for instance, the labor of tribal members as river guides for Henry Thoreau. Finally, the timeline illustrates that throughout these many centuries, Penobscot people have taken every conceivable step—legal, economic, cultural—to reassert their connection to their river. This timeline is not a one-off; it offers dates and ways of seeing Penobscot history that are recirculated in other arenas, including Penobscot uses of new media.

Some other New England tribes have chosen more narrative histories for their websites rather than bulleted chronologies. Under a tab for "History," the Narragansett Indian tribe offers links to short essays emphasizing tribal persistence amid illegal colonial actions. The first, "Early History," echoes the assertion of long and continuous presence articulated on the Wampanoag and Penobscot websites: "Archaeological evidence and the oral history of the Narragansett People establish their existence in this region more than 30,000 years ago. This history transcends all written documentaries and is present upon the faces of rock formations and through oral history." As I discussed in chapter 2, Narragansett people deploy multiple literacies— oral, alphabetic, and geographic—to tell and sustain their history; this website adds digital literacy to that rich mix of media ecologies. The Mohegan Indian tribe also uses narrative history on its website but chooses to organize this history around individual leaders rather than periodicity.[4] Unlike many Western histories organized around the stories of great men, however, this one embraces both the male leaders and intellectuals recognized by colonial authorities and the female leaders recognized by the tribe. It is an intriguing intervention, as Indigenous and settler historians have insisted that in many tribes the world over women exercised significant leadership roles before colonization. The Mohegan timeline, however, emphasizes male representatives *earlier* in tribal history and female leaders later. One set of links for "Our History" leads visitors to Sachem Uncas, Samson Occom, and Fidelia Fielding. A link for "Our Ceremonial Leaders" takes visitors to short descriptions of the roles of lifetime chief (currently Dr. Lynn Malerba) and medicine woman (currently Melissa Tantaquidgeon Zobel), followed by pipe carrier and firekeeper. The effect, visually and narratively, is to balance male and female, and even to emphasize female leadership in the present and future. This arrangement is undoubtedly informed by what Tantaquidgeon Zobel has described as Mohegan women's sociocultural leadership, a system wherein women exercise profound power within the tribe, whether or not they have been recognized by settlers as leaders (Fawcett-Sayet). The arrangement of links and information also cannily suggests that gender equality is at the heart of Mohegan tribal sustainability.

Jodi Byrd (Chickasaw) has urged us to consider critically the ways that forms of colonialism persist on the internet, riddled as it is with metaphors of "digital natives" and "new frontiers." She excoriates "the illusion that new and improved American tribal interests have superseded if not entirely replaced Indigenous peoples. Tribal 2.0 if you will" ("Tribal 2.0" 59). Tourist websites create such tribes, often without any reference to even romantic stereotypes of autochthonous inhabitants. The website for visitors to Plymouth Rock, stunningly, elides the whole story of the first Thanksgiving, blithely asserting that whether or not historical records are accurate, this "simple glacial erratic boulder has become a world famous symbol of the courage and faith of the men and women who founded the first New England colony."[5] These myths persist as well on both sides of the international border that divided northeastern tribal peoples from their kin: the website Discover St. John invites new explorers to "discover Wolastoq," a term "that means 'the beautiful river' in the language of the Maliseet people who once lived on *our* shores" (italics mine)—something contemporary Mali-

seet people would surely be interested to know.[6] Tribal timelines remain, as Byrd would have it, "a powerful analytic tool
with which to confront, challenge, and reconfigure the stories colonizers like to tell about themselves and their place in
the world" ("Tribal 2.0" 62). Like the Wampanoag books and
pamphlets that challenged federal disclaimers of Wampanoag
survivance, these electronic timelines challenge the obsessive
colonial "firsting and lasting" (to borrow Jean O'Brien's terms)
that persist in supposedly new frontiers.

Language Projects

After official tribal websites, language documentation and revitalization initiatives probably represent the largest proportion
of currently visible Indigenous digital activity based in New
England, and they show how Native linguists, activists, and
writers are working to sustain their languages in concert with
their material culture, histories, and land bases. Language revitalization movements have been growing worldwide, and many
regional tribal nations now offer real-time classes, immersion
schools, and print resources as well as online dictionaries and
web portals. Probably the best known is the Wôpanâak Language Reclamation Project (wlrp.org), founded by the MacArthur
scholar Jessie Little Doe Baird and the subject of the award-
winning documentary *We Still Live Here*. Perhaps emboldened
by the success of this project, which now has a dozen certified
Wampanoag-language teachers and an immersion school, others have followed suit. The Passamaquoddy have a new immersion school; a language portal of their own (pmportal.org), which
includes a dictionary, videos, and reference documents; and
a mobile app, available only to tribal members, that includes
audio examples, quizzes, and games.[7] The Mohegan Language
Project (moheganlanguage.com) includes lessons, exercises,
and audio. Like the Wôpanâak Language Reclamation Project,
it was started by a graduate of MIT's Indigenous Language Ini-
tiative, Stephanie Fielding.

   As these examples suggest, current language sustainability
efforts are heavily digitally mediated. One linguist argues that,

while in and of themselves, digital media "cannot secure the future of [Indigenous] languages, their role in language maintenance and revitalization cannot be ignored" (Moriarty 447). We might reiterate that Indigenous people have always known they could not look to a single technology as the savior of any facet of culture, that they have always seen language revitalization as deeply embedded in other cultural *and* ecological efforts. Consider the work of Jesse Bruchac, discussed in the previous chapter. Bruchac has been republishing historic Abenaki dictionaries and language primers not simply as language preservation tools but also as tools for reuniting Abenaki people with their land bases (which are quite literally mapped in these dictionaries) and their ecologies (e.g., the dictionaries help recirculate Indigenous terms for humans and other-than-humans).[8] In so doing, Bruchac is capitalizing on what the digital theorist Alan Liu calls "thick affordances between media regimes" (11). Despite many scholars' desire for linear narratives of technological and communicative progress, Liu argues, different media—orality, writing, broadcasting, internet, and so on—have historically always overlapped, contradicted, and worked with and against each other in multiple and simultaneous directions.

In keeping with Loft's notion of a media cosmology, we might consider how these affordances work not only across media regimes but also in concert with "language, culture, technology, land, spirituality and histories." For instance, Bruchac's website, westernabenaki.com, offers online language lessons and also brokers face-to-face language camps. The radio show includes fifteen episodes, each ten minutes or less, entirely in Abenaki. Bruchac assures his listeners, "Chaga nda kd'aln-8ba8dwaw, chaga nda k'wawtamowen, akwi saagidah8ziw! If you don't speak Indian, if you can't understand, don't worry! K'kizi askwa ibitta tbestam ta wig8damen. You can still just listen and enjoy it." The goal is nothing less than an Abenaki soundscape. You can hear a traditional Gluscabe story, an announcement for a powwow, a recorded phone call between Bruchac and his father, an interview with elder Cecile Wawanolette. You can also hear Bruchac read a story about Turtle written by

Wzokhilain in 1839, never before translated into English (or, as Bruchac says, "Kwin8gwi / 8da kizi n'namitowen, / At least / I haven't seen it, / askwatta/ yet" (episode 10).[9]

In effect, the website is an intergenerational gathering space linking Abenaki people across their traditional territory. With his family and elders, Bruchac stages conversations whose participants extend beyond different media forms (video and audio); these are conversations among distant ancestors and future generations. This implies a view of the internet itself as (to quote Loft once more) "a space populated by our ancestors, our stories, and, in a wider way, ourselves" (Loft and Swanson 172). "Cyberspace," Loft continues, "connects the past to the present and the spiritual to the material in ways that would make our elders laugh. They've always known this" (175). Indeed media theorists today like to celebrate the ways that digital and especially mobile technologies are amplifying the affordances among media regimes, conferring agency to objects.[10] Bruchac and his Abenaki relatives seem to have anticipated these circulations. Joseph Laurent, documenting the transition in the word *awikihiganak* from originally denoting birchbark maps to also referring to print books, clearly saw the intimate connections between trees and humans, between cartographic and alphabetic literacies, and between cultural and ecological sustainability. Bruchac's books, CDs, and hyperlinks are thus participants in a much broader network that includes Abenaki community members and Abenaki landscapes, which create a community around these books, CDs, hyperlinks, and physical links in language camps.

Sound obviously plays an important role in language instruction and acquisition, but it is important too in sovereign and sustainable media cosmologies and Indigenous ecologies. As one Indigenous language activist puts it, "The spoken language is a cherished intellectual treasure. Each sound captures how we see the world" (Ernest). In his performances, language camps, and digital communications, Bruchac apprehends the importance of *hearing* a language—even piecemeal—as a powerful affective experience. His radio show and YouTube channel aim to effectively create or contribute to an Abenaki soundscape. As we saw in the previous chapter, he teaches people how the language reconnects people to their land bases; he also teaches them to recognize how it connects them to each other: "Aln-8banaki waj8nemak kwinatta wd'alamitoal lintow8ganal. The Abenaki have many greeting songs. Kw8gweni gez8wado wji maahl8mek. Because of the importance of gathering together" (episode 3).

It is purposeful that, like the Indigenous language primers in print, so many of the digital language projects make a point of teaching words about nature. The Mohegan language project has a link devoted to a list of animal names, with MP3 files of the words being spoken; the Wôpanâak Language Reclamation Project site has a "Fun with Words" page that emphasizes place names as well as "pumpkin," "skunk," "moose." Its home page quotes Jessie Little Doe in an articulation of Wampanoag media cosmology: "This is but one path which keeps us connected to our people, the earth, and the philosophies and truths given to us by the Creator." These exercises might strike some scholars raised on Shephard Krech's attack on "the ecological Indian" as unduly romantic or infantilizing, but it is impossible to deny that the destruction of Indigenous languages was a colonial tool for destroying Indigenous communities and expropriating Indigenous lands. Teaching a Native word for "water," for "the people," and holding language classes in Native space are ways for these communities to do what Leanne Simpson says is the most radical act of all: "The only thing left to do is to put our bodies on the land."

Facebook: Protest and Archiving

To put their bodies on the land, Indigenous people in New England have also used that now universally loathed platform: Facebook. But while critics of social media have long (and rightly) worried about their promotion of antisociality, many marginalized communities do continue to use it to convene people for real-time events.[11] Indigenous people in New England are now using it, as they have used their historic newsletters, to reconvene lost communities. The most dramatic example may be the St. David's Islanders and Native Community Facebook group. This formed after a series of physical reunions, dating back to 2001, between Wampanoag and Narragansett people with their relatives in the West Indies, where so many had been sold into slavery in the seventeenth century (Jim Adams), and it has been documenting and facilitating further reunions and kinship rebuilding.

In Maine the page for the Dawnland Environmental Defense served as a prompt to and record of Indigenous resistance to state assaults on Indigenous sovereignty and sustainability. In 2012 the Maine state attorney general attempted to assert that the Penobscot reservation (which, under terms of the 1980 Maine Indian Claims Settlement Act, includes over two hundred islands in the main stem of the Penobscot River) does not include the *water* surrounding the islands. The Penobscot tribe sued the state on the grounds that the tribe has "relied upon subsistence fishing and hunting on the river from time immemorial." In so doing, the Penobscots were quite deliberate about the inextricable connection between ecological sustainability and "the right to continue to practice our culture as a riverine people." They noted, "Part of that culture is that we take our sustenance from the river and its resources, as well as the lands which form our Aboriginal territory" (Chavaree). Reinforcing the connection between their lands and their identity as distinctive people, they have a locally popular refrain: "When the river's gone we are gone."

On December 28, 2014, the tribal historian Maria Girouard launched the Dawnland Environmental Defense Facebook page. It called the group "an alliance of Native and non-Native peoples united in the protection of the Dawnland with particular focus on the sacredness of Water," and its success has been striking. Like many Facebook pages, this one enabled virtual activism (e.g., MoveOn petitions), but it also announced and convened face-to-face gatherings like rallies and festivals. It alerted people when a particular issue was up for discussion at a local town meeting, and it reported on results. For instance, the page helped organize and celebrate a series of flotillas, groups of Penobscot paddlers and their allies bringing awareness to the cause. They were putting their bodies on the land, in this case, *in* and along the river—a *grounded* action that highlighted the absurdity and violence of the state's attempt to divide an ecosystem into land versus water, territory versus culture.

The Facebook page took full advantage of multimedia to reinforce this understanding. For instance, it posted a link to a 2014 video, *In Our Veins*, which interviews tribal leaders about the relationships between the people and the river. John Banks, director of the tribe's Department of Natural Resources, reflects on Penobscot sustenance fishing as a way of life that worked for twelve thousand years and that has really only been "dormant," in his words, for about one hundred. Banks sees the river "coming back" due to restoration efforts, including dam removal. This again is the Indigenous longue durée: a sense that it is indeed possible to reverse some of the disruptions of settler colonialism, to reclaim older ways of being with and in this river system.

Like the tribal newsletters discussed in chapter 2, the Dawnland Environmental Defense Facebook page also participated in the recirculation of a very old Penobscot story. The story describes the origin of the Penobscot River: after a severe drought that was starving the people, the culture hero Gluskabe clubbed the frog monster who had been hoarding all the water, releasing its mighty flow. Recorded in the early twentieth century by the anthropologist Frank Speck (7), this story began appearing in a variety of new media at the end of the century. In 1994, for instance, Penobscot children (grades 3–8) at the Indian Island School featured it in an animated video using clay and paper cutouts. Four years later, in an interview with a local paper, the tribal elder Arnie Neptune told the story in the context of the Maine tribes' lengthy battles with the state over water quality issues. The reporter noted that Neptune "compare[d] the state to the giant frog."[12] In January 2015 the Dawnland Environmental Defense page announced, "Like the Frog Monster who gobbled up all the Water, Nestle is hellbent on gobbling the Water of the Dawnland. . . . Below is important information from Dawnland Environmental Defense's partner in Water respect & protection, Community Water Justice. . . . 'Water sovereignty,' ~ a term worth having in our vocabulary as we move into the future."

The Potawatomi biologist Robin Kimmerer asserts that Indigenous sustainability methods depend as heavily on *narrative* as on living, ecologically minded practice: "Cautionary stories of the consequences of taking too much are ubiquitous in Native cultures" (179). Settlers often mis-hear Indigenous origin stories as charming etiological tales or as depoliticized representations of the idea that Indians took only what they needed, as though Native people's practices existed in the remote past and might, in relatively vague terms, somehow save modernity from itself. The Penobscot multimedia circulations of the frog monster story, however, suggest that, in addition to teaching Penobscot people how to relate to their river reciprocally and therefore sustainably, the story has also come to signify tribal sovereignty, a twentieth-century allegory for relations with the state and/or transnational corporations. Such resignifications are by no means unique to Indigenous stories, but what is unique here is that the meanings of this story also go beyond mere allegory, where the frog simply stands in for something else. As the story re-places Penobscot people not just imaginatively but also politically and physically in their river, it enlists a vast communicative network in which actual water and actual frogs have communicative agency as surely as humans and Facebook pages do. Whereas media ecology may understand "ecology" as more or less a metaphor for the ways that media systems interact, media cosmology sees human communication as reciprocally embedded in those natural and spiritual ecologies.

Political theorists who have studied social media and protest movements are often concerned about whether such movements represent only short-term disruptions to global power. "In the long run," says one, "it is new institutional actors that are needed if new directions of political action are to be sustained" (Couldry 43). My guess is that Penobscot people might counter that they already have their institutional actors, in the form of their river, their oral traditions, and their long-standing reciprocal practices of land and community care—that institutions like the attorney general's office and even the Department of Education, while they can be fruitfully engaged or challenged, are relatively recent arrivals in the Indigenous longue durée. Thus what another theorist calls "augmented revolution" (Jurgenson)— the heady combination of social media and aggregated physical protests in geographic space—is arguably not new at all, from an Indigenous perspective, if we consider that material "codes" like wampum belts and "virtual" stories like oral traditions have historically connected people to their lands and to each other while also being mobilized for political protest. "New" networks like those found on Facebook and Twitter may feel like they represent a departure from what has gone before, but Native people, as I have been arguing, have never overinvested in a single technology—not Twitter, newsletters, or for that matter wampum belts—nor have they even overinvested in the human. Networks with the other-than-human, and with their distant ancestors and future generations, are what have formed the basis of their sustainability and their sustainability politics.

Reviled and problematic though it may be, Facebook, for a host of reasons, is at this time something of a preferred digital gathering place for Indigenous New England. Such authors as Melissa Tantaquidgeon Zobel (Mohegan), Donna Roberts Moody (Abenaki), and Maggie Dana (Passamaquoddy) post regularly; they debate tribal politics, share notices about upcoming gatherings, and post photographs of family and tribal events. Certain newsletters, including *Nipmucspohke*, now exist as Facebook groups, this format being much easier to maintain and likely better-read than some print formats.[13] Additionally, tribal museums and historic preservation officers use Facebook to inform their communities of events. Periodically they will post images from their collections—historic documents and photographs, even MP3s and video—and invite tribal members to identify the people in the pictures, fill in the context for historic events, and share their enthusiasm for tribal history and documentation. Cheryll Toney Holley, the Nipmuc chief and historian, regularly posts photographs of items from her archival searches, including a 1930 letter from Gladys Tantaquidgeon (Mohegan) to the mother of Zara Ciscoe Brough (Nipmuc).[14] For a time, the Tantaquidgeon Museum in Connecticut offered "Facematch Fridays," quizzing community members to identify people in historic photos. The Passamaquoddy Cultural Heritage Museum similarly posts pictures of important tribal leaders, as well as cherished tribal places.

In many of these cases, the tribal historians posting these images already know the identities of the people in the photographs, the dates on which they were taken, and other basic cataloguing information. What they are really trying to elicit are community memories and community investment in their collections. As Ramesh Srinivasan and a team of researchers including the Zuni archivist Jim Enote have argued, digital objects can serve "as a key rallying point for cultural revitalization." They "offer a flexibility, mobility, and extensionality," and as such they are "ideal for projects related to cultural revitalization and collaboration" (Srinivasan et al. 758). Everyone looking at these objects on Facebook realizes that they are not "the real thing"; the occasion of sharing photographs of tribal elders or treasured objects, of gathering stories about these, and of infinitely sharing that multimodal information contributes to the larger project of sovereignty and sustainability. Indeed there is a growing awareness among many museums and heritage institutions these days that "the usual metadata approach is insufficient," as it is geared only toward "management of [these objects] within an institutional paradigm, and [thus] omits the possibility of sharing diverse narratives and knowledges" (Srinivasan et al. 760). Conversely, digital copies can actually do things that physical collections sometimes cannot: they "can stimulate grassroots participation and enable previously marginalized communities to actively lead and take ownership of cultural heritage objects on their own behalf" (747–48).

The Tantaquidgeon and Passamaquoddy Facebook pages are examples of *indigenizing* metadata. They are gathering not

Library of Congress–ready and machine-readable fields but tribally specific ways of remembering, seeing, and categorizing these items. Facebook is obviously fraught in other ways, not least of which is the monetization of personal data and the fact that it does not make all of this information readily searchable or storable by tribal museums. This is a sustainability and sovereignty issue of a different kind, one to which I return toward the end of this chapter.

Decolonizing Archives

With tribal museums' use of Facebook to share their images, we have entered the world that some have called "Archives 2.0," where electronic innovation and social media meet the desire for more democratic record-keeping and public memory.[15] Antoinette Burton says there are now "hundreds, perhaps thousands of . . . archive enterprises taken up by groups who believe that their histories have not been written because they have not been considered legitimate subjects of history—and hence of archivization per se" (Burton et al. 2). Local communities, families, and special-interest groups have always pursued the impulse to collect their own materials, but the presence of new digital media—and of new digital tools designed to help people store and share such materials—seems to offer exciting new possibilities for recirculating community content, maybe even for redistributing the power to curate that content. It should be readily evident that, for Indigenous people, "the power to curate" is a sovereignty issue; it involves what Angela Haas and Scott Lyons refer to as Native peoples' "inherent right and ability . . . to determine their own communicative needs and desires." It is also a sustainability issue, insofar as digitally curated materials, like print materials, speak to the centuries-long endurance of Indigenous people in their homelands. The fields of cultural heritage management and historic preservation now routinely talk of "cultural sustainability," partly because "management" and "preservation" are such vexed and loaded terms, but more substantively because cultural preservation so often butts up against ecological and economic concerns: extreme weather wreaking havoc on historic sites, community trauma and economic crisis wreaking havoc with cultural nonprofits' budgets. Given that New England is a region built so deliberately on the myth of Indian disappearance, any digital engagements and archives that involve Indigenous people here must keep the *relational* aspects of sustainability—the interconnections among cultures and ecologies—in mind.

Countless scholars have explained that archives are far from culturally or politically neutral.[16] Historically many were built by the most imperial of impulses, and the problem with respect to Indigenous cultural heritage is profound. Many treasured and even sacred Indigenous items reside not in the communities that produced them but in non-Native museums, libraries, and antiquarian societies. Too many of those institutions came by those objects as part of a global, imperial enterprise to steal cultural materials wholesale from Indigenous communities. In North America the practice began almost as soon as colonists arrived, a point of which Cheryl Savageau wants us to remain cognizant in her poem "Before Moving on to Plymouth from Cape Cod—1620," with its haunting refrain:

> they find what looks like
> a grave
> what looks like a grave
> a grave and they
> dig it up. (in Senier, *Dawnland Voices* 322)

Cultural plundering escalated during the nineteenth century, when so-called salvage anthropologists fanned out in search of the ever-coveted "last of the tribe." Anthropologists collected those objects that suited their conception of Indigenous people as both exotic and dying—funerary objects or sacred objects, human remains—in extractive violence that is now so widely acknowledged that legislation like the Native American Graves Protection and Repatriation Act seeks to return many of those objects to their rightful owners.[17]

Historically, then, much of the archiving of Indigenous materials by non-Indigenous people has been enacted in direct service to vanishing-race mythologies. Collecting institutions have been far less interested, for instance, in tribal newspapers, records of Native businesspeople, political testimonies. Thus, if archives are imperial, they are also necessarily partial. Verne Harris, the archivist for Nelson Mandela, has characterized the archival record as "but a sliver of social memory . . . [and] but a sliver of the documentary record," adding, "If, as many archivists are wont to argue, the repositories of archives are the world's central memory institutions, then we are in deep, amnesiac trouble" (64). In short, dominant cultural heritage institutions have generally been uninterested in stories of Indigenous sovereignty and sustainability, and Archives 2.0 seems to offer the possibility of charting new paths.

It hasn't always worked out this way. Considerable prestige—and considerable funding—now accrues to projects like the Perseus Digital Library of Greco-Roman classics, the Benjamin Franklin papers, the Shakespeare folios, the Rossetti Archive, and other canonical collections.[18] These are innovative, vital collections, led by scholars who have generously sought to share their knowledge and expertise in building such collections with others. But the rush to digitize—which Roopika Risam deliberately calls "the race for digitality"—has resulted in some tiered (and tired) systems, just as we saw in print canons. Adeline Koh, Amy Earhart, and others have observed that, after an initial burst of optimism in the early 1990s around digital collections, especially small-scale projects devoted to writers of color, many of these projects fell into obsolescence, and the field of digital humanities seemed to retrench around canonical figures and tool-building.[19]

One effort to democratize Indigenous digital collections comes in the form of so-called digital repatriation, in which libraries, museums, and other heritage institutions create electronic surrogates of original materials, which are then theoretically available to the source communities that created them. The practice is not confined to textual documents; in some cases, electronic copies of everything from sacred masks to architectural structures are being created in the spirit of access.[20] An exceptional

model is *Gibagadinamaagoom*, led by Tim Powell in cooperation with several Ojibwe elders, which leverages the power of
the web to create thick contextualization for material items: it
surrounds an image of a thunderbird on birchbark with MP3
files of Ojibwe elders speaking and contextualizing this image
on their own cultural terms.[21] Another is the Yale Indian Papers
Project, which is creating new access to valuable primary source
materials that can help change New England Indian historiography and is also involving tribal historians in the selection,
transcription, and annotation of these documents.[22]

In addition to digital repatriation, many electronic archives
that include Indigenous materials are also newly mindful of
culturally specific protocols for the sharing of knowledge. The
anthropologist Kimberly Christen, who has been a leader in this
field, has put the question pointedly: "Does information want to
be free?" Originally working with Warumungu people in Australia, Christen found that Aboriginal community members had
a complex rubric for what images should be shared and with
whom. In response, she and her colleagues designed a justifi-
ably acclaimed content management system called Mukurtu,
expressly to let Indigenous communities build digital exhibits
based on their own culturally specific protocols. A Mukurtu pro-
tocol may, for instance, restrict access to a photograph to members of a particular kin group, let only tribal members view a
certain document, or confine access to an MP3 to people with
specific ritual knowledge.[23] Additionally, Christen's frequent
collaborator, Jane Anderson, an intellectual property scholar,
has developed "traditional knowledge" or "TK" labels, intended
as legal and pedagogical instruments to "help non-community
users of this cultural heritage understand its importance and
significance to the communities from where it derives and continues to have meaning."[24] TK labels may indicate, for example,
that particular web content is "community only" or "men only"
or "commercial use only." Taken together, technical solutions like
these seek to decolonize archives by prompting critical reflection on settler colonial epistemologies themselves, rather than
by proffering unmediated access to an imagined full corpus.

It's worth noting that the need to protect Indigenous materials from misuse by outsiders is not new to the digital age. The Tomaquag Museum in Rhode Island has long used a paper filing system that includes "the red dot"—a flag on a file indicating that the material is sensitive and for in-house or tribal use only. The Mohegans have taken a fascinating approach to their intratribal newsletter, *Wuskuso*, instructing tribal members to dispose of this publication (eight pages on glossy stock, with color photographs) after reading it. The tribal archives retains copies for descendants to view on-site.[25]

Decolonial archiving practices thus stand in direct opposition to the usual ways that colonial archives disseminate knowledge and envision cultural ownership.[26] The Cherokee scholar Ellen Cushman, who is working with the Cherokee Nation on a digital archive of Cherokee-language stories, suggests:

> Decolonial archives operate through an understanding of *time immemorial* that belies the imperial creation of tradition marked along Western timelines. They operate by relocating meaning in the context of its unfolding that opposes the imperial archive's penchant for collecting, classifying, and isolating. They operate through the co-construction of knowledge based on interactions between storytellers and listeners that counter the imperial archive's insistence on expert codification of knowledge. And they operate through linguistic and cultural perseverance rather than the imperialist agenda of preservation of cultural tradition as hermetically sealed, contained, and unchanging. ("Wampum, Sequoyan, and Story" 116)

Digital repatriation is only a first step in decolonizing archives. It does not (and perhaps cannot) address the physical return of original items taken illegally or unethically from Native communities, although some scholars see it as opening a door to further repatriations.[27] Moreover digital repatriation does not, in and of itself, reverse the politics of the initial archive. Indeed digital repatriation assumes that "the Indigenous archive" is already extant, *somewhere*—and in the best-funded, most visible Indigenous digital archives so far, that somewhere is a non-Native museum, university, library, or historical society.

Institutions like Yale and the American Philosophical Society indisputably hold materials of great interest and value to tribal communities; that is the whole point of the repatriation movement in the first place. Still, as colonial and/or ethnographic archives, they tend to contain very different material from those collections stewarded for centuries by Indigenous communities themselves.

Digital Literary Stewardship in Indigenous New England

Thus far, conversations about digital Indigenous archives have generally sidestepped the simple fact that most tribal people do *have* archives of their own.[28] They have generally not acknowledged the long history of Native people's *own* archival methods—methods of memory-making that include oral and material cultures, as well as tribal offices, tribal libraries and museums, tribal members' homes, and other spaces. To non-Native people and funding institutions some of these archives remain unintelligible as "archives" at all. One of the first books about Native American archives argued that, traditionally, "archives did not reside in a building but lived, on a daily basis, among, interconnected with, and interpreted by" members of the tribal community (Roy et al. 177). In New England this is still very much the case. Mountains of writing can be found in tribal elders' garages or piled on living-room floors. Important documents are retained in family collections, as well as in tribal historic preservation offices and small tribal museums. Tribal members have saved historic letters to colonial officials, diaries and newspaper clippings, and rich community publications like tribal newsletters, histories, dictionaries, and children's books. They have compiled their own histories, crafted their own newsletters, and sustained oral traditions *about* those very writings—partly because these methods extend and sustain much older ways of gathering, describing, and circulating materials deemed important to the survival of the tribal nation and partly because tribes have seldom had access to the political capital and material resources needed to build what typically looks like a physical archive or cultural heritage institution.

This was a central conundrum revealed in the process of compiling *Dawnland Voices*. As the tribal editors and I were finalizing the print anthology for publication we were chafing at the limits of the codex itself. As hefty as this tome was, it still felt too small. We had much, much more material we wanted to include—more historic documents, more contemporary writers, more *context* for these writings, which are so new and unfamiliar for most readers. The book also felt too final. Putting something in print means giving it a fixity with which many of us were uncomfortable, particularly because we had made a point of eliciting as much input (and, inevitably, as much disagreement) as we could from tribal members and scholarly experts. Finally, and perhaps ironically, the print anthology also felt too ephemeral, something that Indigenous people have always been aware of. Louise Erdrich once said that publication is "temporary storage" (Erdrich et al. 232). She was referring specifically to an author's prerogative to revise and change stories with new editions, but we might also remember that books themselves are temporary storage. Eventually most books do go out of print, if they do not get lost or destroyed, and all of that work, all of those stories become much less readily available. At *Dawnland Voices* we turned to the web not because we expected it to be more permanent but because, considering the long-term sustainability of Indigenous writing, we knew that Native people have continued to produce in a wide range of media, making use of the tools given to them at any particular moment.

We began building dawnlandvoices.org slowly. One virtue of a website or electronic archive is that, unlike a print book, it is more easily extensible and revisable; for creating collaborative projects, it is easier to produce pages, show them to the community, and make changes.[29] I was particularly interested to see how we might leverage university resources—labor and technical assistance, equipment, and even funds—to help tribal communities take their physically archived stories online, making them more searchable and accessible. We began with Omeka.net, a free and open-source content management system developed by public historians at George Mason University's Center for History and New Media. Omeka was built out of a desire to help even the smallest museums and archives (really, anyone with a story to tell) easily upload material to the web, mark it with the metadata that will make it easy to find, and create rich narratives around that content. Initially some students working on independent studies began building individual author entries, so the site was functioning more or less as a glorified annotated bibliography.

But I was then approached by the Mt. Kearsarge Indian Museum in Warner, New Hampshire, to create an online version of a 2011 traveling exhibit their curators had produced in collaboration with several area Abenaki basket makers and historians. *Along the Basket Trail* became a model for student-community research, writing, and editing, as the curators gave us some historical outlines and background; students did documentary photography, interviewing, archival research, and writing; the basket makers and historians edited and made suggestions on the web pages before we made them public.[30] Students in subsequent courses have continued adding to the archive, both historic and contemporary material, again while interviewing and consulting with authors and tribal historians.[31] As the project grew and I was able to secure some internal funding from my university, we migrated the site to omeka .org, the nonhosted and more robust version of the platform. We gave it a more succinct URL (originally indigenousnewengland .com, it is now dawnlandvoices.org) and some improved design, including a bipartite structure: *Dawnland Voices 2.0* is now an online literary magazine, published twice a year, for contemporary and emerging regional Native writers; *Indigenous New England Digital Collections* is an archive for the digital preservation and accessibility of more historic materials. This bipartite structure was purposeful for emphasizing the continuous presence and vitality of Indigenous literary traditions in New England: ultimately visitors to the site can search for, say, "Passamaquoddy" texts and find both older tribal newsletters and contemporary poetry. Given that New England is built on the dispossession of Native land and the continued exploitation of

Native resources, both ecological and cultural, this site allows us to document and hopefully extend the efforts of regional Native *writers* to challenge that exploitation.

The kinds of materials that have been entering this born-digital archive often speak, thematically, to issues of sovereignty and sustainability. A Passamaquoddy-language poem by Stephanie Francis (Passamaquoddy) proclaims, "the earth is our mother." An essay by Rachel Sayet (Mohegan) discusses regional approaches to food sovereignty. A personal reminiscence by John Dennis (Mi'kmaq) ponders the meanings of "reconciliation" for families, tribes, and state governments. An audio recording by Suzanne Rancourt (Abenaki) celebrates the Wabanaki homeland. A newsletter published by Donna Loring (Penobscot) and Donald Soctomah (Passamaquoddy) records tribal interventions in the workings of the Maine state legislature at the beginning of the twenty-first century. Rather than inventory or close-read these writings, however, I would like to wind down this discussion of digital literary stewardship with some further reflections on sovereignty and sustainability.

Duarte's formulation of "network sovereignty" is appealing precisely because it redirects our attention to the ways that Indigenous people have used communication systems to survive settler colonialism over many centuries and to the *embeddedness* of these communication systems in much larger webs of human and other-than-human relations. In Duarte's observation, tribal leaders and information and communication technology professionals "view their work deploying broadband as a social enterprise—a matter of governance, sovereignty and self-determination—rather than primarily as a profit-making enterprise" (64). Even their approach to building physical infrastructure, she finds, is deeply place- and culture-based, as they make "decisions about where to build towers shaped by seasonal rhythms of hunting, wildfires, and prayer, not to mention the matter of land and edifice allocation" (53–54). To many people working in the digital humanities, sustainability is "the elephant in the room," meaning we are all intensely worried about what happens when our grant runs out, our institutions run out of server space, our graduate assistants move on.[32] But Duarte's notion of "network sovereignty," while acknowledging these material questions of infrastructure, insists that *relationships* are at the center of any sustainable Indigenous digital enterprise because relationships have always been at the center of sovereignty and sustainability.

As a non-Native scholar working in the field of Indigenous literature, I have made countless mistakes. One of the biggest, early on with dawnlandvoices.org, was imagining that the affordances of the tools themselves might help promote and disseminate Indigenous literature. I honestly imagined that I could build our site in Omeka, give the tribal editors their own passwords, and they would begin magically populating the site with all of the material we couldn't include in the book. This is stunningly obtuse. Some of the tribal editors are underemployed and lack access to scanners and reliable internet connections. Others have full-time jobs outside of the heritage field and lack the time to do much more than upload the occasional jpeg (hence, perhaps, the appeal of Facebook).[33] Even those who work as tribal historic preservation officers or museum curators lack staff. They could apply for outside funding, of course, but some of the local archives do not even have 501c3 designations, and even if they were to devote precious resources to such applications, many of them honestly have more pressing concerns: wear and tear on their buildings, community emergencies, elders providing endless unremunerated labor.[34] Above all, everyone lacks *time*.[35]

The National Endowment for the Humanities provided dawnlandvoices.org with a short-term Preservation and Access Grant to look at some of the barriers to digitization among the kinds of local, precarious, and tribally governed collections represented in the book *Dawnland Voices*. The Tomaquag Museum, the Passamaquoddy Tribal Historic Preservation Office, and the Indigenous Resources Collaborative in Mashpee, Massachusetts, collaborated on this project.[36] They all have collections that, to borrow from Burton, have "not been considered legitimate subjects of archivization per se." They are often uninventoried or uncatalogued, or inventoried and catalogued only in elders' memories. In library parlance (and with irony duly noted), these materials are "undiscoverable"—not easily searchable even in-house, much less in larger systems like electronic catalogues. We knew that digitization would not be easy for any of these collections, but we believed that they deserved to try. We wanted to see what could happen if we trained tribal historians to scan and upload their own materials.

Other grant recipients will know how quickly a team can spend down $40,000. We were able to host a two-day planning meeting with leading experts on digital collections and Indigenous intellectual property issues.[37] Digital librarians visited each of the three tribal collections, setting them up with scanner, laptop, software, and two days of rudimentary training. Two days of training proved to be barely enough to handle the scanning; nobody felt particularly ready to learn or wrangle Omeka during this stage of the project. We have enlisted students at the University of New Hampshire, the University of Maine, and Bryant University to do some of the work of uploading and curating items. We created an initial exhibit, *Tribal Archives: Untold Stories of Activism and Survival*, and we have continued to upload and curate other archival items, most notably tribal newsletters, which regional tribal archives have in abundance.[38]

A digital project like this is always unfinished, and it's always breaking and stalling. It also has its merits. Students have benefited tremendously from the opportunity to collaborate with tribal authors, to learn about digital writing and project management, and in some cases even to have polished pieces they can list on their résumés. Tribal authors have benefited from the additional access to publication opportunities; some, including Natalie Dana (Passamaquoddy) and Sherri Mitchell (Penobscot), have secured their own book publication contracts since publishing in the print and online versions of *Dawnland Voices*. On the other hand, we are not necessarily in a position to return to the National Endowment for the Humanities or a similar granting agency at this point and say that we are ready for a much

larger grant. The Tomaquag Museum continued to scan documents after the end of our grant, but they prefer to store most
of their digital objects in-house—an aspiration that will need
much more funding. Donald Soctomah, the Passamaquoddy
tribal historic preservation officer, continues to scan items as
he is able, but he is stretched thin and pressed for time. The
Indigenous Resources Collaborative seemed to be discouraged
by the labor-intensiveness of scanning and has not continued;
they are much more interested in the idea of curating a small
handful of items with rich metadata like video and oral history,
but this too will require additional resources.[39]

More pointedly, it is not clear that the tribal editors aspire
to the same things to which the large granting institutions and
the field of digital humanities aspire. One major aspiration
these days is *scale*: the pressure, when you write grant proposals especially, is to demonstrate that you are digitizing to scale,
such that you make sizable databases that then become ripe for
distant reading. Computer-assisted interpretation has yielded
some genuinely exciting work, but in the case of Native American and Indigenous literary studies, a term like "text mining"
ought to give us pause. There is, as of this moment, not much
evidence that digitization at scale is necessarily what Indigenous communities want or need.[40] There is not a significant
digitized Indigenous textual corpus in the first place, but more
interesting, perhaps, there's not an overwhelming stated *desire*
for such work among tribal communities. Indigenous people
are rightly cautious about putting their cultural heritage materials out there for free and open access, even texts like books
and poems that were originally intended to be public. They have
serious questions about who is going to use this material, why,
for what purposes, and what's in it for them.

Another major aspiration of digital humanities is what you
see in those highly sophisticated textual editions like the Rossetti
Archive and the Blake Archive: literature encoded, edited, and
contextualized to the highest scholarly standard, fully searchable and interoperable with other systems. There is no question
in my mind that the kind of treatment Dante Gabriel Rossetti

got is the kind of treatment that Indigenous literature deserves, but it is actually an open question whether that is a high priority for tribal communities. It does not seem to be a high priority for the contributors to dawnlandvoices.org, and that is not necessarily a failure of the project. Rather our experience highlights something that Duarte observes, regarding assumptions about Indigenous uses of information and communication technologies:

> With regard to the Internet in Indian Country, previous studies were diagnosing limited Internet access on American Indian reservations as an outcome of inadequate infrastructure, remote geography, and insufficient market demand endemic to reservation life—in other words, limited Internet access on reservations was an "Indian problem." But these descriptions of Native uses of ICTs did not account for the legacies of colonialism, exigencies of tribal sovereignty, histories of self-determination, and the realities of day-to-day reservation life. . . . Supposedly, connectivity would be possible, under the right conditions: sustained local capital, sufficient demand, technical know-how, nearness to urban centers, and the adoption of the values of a technological society. (29–31)

She is talking specifically about broadband infrastructure, but her observations could apply just as well to many assumptions in the digital humanities. In thinking that I could just build an Omeka site and crowdsource the continuation of the anthology, I was thinking that the affordances of the technology would make literary stewardship happen. I was failing to understand what the tribal editors and these very writings had been trying to tell me all along: that Indigenous communities have their own, long-standing and highly successful mechanisms for remembering their most important stories, texts, and authors, and that these mechanisms succeed because they are dependent on relationships.

One of the premises of this book has been that while sustainability is on everyone's lips these days, it too seldom acknowledges Indigenous histories, specifically Indigenous histories of colonial dispossession and Indigenous sovereignty. Sustainability discourse too seldom acknowledges Indigenous people at all, except in the most stereotyped, primordial way. But Indigenous people have in fact been *theorizing* the relations between humans and other-than-humans for a very long time now— not because they are romantically hardwired to be one with the earth but because they have centuries of practical experience trying to opt out of extractive colonialism. From an Indigenous perspective, sustainability is always a question of the long-term survival of both ecological and cultural systems, precisely because Indigenous people's land bases sustain their distinct cultures, which in turn sustain their lands, waters, and other forms of life.

In this view, Native literature is an integral part of much larger networks of meaningful and sustainable relations (to borrow from Niigaan Sinclair) or "coupled human-natural systems" (to borrow from the sustainability scientists)—networks including humans and other-than-humans, natural and human-made structures, ancestors and future generations. Native literature helps steward these networks, exercising a fiduciary duty of care toward them, and is in turn stewarded by them. It reflects and enacts what Carpenter and her colleagues call "a notion of mutual trusteeship—enriched by a view of interdependence between present and future generations and between different peoples—that acknowledges the fact of global cohabitation and mandates a sense of shared responsibility" (1079). This understanding of sustainable sovereignty, or sovereign sustainability, calls for a style of reading that is a little bit different from parsing texts for evidence of traditional ecological knowledge. It calls for something more akin to media ecology, where we consider the relationships among different generic forms, institutions, landscapes, and communities, even as we value the language of the texts themselves. We cannot keep *extracting* from the earth and from Indigenous cultures; we can't *extract* literature from its webby ecologies, histories, and politics.

Waziyatawin refers to "the paradox of Indigenous resurgence": that just as a global economy based on extraction and exploitation seems ready to implode, Indigenous people are rising up to insist on their sovereignty and sustainability—their right to free prior and informed consent over what happens on their lands and with their cultural practices. That this resurgence is happening in New England, a region built on the very notion of Indigenous disappearance, registers a powerful vision for the future.

Notes

Preface

1. In keeping with current practice in the field of Native American and Indigenous studies, I use the contested terms "Native American" and "Indigenous" interchangeably. Tribally specific designations are preferred whenever possible; otherwise, many scholars and activists choose "Indigenous," especially in discussions of global ecological and social justice, to highlight prior occupancy and political claims. Albeit imperfect, "Native American" still sometimes proves useful for evoking the particular colonial history and ongoing violence of what is now called the United States.

Introduction

1. Ethel Boissevain describes the 1880 detribalization; for a brief explanation of *Carcieri v. Salazar*, see Klopotek.

2. The Penobscot River case received extensive coverage in the *Bangor (ME) Daily News*; see, for instance, Gagnon. Penobscot elder Donna Loring provided some of the best discussions of the case from a tribal perspective on her radio show, *Wabanaki Windows*, archived at http://archives.weru.org /?s=Wabanaki+Windows.

3. The notion that Native people have or do not have a requisite level of "Indian blood" comes not from any biology but from the U.S. government, which has needed to find ways to restrict the number of people to whom it owes its treaty obligations. For thorough deconstructions of blood quantum by Native scholars, see Garroutte; Sunray, "Blood Policing"; Tallbear.

4. Today those old Massachusett-language documents continue to provide invaluable material for contemporary Wampanoag political and cultural projects, including the language revitalization project begun by the tribal member and MacArthur Fellow Jessie Little Doe Baird. For the seventeenth-century documents, see Goddard and Bragdon. The Wampanoag Language Reclamation Project is at http://www.wlrp.org/. Anne Makepeace's film about this project, *We Still Live Here*, is well worth seeing.

5. This practice undoubtedly preceded the arrival of Jesuit missionaries but was quickly commandeered for instruction in Catholic catechism and continued at least into the twentieth century in the form of hieroglyphic prayer writing; hieroglyphs are still taught, in fact, as part of the Mi'kmaq language program at Cape Breton University. For a history of hieroglyphic prayers, see M. Marshall and Schmidt. Cape Breton University's Mi'kmaq-language course listings appear at https://www.cbu.ca/indigenous-affairs/unamaki-college/kji-keptin-alexander-denny-lnuisultimkeweyokuom/mikmaq-language-teaching/.

6. In the interest of space I am being enormously reductive here; federally recognized tribes do not get anything like free rein, as they are subject not only to federal laws but also to laws and policies in the states in which they reside. For a lucid discussion of this "triangulated power" of tribe, state, and federal government, see Weaver 189–200. Federal recognition is pursued by tribes across the continental United States, for a variety of reasons; however, because, prior to 1980, *no* New England tribes had it, recognition battles have had something of a defining force in Indigenous politics regionally. For a good critique of how the very term "federally recognized" plays out, politically and personally, for Native people around the United States, see Sunray, "'Federally Recognized' Often Misused."

7. The draconian Rhode Island state police raids on a Narragansett smoke shop in 2003 and the clashes between Passamaquoddy people and Maine state authorities over elver fishing in 2013–14 are only two examples.

8. For a first-person account of this history, see tribal member Ruth Garby Torres's essay "How You See Us, Why You Don't" in Den Ouden and O'Brien. Brian Klopotek describes it as part of the Connecticut backlash, recalling that two senators from Connecticut allegedly threatened to fire the secretary of the interior if she didn't reverse the decision (4).

9. For an excellent bibliographic essay on sovereignty, as well as newer discussions of the term, see Teves et al.

10. A brief but widely cited introduction to sustainability science is Clark and Dickson. For a helpful annotated bibliography of readings in the field, see Kates. A lucid and useful approach to sustainability as an epistemological concern is Donella Meadows's *Thinking in Systems*.

11. For example, the popular contention that "Indians had [no] fundamentally different understanding of the environment than any other people on Earth" (Riley), as well as the assertions noted by Kauanui (above) that because Indians have casinos, they have somehow forfeited any right to challenge environmental depredation. Clint Carroll (Cherokee) sums up the Indigenous response to Krech nicely: "I reject the debate as a starting point for thinking about environmental issues in Indian country. . . . Discourses on the ecological Indian often mask the politics of what is at stake in indigenous environ-

mental activism which entails counteracting histories of dispossession by reasserting sovereign claims to land" (xv).

12. Adamson makes a similar point (47–50).

13. There are scholars like Stephanie LeMenager who, in analyzing both the content and the material incarnation of literary texts, do both. I do not mean to imply a completely clean binary, but in general, conversation between environmental humanities and cultural heritage preservation has been relatively halting. Literary critics who have called for a reclamation of the term "sustainability" from the point of view of the humanities include LeMenager and Foote; Keller. Scholars thinking about cultural heritage preservation or sustainability cross a wider variety of disciplines: economics (e.g., Throsby); urban planning (e.g., Vallance et al.); historic preservation (e.g., Kaufman). Barthel-Bouchier offers a useful introduction, as does the journal *Heritage and Society*. There is an equally vast literature on intangible heritage and sustainability since UNESCO's determination of "the importance of the intangible cultural heritage as a mainspring of cultural diversity and a guarantee of sustainable development" (United Nations Educational, Scientific and Cultural Organization). L. Smith and Akagawa provide an indispensable introduction to this field. For thoughtful considerations of the interactions among race, power, and the environment, see Marmion et al.; Naguib; Ortega; Vecco; Nieves. Jon Hawkes, writing for the Creative City Network of Canada, adds yet another dimension to the discussion of culture and sustainability: the need to promote a "culture *of* sustainability," or the idea that economic and ecological sustainability require concomitant shifts in people's belief systems, values, and practices.

1. "We're Still Here"

1. Often uttered by Wampanoag people in interviews and at public events, "We're Still Here" was the title of a Boston Children's Museum exhibit in the 1970s and later a book compiled by the curator, Joan Lester. *We Still Live Here* is the title of a documentary by Makepeace Productions and Cultural Survival about the MacArthur Genius Grant winner Jessie Little Doe Baird and the Wôpanâak Language Recovery Project.

2. Linda Coombs's blistering review "*Mayflower: A Story of Courage, Community and War* by Nathaniel Philbrick" appears in *Cultural Survival Quarterly*. Debbie Reese (Nambé Pueblo) has written critically about *Caleb's Crossing* on her widely read blog.

3. Hayden White was one historian who gave a more generous reading of date lists or *annals*, which he distinguished from *chronicles* (which were narrated but "not yet *narrative*") and modern historiography (which is driven by such imperatives as plot, morality, and aesthetics). To White there was nothing rudimentary about assembling a chronology, and even the most ellipti-

cal medieval date lists could reveal a great deal about the period and culture in which they were produced. Some of the Wampanoag writings I discuss might oscillate, if we cared to create such a taxonomy, between the annal (in which, White says, agency is attributed less to humans than to events) and the chronicle (in which there is a distinct "social center," or point of view). See White 1–25.

4. A phrase she uses several times throughout *Firsting and Lasting* to summarize colonial historians' master narratives.

5. The court began with language from a 1901 case, *Montoya v. United States*: "a body of Indians of the same or a similar race, united in a community under one leadership or government, and inhabiting a particular though sometimes ill-defined territory" (Campisi 23). During the course of the trial, a variety of ethnographic and legal definitions were presented that could either finesse or restrict this definition. But as the anthropologist Jack Campisi describes it, "in the end the conflicting views led [Judge Skinner] to discount all the alternatives for one of his own creation, one founded on less substance than those he discarded" (52). For instance, he interpreted Mashpee intermarriage with non-Indians as a form of racial "dilution"—a popular misconception having nothing to do with Wampanoag conceptions of identity or, for that matter, with any scientific or ethnographic evidence. He also instructed the jury to evaluate historically shifting definitions of "community" and land "ownership," regardless of the fact that these definitions were imposed on—and revoked from—the Mashpees by the state in the first place. For thorough accounts of the case, see Campisi; Clifford, *The Predicament of Culture*; and Brodeur.

6. For other examples, see Klopotek.

7. As long as we are on the subject of sustainability and politics, this is the same judge who in 1982 exonerated W. R. Grace and Beatrice Foods of poisoning the water supply in Woburn, Massachusetts.

8. Campisi describes Skinner's response to accusations of inconsistency in the verdict thus: the judge pointed to "the absence of any self-identification as Indians and because of the failure of the group to establish common lands after 1869. One wonders how they might have accomplished the latter given that the state had acted unilaterally in the same period to sell the lands the tribe held in common" (61).

9. See, for instance, Torres and Milun; Campisi; Brodeur.

10. In 1970, the centennial of Massachusetts's incorporation of Mashpee and Aquinnah as towns, Amelia Bingham (Mashpee) and Helen Attaquin (Aquinnah) each published a foundational history of their respective communities, based on assiduous research in local archives. See also *Moshup's Footsteps* (2001), a memoir by Helen Manning, also from Aquinnah. Manning includes a timeline at the end of her book, beginning at 12,500 BC—a powerful way of suggesting just how brief European presence has been, after all—

and traces the relations between the Commonwealth of Massachusetts and Aquinnah, which received federal recognition in 1987.

11. Email communication, September 26, 2013.

12. Exceptions being the passing reference in Campisi and a brief interview in Brodeur.

13. For more on this history, see Mills's *Talking with the Elders of Mashpee*, especially 134–35. See also David Silverman's *Faith and Boundaries*, which illustrates how, very early on, Wampanoag people saw conversion to Christianity as providing certain opportunities to protect their lands, have a voice in the new colonies, and keep their communities together.

14. See especially Cooper's chapter "Thanksgiving Mourned" in her book *Spirited Encounters* (121–30).

15. Founded in 1913, Boston is the second oldest children's museum in the country, after Brooklyn (1899). For more on its history, see Din.

16. Some of this history is recounted in Steuert, Jenness, and Jones-Rizzi; see also Lester, "Working Together to Get It Right."

17. For more on the history and varied meanings of powwow, see the excellent anthology of Native scholars' writings edited by Ellis et al.

18. Avant 19. Mills says there was no powwow from about 1940 to 1957, when Mashpee held the Four Directions powwow.

19. For more on the DeVries homestead and ACC, see Dresser 173.

20. Its first director was Nanepeshemet (d. 1995), another Wampanoag writer of great interest, whose work remains in the Plimoth archives.

21. Kirshenblatt-Gimblett; Lowenthal. Magelssen appears to have talked only to one "Plimoth PR worker."

22. For example, "WHEREAS, the Plymouth settlers came to the United States to realize religious freedom, an essential tenet of democracy," and "WHEREAS, Plymouth has served as the location of several prominent events, the most notable being the First Thanksgiving feast, when Native Americans and the Plymouth settlers joined together to enjoy their harvest" (*Executive Order No. 502*).

23. Coombs's use of the phrase "stuck with it" to describe the national holiday ("First Thanksgiving") is no joke. As a national origin myth it is exceptionally stubborn, despite widespread efforts to challenge it, as in James Loewen's popular book *Lies My Teacher Told Me* (70–92) and the emergence of alternative curricula and even children's books that purport to debunk the myth, like Gunderson. In 1970 a group of Wampanoag activists famously declared Thanksgiving a National Day of Mourning; Frank James's (Wamsutta's) speech from that day has achieved a kind of canonical status among Wampanogs: "You the white man are celebrating an anniversary. We the Wampanoags will help you celebrate in the concept of a beginning. It was the beginning of a new life for the Pilgrims. Now, 350 years later it is a beginning of a new determination for the original American: the American Indian. . . .

The important point is that along with these necessities of everyday living, we still have the spirit, we still have the unique culture, we still have the will and, most important of all, the determination to remain as Indians. We are determined, and our presence here this evening is living testimony that this is only the beginning of the American Indian, particularly the Wampanoag, to regain the position in this country that is rightfully ours" (458). James speaks to the paradox of Indigenous resurgence: that while national and state narratives assiduously erase (and re-erase) Wampanoag presence, the tribal nation has nevertheless endured, and is in fact poised for renewal. This has been a recurring theme of efforts to unteach the Thanksgiving story. For some additional, indispensable Indigenous perspectives on Thanksgiving, see Seale and Slapin 201–8; Grace.

2. Tribal Periodicals

1. Daniel Littlefield and James Parins have documented hundreds of publications in their two-volume reference, *American Indian and Alaska Native Newspapers and Periodicals* (1986). But most of these periodicals remain inaccessible and unknown outside of the communities that produced them. Only seven are included, to date, in the Library of Congress's digital newspaper project, *Chronicling America* (three papers from Minnesota, four from Oklahoma; http://chroniclingamerica.loc.gov/newspapers/?state=&ethnicity= Indians+of+North+America&language=). And few have been the subject of any scholarly research. The *Cherokee Phoenix* (1828–34) has received some attention as the "first" Indian newspaper, as have the student papers published by the infamous Carlisle boarding school during the late nineteenth and early twentieth centuries. See Cushman, *The Cherokee Syllabary*; Katanski. Some research has been done around the periodical writing of activists associated with the Society of American Indians (including Zitkala-Sa and Carlos Montezuma) in the late nineteenth and early twentieth centuries, but many of these "have become lost to history" (Zuck 73). Other notable studies include Terri Castaneda's discussion of the *Smoke Signal*, edited from 1948 onward by Marie Potts (Maidu); and Loew and Mella's survey of Native environmental journalism in Wisconsin tribal newspapers between the 1970s and 1990s. In short, periodical literature is a much richer record of Native conversations around a host of topics, including sovereignty and sustainability, than scholars have fully appreciated.

2. A link to an evolving spreadsheet of regional periodicals is kept at the Periodical Literature exhibit on dawnlandvoices.org: https://www.dropbox .com/s/gaxlud1qe3llnsw/New%20England%20Newspapers.xlsx?dl=. My claim is not necessarily that Indigenous people in New England produce more of these kinds of periodicals than those in other regions but that, in a region whose people are generally excluded from literary history, these texts

are an important source of writing. A promising (though proprietary) new collection of such publications is *The American Indian Newspaper Project,* compiled in cooperation with the Sequoyah Center: https://www.amdigital.co.uk/primary-sources/american-indian-newspapers.

3. The popular electronic search tool that catalogues the contents of some seventy-two thousand libraries.

4. "Skitemiq Nutacomit," or "Earth Speaker." Begun in December 1999 and archived at http://www.maliseets.com/Newsletters/.

5. The classic text is Ong's *Orality and Literacy,* which has prompted decades of new scholarship as well as criticism. A full review of those debates is beyond the scope of this chapter; interested readers may consult the works of Street and Brandt for some strong critiques, and Cushman, *Literacy* for a useful overview of the field. Most germane to my discussion here, the Ong school has been accused of "plac[ing] non-Western cultures in the collective past of the settler nations that surround them" (Sterne 219). In the context of Native American history, it is probably also worth noting that the anthropologist Lewis Henry Morgan promoted the idea of cultural "progress" in *Ancient Society* (1907).

6. The placement of those oral traditions in American literature anthologies is doubly misleading, since most of these selections were actually transcribed in the late nineteenth and early twentieth centuries. It's a beautiful irony that while anthropologists believed they were documenting vanishing races, tribal intellectuals were also running their own magazines, transcribing and recirculating oral traditions themselves.

7. This includes scholars like Lisa Brooks but also scholars in rhetoric and communication; see Haas; M. Powell; King et al.

8. In particular, this act intended to reverse the 1887 Dawes (General Allotment) Act, which had divided tribally held lands into individually held parcels, and which had the effect of divesting Indian people of a further two-thirds of their total land base at that time. The IRA was not uncontroversial, in its own day and now, because whatever its good intentions, to some degree it made tribes beholden to practices that might not conform with Indigenous structures of governance (e.g., it required them to adopt tribal constitutions by a majority vote). Jodi Byrd (Chickasaw) puts it bluntly: "[Under the IRA] citizenship was determined through blood quantum and enrollment, and traditional government and values were subsumed within a corporate model that set the stage for termination in the 1940s and 1950s and the struggles of the 1970s" (*Transit of Empire* 160). For a concise introduction to these federal policies, see Kidwell. For a detailed examination of the IRA in its positive and negative ramifications, see Taylor.

9. To some extent this was symbolic. New England tribes got none of the federal benefits of the IRA back in 1934 (e.g., funds for land repurchase). This has pursued them, cruelly, into the present: in the 1990s, when the Narra-

gansetts bought back thirty-one acres for elderly housing and tried to get that land put into federal trust, *Carcieri v. Salazar* ruled that they were ineligible to do so because they were not federally recognized at the time of the IRA.

10. See Boissevain; Herndon and Sekatau.

11. "Ella Peek took two years at the New York Art School after finishing normal school. Last year she did two large panels in oils, in the Long Acre Building, Times Square, New York. She also painted, for two years, for the Gorham Co. 5th Ave., New York" (*Narragansett Dawn*, July 1935, 7–8). According to the Tomaquag Museum, Peek was "born Mary Congdon"; her father was Walter Peckham Glasko (Narragansett), and her mother was a Weeden (possibly Narragansett or Wampanoag) (Lorén Spears, personal email communications, January 9 and April 29, 2014). Walter Peek, her first husband, coedited an interesting anthology of Native American literature in the 1970s, one of the rare anthologies to include New England writers, including his wife (Sanders and Peek).

12. Not to be confused with the Winnebago silent-film actress who performed under the same name. The modern ambivalence over Indian names and their political utility, especially in early twentieth-century New England, has been discussed at considerable length elsewhere. Some of the more thoughtful commentators include Debbie Reese (Nambé Pueblo), who admits upon first reading about (the Narragansett) Red Wing, "Given that notions of royalty were placed onto Native societies by Europeans, the word 'princess' always gives me pause. . . . From my perspective, [these phrases] play to an audience that reveres the image of the romantic Indian. As a Native woman and scholar studying literatures and representation at this moment in time, I am, perhaps too often, critical of activities by Native peoples whose work affirmed—and affirms—negative or positive stereotypes that I view as harmful to our well-being as Native peoples in the present day" ("Native Literary Nationalism"). In a very good undergraduate thesis for Brown University, Mary Jean Sia Uy conducted an analysis of the *Providence (RI) Journal* during this period, immediately before and after Narragansett people began to use Indian names, and found that the newspaper went rather quickly from talking about the tribe as though it were nonexistent to celebrating its power and nobility. In this case, she concluded, it is "not that the Narragansett deliberately constructed 'false' identities, but rather that the terms of legitimacy with respect to 'Indianness' were controlled and repeatedly revised by whites" (79).

13. The University of Rhode Island's library has made the magazine available in pdf at http://digitalcommons.uri.edu/sc_pubs/5/. The Indian & Colonial Research Center in Old Mystic, Connecticut, has created an index of names that appears in the magazine and can send photocopies: http://indianandcolonial.org/databases/narragansett-dawn.

14. In some of our personal conversations, Paulla Dove Jennings has speculated that they ran out of money.

15. W. S. Simmons 143.

16. January 1936, 206. These stories are unattributed and may or may not reflect heavy editing by Red Wing and her colleagues.

17. Tomaquag Museum, John Onion Worksheets, 2013.

18. There is a vast literature on Indigenous language revitalization. In New England and the Canadian Maritimes, this work includes scholarly studies like the Maliseet linguist Bernard Perley's *Defying Maliseet Language Death*; new print dictionaries like the *Passamaquoddy-Maliseet Dictionary* (Francis and Leavitt); reprints of primers that have long been in quiet community circulation, like Bowman Books' reissues of Laurent and Masta; online initiatives like the Mohegan Language Project maintained by Stephanie Fielding and Jesse Bruchac's Abenaki Radio and YouTube stations; as well as community projects, including the Wôpanâak Language Recovery Project (mentioned in chapter 1), and many more.

19. It is actually not surprising or uncommon in literature from the turn of the century, even that written by Native people themselves, to use "vanishing" tropes right alongside appeals to "the future years." The language of Indian disappearance and assimilation was so entrenched in public discourse of the period that it became available for a variety of meanings. As one historian has put it, American Indian intellectuals "defended Indianness in ethnic terms, especially during World War I and beyond. For them the Indian was a 'vanishing race' in purely full-blood biological terms, but not in intellectual, social, or cultural terms" (Rosier 44).

20. See James Wherry, "Of Micmacs and Maliseets." Wherry neglects to mention Tom's sister Marie Battiste, now a highly prolific scholar.

21. For a fascinating parallel, see Elizabeth James's study of the *Tundra Times*, published by Alaska Native groups for three decades between the 1950s and 1980s. The newsletter started in 1958 in opposition to Project Chariot, a proposed nuclear testing ground that the Atomic Energy Commission wanted to build on Cape Thompson in Iñupiat territory. Chariot was suspended in 1962, thanks in no small part to Iñupiat activism. James argues that the paper "helped set the [geographically dispersed and linguistically and culturally varied] Native population of Alaska on a course of activism and political clout predating the more well-known activities of the American Indian Movement" (287).

22. In her study of Carlos Montezuma's *Wassaja*, Rochelle Raineri Zuck argues that reader letters helped mediate the intertribal hostilities fanned by institutions like the Bureau of Indian Affairs: "The function of Indian papers was the transmission of information and the formation of networks of communication that crossed geographic and tribal borders, not to represent an authentic 'Indian' voice or to speak the 'truth' about Indian identity" (74). At present, the *Narragansett Dawn* archives remain mainly inaccessible, as they await proper curation and cataloguing. Jennings, however, agrees that

Red Wing would have been a relatively assertive editor (personal communication, July 15, 2014).

23. One classic introduction to the field is Counihan and Esterik. Winona LaDuke has also written a great deal about Indigenous food sovereignty. On the history of American scrapbooking, see Garvey.

24. For a concise North American Indigenous food history, from colonial destruction of subsistence land bases to forced reliance on government commodities to the reclamation of traditional food practices, see LaDuke's important chapter "Food as Medicine" in her book *Recovering the Sacred*.

25. The term is usually attributed to La Via Campesina, a global coalition of peasant farmers that emerged in the 1990s in support of small-scale sustainable agriculture against the hegemony of multinational corporations. The food sovereignty movement has been characterized by Emily Johansen as "territorialized cosmopolitanism," a movement highly attuned to transnational and planetary concerns while remaining at the same time firmly rooted in place. "Food and place," she says, "are explicitly part of a program of responsibility and obligation to others throughout the world" (2). For a discussion of the "malleable discourse of food sovereignty"—its broad appeal to activists working on issues from agriculture to women's rights, from large-scale protests to everyday resistance—see A. Mann 7.

26. For an account of the Passamaquoddy tribe's fight with the state to exercise their sovereign fishing rights, see Toensing. The Maliseet poet Mihku Paul has a witty triolet with the refrain "When fiddleheads cost eighty dollars a pound / Will Indians get a fair price?" ("Trade in the 21st Century" in Senier, *Dawnland Voices* 153).

27. Kenneth Lincoln wrote a book with this title in 1985, and the term is still widely used to refer to Native literature from *House Made of Dawn* onward.

28. For an excellent discussion of the way the very term "federally recognized" gets used *against* certain groups, see Sunray, "'Federally Recognized' Often Misused."

29. The Nipmuc Nation is recognized by the state of Massachusetts. The *Maine Indian Newsletter* is archived at http://dawnlandvoices.org/collections /exhibits/show/newsletters/maineindiannews. *Nipmucspohke* is archived at http://nipmucspohke.homestead.com/Past-Issues.html.

30. Lecture, University of New Hampshire, March 28, 2013.

31. This history needn't be limited to tribal newsletters; mainstream newspapers are also great sources of regional Native writing. Indigenous contributions to newspapers date back at least to the 1870s, when Joseph Nicolar (Penobscot), writing as "Young Sabbatus," contributed pieces on Penobscot history and culture to local Maine newspapers (Shay). In the twentieth century through the present, newspaper contributors have included Joan Tavares Avant (Wampanoag), who writes periodically for the *Cape Cod Times* and *Mashpee Enterprise*. Much of this writing, produced before the electronic era

or in small papers that will not likely be fully digitized any time soon, remains buried on microfilm or in local libraries. It takes a determined researcher to root them out. For example, Maria Girouard (Penobscot) has assiduously combed through issues of Maine's *Bangor Daily News* from the early 1980s, when recognition was being debated for the Maine Indian tribes, and has found numerous letters to the editor written by tribal people, challenging local misconceptions about Indians and making the case for tribal sovereignty. The radio show *Wabanaki Windows*, hosted by *Dawnland Voices* author Donna Loring (Penobscot), is well worth a listen on this subject: archived at http:// archives.weru.org/wabanaki-windows/2014/08/wabanaki-windows-81914/. These are radical literary histories, forgotten by most people outside the tribes. Additionally, the late twentieth century saw the rise of professional Native journalists in New England and elsewhere. The Native American Journalists Association was established in 1984 "to develop and improve communications among Native American people and the non–Native American public" and to "encourage Native Americans to enter the field of journalism" (Native American Journalists Association). Regionally, some of the writers who have entered that field have included Paula Peters (Wampanoag), Donna Laurent Caruso (Abenaki), and Rhonda Frey (Penobscot), who unfortunately passed away before her career was fully realized.

3. Novels of the Anthropocene

1. For a fascinating take on the literary caste system, see Berry.

2. July 29, 2017.

3. Angela Bennett.

4. Cord Whitaker.

5. An excellent collection of essays about the novel—from arguments over what actually constitutes it to analyses of how novels function as commercial, national, and transnational objects—is Lynch and Warner's 1996 volume, *Cultural Institutions of the Novel*. An incisive critique of the idea that the novel is dying comes in Fitzpatrick's *Anxiety of Obsolescence*.

6. "Anthropocene" was coined by the chemist Paul Crutzen and the ecologist Eugene Stoemer, who identified the rise of the steam engine in 1784 as the beginning of human- and fossil-fuel-driven climate change. That date has been subject to extensive debate, with some scholars suggesting instead 1610 for the Americas since that year ushered in the deaths of tens of millions of Indigenous people. The rise of the novel was most famously defined by Ian Watt as an individualistic form connected to the emergence of nation-states. For useful background on the debates surrounding the Anthropocene, see Short and Lennox 182; Davis and Turpin; and selected essays in Adamson and Davis, most notably Tony Birch's discussion of Indigenous knowledge and the Anthropocene.

7. James McKay.

8. See, for instance, K. Marshall; Trexler; the essays in Siperstein et al.; and Heise's classic *Sense of Place and Sense of Planet*.

9. In 2001, when he was reading about the Spanish Main, Hopkins said, "Suddenly the dates seemed to leap out at me. I realized that they dovetailed nicely with the end of King Philip's War. I had been thinking of writing some story about New England Indians as most books and movies focus on a handful of tribes—Sioux, Apache and Cherokee" (personal communication, November 10, 2011).

10. July 14 has taken on enormous significance for Narragansett people; they continue to gather on this date at the site of the former cigarette shop, which was violently raided two days after its opening by dozens of state police. The raid came on order of Rhode Island's governor Donald Carcieri, who was consistently hostile to any exercise of tribal sovereignty, blocking tribal efforts to build a casino and even to open elderly housing.

11. He continues to write prolifically, keeping a blog, writing poetry and an array of genre fiction. His published books include *Rhyme or Reason: Narragansett Poetry* (2013); a western, *Nagocdoches* (2004); a paranormal thriller, *Twilight of the Gods* (2012); and a collection of some of his humorous and satirical newspaper writing, *Writer on the Storm* (2014).

12. See, for instance, Adams.

13. Hopkins gives him the Indian name Pokanoket, an earlier name for Metacom's Wampanoag people. No scholar seems to have traced what became of Metacom's son and wife, and I have been unable to find oral histories that retain this knowledge.

14. When I was emailing him about this chapter in progress, Hopkins wrote a long account of *Carlomagno*'s publishing history and posted it to my Facebook wall (December 17, 2014). His story was one of utter despair: he tried a university press, which rejected it for a "lack of a bibliography and footnotes. I pointed out that it was a work of fiction. They did not respond." Finally, he says, "in a fit of depression I threw [the first version of the manuscript] in the woodstove." The melancholic artist is a common trope, but depression among Native writers is serious business, fueled by poverty and institutional racism. Many, if not most, of the writers in *Dawnland Voices*—including Hopkins—have stories of being tracked in school, of being cruelly discouraged in their writing, and of being advised that they should consider more "vocational" careers. What is amazing is that so many have persisted with so few resources and so little help. Meanwhile histories like Nathaniel Philbrick's *Mayflower* and novels like Geraldine Brooks's *Caleb's Crossing* make big money, despite the thorough critiques they have received from Native intellectuals. For a searing review of *Mayflower* from a Wampanoag perspective, see Coombs, "*Mayflower*."

15. Duckworth-Elliott announced the opening of wampumbooks in 2009, with great ambitions to nurture Native authors, especially regional writers targeting readers of all ages. Using print-on-demand technologies, she published her own young-adult novel, *Poneasequa*; the *Carlomagno* reprint; and a book by the singer Jana Mashonee. Unfortunately wampumbooks dissolved after only these three publications.

16. DeMeyer founded Blue Hand expressly to help educate Indigenous authors about the publishing process and to help them reach readers. DeMeyer encourages the e-book format and, using a blend of electronic and print-on-demand publishing technologies, has hopefully found an affordable, sustainable model for keeping books like *Carlomagno* available for readers. On October 25, 2017, DeMeyer announced on Facebook that Blue Hand would have to cease publishing due to lack of revenues (she had been sustaining it with their own income) but that the books would continue to be available at bluehandcollective.com.

17. For example, Seale and Slapin 113.

18. The forced sterilization of Indigenous women—widespread globally throughout the twentieth century—has been the subject of many studies. Some of these are cited and aggregated in A. Smith; Mihesuah.

19. Some scientists, it's worth noting, consider the post–World War II period a major milestone in the Anthropocene (e.g., Steffen et al.).

20. Debbie Reese, a Nambé Pueblo scholar who maintains an extensive database of reviews and commentary on American Indians in children's literature, sharply criticized Scholastic for letting the book go out of print. See Reese, "American Indians in Children's Literature (AICL)."

21. *Anthropocene Fictions* is the title of an excellent survey of climate-change fiction by Adam Trexler.

22. See, for instance, essays in the collection edited by Wigley et al.

23. Fielding's original Mohegan-language diaries have been digitized at Cornell University Library's Native American Collection, http://nac.library .cornell.edu/exhibition/writtenword/writtenword_5.html. Weather information can also be found in the diaries of Joseph Johnson, a contemporary of Occom's (Johnson and Murray). For a poetic transliteration of Fielding's weather notes by one of her descendants, Stephanie Fielding, see "Weather" in Senier, *Dawnland Voices* 575–76.

24. In Australia these conversations have taken an interesting direction: the Indigenous Weather Knowledge Project (http://www.bom.gov.au/iwk/about /index.shtml) is documenting Aboriginal calendars based on meteorological factors (wind, temperature) commonly associated with seasons and on cultural factors like ceremonies and food procurement. One scholar has gone so far as to suggest that Australia revise the European four-season calendar to acknowledge a six-season Aboriginal calendar. See Ryan.

25. Without making the naïve mistake of conflating climate and weather, Mark Carey makes a helpful distinction between historical climatology (the collection of data about past climates) and climate *history* (the study of society-climate interactions). The latter, he says, can include examinations of weather and meteorology (24).

26. Cheryl Savageau tells an amusing story about hearing her French Canadian mother on the phone, relaying a story that she had picked up via Louise Erdrich. When I asked Cheryl about this recently she said, "I'm thrilled that you remember the story about my mother. It's even funnier than what you remember. I was teaching at Holy Cross and my mother asked me what exactly I did in my job. We'd been reading *Love Medicine*, and I ended up telling her about Marie and Lulu and Nector and the house burning down, about Marie peeling every potato in the house, Lipsha and the love medicine and Nector dying from store-bought turkey? chicken? hearts, and then Marie giving Lulu eyedrops when they were in the senior housing, and Lulu telling Marie that she didn't regret anything. I left the room for a minute and when I came back my mother was on the phone with her sister, telling her the stories with exclamations of 'can you imagine her saying that?' etc. What I love about this is the idea that our written stories can become part of oral tradition and not just vice versa" (email, July 31, 2018).

27. Interestingly for this discussion of Mohegan weather lore, that article includes discussions of erotic relations with wind and thunder.

28. Trexler calls floods and deluges "the dominant literary strategy for locating climate change" (82). In his reading, "we simply do not know how to think about methane, ocean acidification, and biodiversity, but twentieth-century reinterpretations of Genesis were popular before greenhouse gases became a matter of public concern" (83). He might be interested in Indigenous novelists' approach to these topics.

29. Wholesale, drive-by dismissals of Indigenous environmental stewardship because of tribal involvement in gaming industries are common; but see, for instance, Krech 219, 225. In Maine, the Audubon Society and other environmental groups were particularly vocal opponents of a Penobscot effort to open a casino for tribal economic development. Since they successfully defeated that casino proposal in 2003, Maine has (unsurprisingly) opened two other casinos to benefit the state. On the Penobscot proposal, see Wanamaker; Donnelly. For a nuanced discussion of Indian gaming and sustainability, using the Florida Seminoles as a case study, see Cattelino, who demonstrates how gaming is simultaneously an extension of long-standing tribal economic practices and a vexed, modern enterprise that creates new forms of economic interdependency.

30. The Mohegans have invested some casino revenues directly in their literary history, for instance. The tribe has published books, including *Makiawisug: The Gift of the Little People*, which Tantaquidgeon Zobel wrote with

Joseph Bruchac. It produced a Claymation video by the same name, and an educational documentary about the historic leader Uncas. Mohegan Sun also built a montage honoring Gladys Tantaquidgeon and sells a small booklet describing the imagery in the casino, to ground visitors in Mohegan space.

31. See, for example, Archetti et al.

32. Of all the unwritten literary histories that a perusal of *Dawnland Voices* might prompt, one would be a history of federal recognition writing. Federal recognition cases are notoriously demanding, time-consuming, and expensive. The U.S. government requires a tribe to demonstrate that they fill seven criteria to prove that they are in fact (in the eyes of the government) a tribe. And this requires thousands upon thousands of pages of historical documentation, testimony, and argument. To compile all of this research and writing, tribes have enlisted attorneys, anthropologists, and their own members.

33. Phone conversation, December 19, 2014.

34. *The Lasting of the Mohegans* also exists in a paradoxically award-winning but unpublished format. Tantaquidgeon Zobel wrote a version that combines tribal history and memoir, winning a First Book Award for Prose in 1992 from the prestigious Native Writers' Circle of the Americas. All too typically, however, the small press that was to have published this memoir folded, and the book has still not appeared in print for wider distribution.

35. If it seems odd that New England's Native authors have turned to academic publishers in the Southwest, that is because university presses in the Northeast have been far less inviting to them. The University Press of New England, now defunct, generally declined to entertain manuscripts from regional Native authors, even after it published Colin Calloway's seminal call to consider Indigenous history, *After King Philip's War*. As the publication of *Dawnland Voices* confirms, university presses like Nebraska and Oklahoma, along with others in the Southwest and Pacific Northwest, tend to have deeper and more developed understandings of Indigenous histories and the importance of Indigenous literatures, and have therefore been more ready to publish Native authors from New England. A similar dynamic obtained in the case of Hobson's important collection, *The People Who Stayed: Southern Indian Writing after Removal*, which was published in 2010 by the University of Oklahoma Press.

36. The term "Native American Renaissance" is from a 1983 book of that title by the literary scholar Kenneth Lincoln. His coinage proved an appealing way to describe the seemingly new outpouring of Native literary production after 1969, when N. Scott Momaday (Kiowa) won the Pulitzer Prize for his novel *House Made of Dawn*. Authors typically associated with the Renaissance include Leslie Marmon Silko (Laguna), James Welch (Blackfeet), Gerald Vizenor (White Earth Anishinaabeg), Louise Erdrich (Turtle Mountain Ojibwe), Joy Harjo (Muscogee), and Simon Ortiz (Acoma). These writers have achieved high levels of prestige: they have won major prizes, including Silko's Pulitzer

and Erdrich's National Book Award, and they are supported by major publishing houses. They appear regularly in classroom literature anthologies and are the subjects of numerous scholarly studies, invited to teach at universities and present at conferences. Although Lincoln himself did explore a wide range of writers, including Joseph Bruchac, "Native American Renaissance" has tended to exercise the same kind of centripetal force that most canons do, always coming down to the same half-dozen writers.

With the exception of Joseph Bruchac, hardly any Indigenous writers from New England have published with major commercial houses. The big houses seem perennially reluctant to take on more than one Indian author at a time. Harper & Row had a Native American publishing series, which, it was felt, unintentionally or intentionally created a two-tiered system, allowing Native authors (James Welch, Duane Niatum) to be published in that series but not elsewhere with Harper & Row. This history is detailed in Wiget.

37. Since she first published her essay in 1993, Cook-Lynn's arguments have been both contested and enriched (e.g., Yazzie and Estes); it is certainly possible to read some of the more successful authors she condemns as deeply invested in decolonization.

38. An instructive alternative I did not discuss in the introduction but that would be well worth exploring vis-à-vis Indigenous environmental literature is *Roots of Our Renewal* by Clint Carroll (Cherokee), who proposes a model of "environmental governance," whereby groups like tribal natural resource offices are finding their own ways to negotiate state power and tribal needs.

4. Sovereign Poetics

1. Robert Dale Parker's indispensable introduction to pre-1930 Indigenous poetry, *Changing Is Not Vanishing*, includes an elegy in Latin, dated 1678, by "Eleazar," an Indian student at Harvard College (47–50). His extensive bibliography demonstrates that poems by Indigenous New Englanders can be found, for instance, in boarding school newspapers, such as the *Carlisle Arrow*.

2. Commuck also wrote hymns (*Indian Melodies*) and a history of the Brothertown Indians, with whom he moved to the Midwest ("Sketch of the Brothertown Indians").

3. From May 1970. This and other issues, including West's verse, are archived at http://dawnlandvoices.org/collections/exhibits/show/newsletters/aroostook.

4. A letterpress run by Diana Prizio out of both Knox and Brooks, Maine, called "Little Letterpress" and "Robin Hood Books."

5. This chapter focuses largely on writers who aspire to write as their primary vocation, but quite a few other regional poets have garnered literary reputations within their tribes through circulation in locally produced booklets and pamphlets, or more recently on the internet. Examples include Rob-

ert Peters (Mashpee Wampanoag), Mary Ellen Socobasin (Penobscot), and Nick Bear (Penobscot).

6. Supported, in this case, at least in part by casino revenues. Casino revenues obviously do not guarantee that tribes will establish publishing ventures for their own members and interests, though. The neighboring Mashanucket Pequots, who did leverage casino moneys for an extraordinary museum and some publishing, have not seen the dramatic surge in tribal literary production that the Mohegans, Wampanoags, or (unrecognized) Abenaki have.

7. The Missisquoi band of Abenaki in Vermont has pursued federal recognition, albeit unsuccessfully. The state of Vermont has recognized four Abenaki bands to date. For a more detailed history, see Wiseman.

8. Alice James, located in Farmington, Maine, was founded in 1973 with the express purpose of publishing and supporting women poets. Curbstone, in Willimantic, Connecticut, was established in 1975 with an emphasis on multicultural literature and social justice. Since its founder, Sandy Taylor, died in 2007, it has been an imprint of Northwestern University Press. Salt Publishing, based in the United Kingdom, is an independent trade publisher that has developed an Indigenous series called Earthworks, which has published such high-profile writers as Kimberly Blaeser, Allison Adele Hedge Coke, Heid E. Erdrich, Carter Revard, and Gerald Vizenor.

9. Created as a companion quilt to "Jazz Autumn," the "Illusion of Ownership" can be viewed, in part, as the header to Savageau's blog at https://cherylsavageaublog.wordpress.com/.

10. It is worth noting that, colonial though they may be, stone walls have also been indigenized in New England: Narragansett people in Rhode Island, in particular, have developed a strong tradition of stonemasonry. There is an excellent 2008 documentary about this tradition, *Stories in Stone*, by Levitt.

11. Clare Barker and I have attempted to spur conversations between Native American and Indigenous studies and disability studies; see our introduction to a special issue of the *Journal of Literary and Cultural Disability Studies* on this topic (Senier and Barker). The work of Joseph Gone (Gros Ventre) on decolonizing mental illness is also much needed and important.

12. This section was previously published in *Studies in American Indian Literatures*. Some newspapers (most famously the *Cherokee Phoenix* and *Awkesasne Notes*) have been around for much longer, but most Native-run literary book publishers have faced serious challenges in achieving long-term sustainability. Some other outfits that arose in the late 1960s and 1970s have since fallen by the wayside, including Rupert Costo's Indian Historian Press and Maurice Kenny's Strawberry Press. Since the early 2000s there has been a new effusion of Indigenous small presses, including renegade planets publishing (MariJo Moore), Mammoth Publications (Denise Low and Tom Weso), Wigawassi Press (Louise and Heid Erdrich), and Blue Hand Books (Trace DeMeyer). Most of these have been dependent

on the financing and labor of one or two extremely dedicated individuals. In Canada, Aboriginal presses like Theytus and Kegedonce have at least had some access to government funding (Chunn), although this has eroded in recent years (Milz). Tribal museums and historic offices have long issued their own books and newsletters for tribal use or local sale. Malki Museum Press opened in 1965, with a focus on California Indians (and on scholarly publishing); the Chickasaw Press, established in 2005, has been publishing Chickasaw-themed books. For a concise history of late twentieth-century literary publishing, including Harper & Row's Native American writers series and the profusion of chapbooks coming out of places like the Blue Cloud Quarterly, see Wiget. I thank my colleagues on the ASAIL-L mailing list for many of these pointers and invite readers to continue updating this information at https://dawnlandvoices.org/a-crowdsourcing-question -indigenous-small-presses/.

13. Electronic formats are not, of course, free of the potential for loss. One thing we already lose with lulu.com is an accurate chronicle of publishing history: a book's publication date will show up as the most recent version, reflecting any edits or changes. Since the books are being printed on demand and are easily updated and edited, it is hard to know when a book first appeared without having a first edition in hand—and, for that matter, knowing that it was the first edition.

14. As of this writing I count no fewer than five facsimile editions of the Laurent book on Amazon's website, some from enterprises committed to increasing access to public domain texts (e.g., Global Language Press in Vancouver) and some by the rapidly proliferating software companies that trawl Project Gutenberg and the Internet Archive looking for public-domain texts to grab and reprint (e.g., Ulan Press, Nabu Press). Although it may be legal— and even ethical—to republish older books like Laurent's, the role of publishers like Bowman Books in properly curating literary heritage cannot be underestimated. For a fascinating history of print-on-demand publishing and its implications for literary history, see Trettien.

15. Writing about the Connecticut River, Lisa Brooks, Donna Roberts Moody (Abenaki), and John Moody say, for instance, "While the settlers of Vermont and New Hampshire designated this river as a boundary, within Native space, Kwanitekw has operated as a major trade corridor, travel route, and gathering place for Indigenous families" (133).

16. Paul, "Artist Statement."

17. See Tantaquidgeon Zobel, "The New York Times Can Do Better."

18. In the back of my mind is Jane Tompkins's classic and brilliant study of Hawthorne's literary reputation.

19. Personal email communication, July 28, 2017.

5. Indigenous New England Online

1. A full engagement with these debates is outside the scope of this chapter. Readers wanting introductions to some of them might consult Gabrys's book on digital waste; librarian Robert Darnton's engaging ruminations on books, technology, and obsolescence; and Maxwell and Miller, especially their chapter "Screens." Discussions of digital labor exploitation are abundant, but Kosnik is particularly astute about digital archives and the endless, *human* labor they require.

2. #IdleNoMore began in late 2012 as a specific protest against Canada's passage of Bill C-45, which, among other things, removed certain protections on waterways and forests in Indigenous territories. The hashtag went viral, adopted by Indigenous people and allies the world over, and remains active as a signifier of Indigenous sovereignty and self-determination. #MMIW calls attention to the extreme situation of murdered and missing Indigenous women. Both hashtags have roots in much older activism; every February 14 for over two decades now, Aboriginal women in Canada have staged memorial marches for missing and murdered women. And each campaign has had ripple effects to further activism, multimedia, museum exhibits, and more. For more on IdleNoMore, see the powerful book *The Winter We Danced* (Kino-nda-niimi Collective); for more on #MMIW, see Native Youth Sexual Health Network.

3. Some of the writers represented in *Dawnland Voices* have kept blogs, although with the exceptions of Alice Azure's (aliceazure.com) and Carol Bachofner's (rockcitypoet.blogspot.com), these have tended to be short-lived. Cheryl Savageau (Abenaki) has started a blog at cherylsavageaublog.wordpress.com. Wunnea Cason (Schaghticoke) has discontinued her blog. Other short-lived blogs have included one written by Lynsea Montanari at the Tomaquag Museum (tomaquag.weebly.com) and another by the talented Penobscot poet Maulian Dana (mauliandana.blogspot.com/). Also of interest, but not discussed in this chapter, is Seven Eagles, the media company run by Donna Loring (Penobscot) that has helped produce film and video, including some Penobscot hip-hop poetry.

4. Mohegan Tribe, "The Mohegan Tribe's History."

5. Destination Plymouth, "Plymouth Rock."

6. Discover St. John, "Discover Wolastoq Park."

7. For a brief description of the smartphone app, see H. Anderson; for an account of the immersion school, see Billings and BDN Staff.

8. See Brooks, *Common Pot* 249.

9. More recently Jesse Bruchac has migrated his recordings to YouTube, where he has an entire channel devoted to language lessons and videos of him speaking Abenaki with his two small children: https://www.youtube.com/user/westernabenaki.

10. "Blogjects," as Julian Bleecker calls them.

11. One of the most recent, Siva Vaidhyanathan, concedes that the "internet generally, and Facebook specifically, lowered the costs of coordination" for things like organizing demonstrations and boycotts and gathering signatures on petitions (127). But he also historicizes this, saying that activists have always "used the communication tools at their disposal" and that Facebook is surely no better—and in many ways more dangerous—than other tools (130).

12. *Lewiston (ME) Sun-Journal*, archived at http://www.bigorrin.org/archive63.htm.

13. The old print issues from 1994 to 2001 have been scanned and archived at http://nipmucspohke.homestead.com/Past-Issues.html. The new public Facebook group is at https://www.facebook.com/groups/65556891253/about/. In Maine, one newsletter and its attendant controversies have carried over onto Facebook. *Keq Leyu* (What's Going On) began as an official publication of the Passamaquoddy tribal government but shut down amid conflict among tribal leaders during the late 1980s (Woodard). In 2012 one tribal member, Stephanie Bailey, tried reviving the newsletter on a volunteer basis, but she quickly found the cost of publishing to be unsustainable and migrated to a closed Facebook group. By the summer of 2014, however, Bailey found herself at odds with the Joint Tribal Council, which ordered her to change the newsletter's name. As one member told a journalist, the Council was concerned about outside parties, including state officials, exploiting information about internal tribal discussions and disagreements. The Council was also worried about quality control, including vulgarity (Woodard). Bailey has so far refused to take the group down.

14. April 20, 2018. Comment by Kristen Wyman (Nipmuc): "Beautiful example of recognition and knowledge exchange among the people!"

15. Some professional archivists bristle at the loose way the term "archive" is being bandied about these days to describe everything from your laptop's backups to large collections of digital surrogates. But many are also now considering much larger questions of public memory and broadening their own roles to include not just accession, ordering, and description but also outreach and community facilitation. For more on this, see Cook; Theimer.

16. The most widely cited tend to include Derrida and Prenowitz; Stoler. I would also point readers to Adeline Koh's important introduction to a special section of *Verge* on Asian digital humanities projects, which asserts that "the existing digital archive is generally deafeningly silent in relation to the representation of peoples and cultures outside of the United States and Western Europe" (21).

17. Some ethnographers were notorious for barging into communities and taking materials (including stories) unethically; others built more reciprocal relations with the communities they worked with and produced materials of some value to Native people today. For more on this history, see Silko.

18. The Perseus Digital Library is at http://www.perseus.tufts.edu/hopper/; Folger Digital Texts is at http://www.folgerdigitaltexts.org/; the Franklin Papers are at https://franklinpapers.org; the Walt Whitman Archive is at http://www.whitmanarchive.org/. These are gorgeous, innovative, and generous archives. The point is that digital humanities funding has retrenched around canonical figures and analytics.

19. The evolving genealogies and contours of digital humanities are being well documented in *Debates in the Digital Humanities*, edited by Matthew Gold and Lauren Klein.

20. Such efforts extend beyond Indigenous archives. For a helpful overview of community-engaged digital historiography, see Enoch and Gold.

21. Available at http://ojibwearchive.sas.upenn.edu/ (accessed February 12, 2014). For more on this project, see T. Powell and Aitken.

22. Available at http://www.library.yale.edu/yipp/ (accessed February 12, 2014). For more on this project, see Grant-Costa et al.

23. Mukurtu's home page is mukurtu.org. See Christen; Jane Anderson and Christen.

24. Labels available at localcontexts.org; see also Jane Anderson, "Indigenous Knowledge, Intellectual Property, Libraries and Archives."

25. *Wususko* means "painted word." Faith Damon Davison, email communication, July 14, 2014. For some years the Mohegans published a separate newsletter, *Ni-ya-yo*, open to nontribal members, though this ceased publication in 2007.

26. In a special section devoted to "the ethnic archive" in PMLA, the editors put the question like this: "Should scholars recover and foreground artifacts that reveal indigenous knowledge, or should they reconsider the archive wholesale, questioning its politics and practices, and implement new practices and methodologies?" (Williams and Lopez 358).

27. For more on this, see Phillips 287; Boast and Enote, who have said point-blank that "virtual repatriation is not repatriation."

28. For a similar argument about Indigenous museum practices, see Christina Kreps's excellent book *Liberating Culture*, which argues that "until relatively recently, collecting and curatorial practices as well as museum-like structures existing outside the western world have largely gone unexplored" (46).

29. Something I heard repeatedly from authors and tribal editors after the publication of *Dawnland Voices* was, "I had no idea," often meaning, "Had I known how big this was going to be, or had I known what other editors and authors were doing, I might have chosen differently." Mia Ridge has observed the value of multiple iterations in crowdsourced cultural heritage projects, pointing out that "crowdsourcing projects are almost inevitably changed (and changed for the better) by contact with the crowd" (7).

30. *Dawnland Voices*, "About."

31. I have written about these pedagogical projects elsewhere. For a fuller discussion of the basket exhibit, see Senier, "Decolonizing the Archive"; for a discussion on adding contemporary writers to the archive, in combination with a Wikipedia assignment, see Senier, "Indigenizing Wikipedia."

32. "Sustainability: The Elephant in the Room" is the title of an essay by Jerome McGann, who has famously said that "the entirety of our cultural heritage must be re-curated within a digital horizon" and has more recently said that he is concluding work on his monumental Rossetti archive and printing the digital materials in their entirety. A fascinating comment on sustainability.

33. Two cultural heritage scholars have suggested that such tools in fact may have already been superseded by more commercial platforms like Facebook (Brown and Nicholas).

34. In their working paper "Digital Access for Language and Culture," Jennifer Carpenter and colleagues make this critical point: "Externally inspired research projects can exert complex pressures on Indigenous communities, diverting community energy and resources away from core tasks and requirements to address outside agendas and expectations. Direct provincial and federal investment in the research infrastructure and human capacity in Indigenous communities is therefore imperative and urgent" (2).

35. The Association of Tribal Archives, Libraries and Museums reports that "Native American tribes remain the most unconnected group of Americans in the country, with fewer than 10 percent having access to broadband, in contrast to roughly 65 percent of all Americans." As a result, the Association has found, the vast majority of tribal libraries and archives are not digitizing anything, even though digitization is now the industry standard, citing reasons of funding, training, staffing, and more pressing priorities.

36. This project is described in more detail in Senier, "Writing of Indigenous New England."

37. A thoroughgoing discussion of Indigenous intellectual property is also outside the scope of this chapter, but I do recommend the April 2014 report of the Penobscot Nation's Intellectual Property Working Group (Newsom and Wobst) as well as all publications by Jane Anderson.

38. Dawnland Voices, "Tribal Archives."

39. Srinivasan et al., working with a team that included the Zuni librarian Jim Enote, found that, for Zuni people, the two most important factors for understanding cultural objects are stories about those objects and their uses, both historical and modern (754).

40. A notable exception is the Nisga'a poet Jordan Abel, who uses digital tools to make new meaning out of source texts (often ethnographic source texts). But this is quite different from digitizing, say, Indigenous writings and mining them for information that may or may not be sensitive or damaging.

Works Cited

Adams, Jim. "Gombey Dancers Mark Reunion." *Indian Country Today Media Network*, 1 Oct. 2003, indiancountrytodaymedianetwork.com/2003/10 /01/gombey-dancers-mark-reunion-89378.

Adamson, Joni. *American Indian Literature, Environmental Justice, and Ecocriticism: The Middle Place*. University of Arizona Press, 2001.

Adamson, Joni, and Michael Davis, editors. *Humanities for the Environment: Integrating Knowledge, Forging New Constellations of Practice*. Routledge, 2016.

Akins, Cynthia. "Summertime on Gay Head." *The Indians Who Met the Pilgrims*. Boston Children's Museum, 1999.

Alaimo, Stacy. *Bodily Natures: Science, Environment, and the Material Self*. Indiana University Press, 2010.

———. "Sustainable This, Sustainable That: New Materialisms, Posthumanism, and Unknown Futures." PMLA: *Publications of the Modern Language Association of America*, vol. 127, no. 3, May 2012, pp. 558–64.

Alfred, Taiaiake. *Peace, Power, Righteousness: An Indigenous Manifesto*. New York: Oxford University Press, 1999.

Anderson, Benedict. *Imagined Communities: Reflections on the Origin and Spread of Nationalism*. Verso, 2006.

Anderson, Heather. "New Passamaquoddy Language App." *Abbe Museum*, 27 Oct. 2015, abbemuseum.blogspot.com/2015/10/new-passamaquoddy -language-app.html.

Anderson, Jane. "(Colonial) Archives and (Copyright) Law." *Nomorepotlucks*, vol. 4, July 2009, works.bepress.com/cgi/viewcontent.cgi?article=1003 &context=jane_anderson.

———. "Indigenous Knowledge, Intellectual Property, Libraries and Archives: Crises of Access, Control and Future Utility." *Australian Academic & Research Libraries*, vol. 36, no. 2, Jan. 2005, pp. 83–94.

Anderson, Jane, and Kimberly Christen. "'Chuck a Copyright on It': Dilemmas of Digital Return and the Possibilities for Traditional Knowledge

Licenses and Labels." *Museum Anthropology Review*, vol. 7, nos. 1–2, 2013, pp. 105–26.

Anderson, Joyce Rain. "Remapping Settler Colonial Territories: Bringing Local Native Knowledge into the Classroom." *Survivance, Sovereignty, and Story: Teaching American Indian Rhetorics*, edited by Lisa King, Rose Gubele, and Joyce Rain Anderson, Utah State University Press, 2015, pp. 160–69.

Apess, William. *On Our Own Ground: The Complete Writings of William Apess, a Pequot*. University of Massachusetts Press, 1992.

Archetti, Marco, et al. "Predicting Climate Change Impacts on the Amount and Duration of Autumn Colors in a New England Forest." PLOS ONE, vol. 8, no. 3, Mar. 2013, p. e57373.

Association of Tribal Archives, Libraries and Museums. *International Conference Program*. Albuquerque NM, 2013.

Attaquin, Helen. *A Brief History of Gay Head or "Aquinuh."* Helen Attaquin, 1970.

Avant, Joan Tavares. *People of the First Light: Wisdoms of a Mashpee Wampanoag Elder*. West Barnstable Press, 2010.

Bachofner, Carol Willette. *Native Moons, Native Days*. Bowman Books, 2011.

Barker, Joanne. *Sovereignty Matters: Locations of Contestation and Possibility in Indigenous Struggles for Self-Determination*. University of Nebraska Press, 2005.

Barthel-Bouchier, Diane. *Cultural Heritage and the Challenge of Sustainability*. Left Coast Press, 2012.

Basso, Keith H. *Wisdom Sits in Places: Landscape and Language among the Western Apache*. University of New Mexico Press, 1996.

Battiste, Marie, and James Youngblood (Sákéj) Henderson. *Protecting Indigenous Knowledge and Heritage: A Global Challenge*. UBC Press, 2000.

Berry, Lorraine. "How the Literary Class System Is Impoverishing Literature." *Lit Hub*, 4 Dec. 2015, lithub.com/the-literary-class-system-is-impoverishing-literature/.

Billings, Johanna S., and BDN Staff. "Passamaquoddy Tribe to Launch Language Immersion Program." *Bangor (ME) Daily News*, 28 Oct. 2015, http://bangordailynews.com/2015/10/28/news/down-east/passamaquoddy-tribe-to-launch-language-immersion-program/.

Bingham, Amelia G. *Mashpee: Land of the Wampanoags*. Mashpee Historical Commission, 1970.

Bleecker, Julian. *A Manifesto for Networked Objects—Cohabiting with Pigeons, Arphids and Aibos in the Internet of Things (or, Why Things Matter)*. 2006, http://nearfuturelaboratory.com/files/WhyThingsMatter.pdf.

Boast, Robin, and Jim Enote. "Virtual Repatriation: It Is Neither Virtual nor Repatriation." *Heritage in the Context of Globalization*, edited by Peter Biehl and Christopher Prescott, vol. 8, New York, Springer, 2013, pp. 103–13.

Boissevain, Ethel. "The Detribalization of the Narragansett Indians: A Case Study." *Ethnohistory*, vol. 3, no. 3, 1956, p. 225.

boundary 2. "Ursula K. Heise—Climate Stories: Review of Amitav Ghosh's 'The Great Derangement.'" *b2o*, 19 Feb. 2018, http://www.boundary2.org /2018/02/ursula-k-heise-climate-stories-review-of-amitav-ghoshs-the -great-derangement/.

Bragdon, Kathleen J. "The Pragmatics of Language Learning: Graphic Pluralism on Martha's Vineyard, 1660–1720." *Ethnohistory*, vol. 57, no. 1, 2010, pp. 35–50.

Brandt, Deborah. *Literacy and Learning: Reflections on Writing, Reading, and Society.* Jossey-Bass, 2009.

Brodeur, Paul. *Restitution: The Land Claims of the Mashpee, Passamaquoddy, and Penobscot Indians of New England.* Northeastern University Press, 1985.

Brooks, Lisa. *The Common Pot: The Recovery of Native Space in the Northeast.* University of Minnesota Press, 2008.

———. *Our Beloved Kin: A New History of King Philip's War.* Yale University Press, 2018.

Brooks, Lisa, and Cassandra Brooks. "The Reciprocity Principle and Traditional Ecological Knowledge: Understanding the Significance of Indigenous Protest on the Presumpscot River." *International Journal of Critical Indigenous Studies*, vol. 3, no. 2, 2010, pp. 11–28.

Brooks, Lisa, Donna Roberts Moody, and John Moody. "Native Space." *Where the Great River Rises: An Atlas of the Upper Connecticut River Watershed in Vermont and New Hampshire*, edited by Rebecca A. Brown, Dartmouth College Press, 2009, pp. 133–37.

Brown, Deidre, and George Nicholas. "Protecting Indigenous Cultural Property in the Age of Digital Democracy: Institutional and Communal Responses to Canadian First Nations and Māori Heritage Concerns." *Journal of Material Culture*, vol. 17, no. 3, Sept. 2012, pp. 307–24.

Bruchac, James. *Be Good.* Bowman Books, 2010.

Bruchac, Jesse. *Mosbas and the Magic Flute.* Bowman Books, 2010.

———. *The Woman and the Kiwakw.* Bowman Books, 2013.

Bruchac, Jesse, Joseph Alfred Elie Joubert, and Jeanne Brink. *L8dwaw8gan Wji Abaznodakaw8gan / The Language of Basket Making.* Bowman Books, 2010.

Bruchac, Joseph. *The Dreams of Jesse Brown.* Cold Mountain Press, 1978.

———. *Hidden Roots.* Bowman Books, 2010.

———. *How to Start and Sustain a Literary Magazine: Practical Strategies for Publications of Lasting Value.* Provision House, 1980.

———. "Indigenous Publishing in New England." *First Nations, Lasting Nations: Community and University Partnerships in Indigenous New England.* Durham NH, 18 Sept. 2010.

———. *Our Stories Remember: American Indian History, Culture, and Values through Storytelling.* Fulcrum Publishing, 2016.

————, editor. *Returning the Gift: Poetry and Prose from the First Native North American Writers' Festival.* University of Arizona Press, 1994.

————. *The Wind Eagle and Other Abenaki Stories.* Greenfield Review Press, 1985.

Bruchac, Joseph, and Jesse Bruchac. *Nisnol Siboal / Two Rivers.* Bowman Books, 2011.

Bruchac, Margaret. *Dreaming Again: Algonkian Poetry.* Bowman Books, 2012.

————. "Hiding in Plain Sight: Abenaki Persistence in VT." *The Abenaki of Vermont: A Living Culture—Teacher's Guide,* edited by Gregory Sharrow, Vermont Folklife Center, 2002, pp. 16–31.

————. *Savage Kin: Indigenous Informants and American Anthropologists.* University of Arizona Press, 2018.

Burton, Antoinette, et al. *Archive Stories: Facts, Fictions, and the Writing of History.* Duke University Press, 2006.

Byrd, Jodi A. "Red Dead Conventions: American Indian Transgeneric Fictions." *The Oxford Handbook of Indigenous American Literature,* edited by James H. Cox and Daniel Heath Justice, New York: Oxford University Press, 2014, pp. 344–57.

————. *The Transit of Empire: Indigenous Critiques of Colonialism.* University of Minnesota Press, 2011.

————. "Tribal 2.0: Digital Natives, Political Players, and the Power of Stories." *Studies in American Indian Literatures: The Journal of the Association for the Study of American Indian Literatures,* vol. 26, no. 2, 2014, pp. 55–64.

Caduto, Michael J., and Joseph Bruchac. *Keepers of Life: Discovering Plants through Native American Stories and Earth Activities for Children.* Fulcrum Publishing, 1998.

Campisi, Jack. *The Mashpee Indians: Tribe on Trial.* Syracuse University Press, 1991.

Carey, Mark. "Beyond Weather: The Culture and Politics of Climate History." *The Oxford Handbook of Environmental History,* edited by Andrew C. Isenberg, New York: Oxford University Press, 2014, pp. 23–51.

Carlson, Richard G. *Rooted Like the Ash Trees: New England Indians and the Land.* Eagle Wing Press, 1987.

Carpenter, Jennifer, et al. "Digital Access for Language and Culture in First Nations Communities." Vancouver, Oct. 2016, http://fnhssm.com/peke/wpcontent/uploads/2017/08/report_2016_digital_language_access.pdf.

Carpenter, Kristen A., et al. "In Defense of Property." *Yale Law Journal,* vol. 118, no. 6, Apr. 2009, pp. 1022–255.

Carroll, Clint. *Roots of Our Renewal: Ethnobotany and Cherokee Environmental Governance.* University of Minnesota Press, 2015.

Castaneda, Terri. "Making News: Marie Potts and the *Smoke Signal* of the Federated Indians of California." *Women in Print: Essays on the Print Culture of American Women from the Nineteenth and Twentieth Centu-*

ries, edited by James P. Danky and Wayne A. Wiegand, University of Wisconsin Press, 2006, pp. 77–125.

Cattelino, Jessica. *High Stakes: Florida Seminole Gaming and Sovereignty.* Duke University Press, 2008.

Center for New England Culture, University of New Hampshire. "The Illusion of Ownership—Quilt by Cheryl Savageau." *"We're Still Here" Online Exhibit*, 2005, http://cola.unh.edu/media-gallery/detail/7591/90950.

———. "Jazz Autumn—Quilt by Cheryl Savageau." *"We're Still Here" Online Exhibit*, 2005, http://cola.unh.edu/center-new-england-culture/quilts -weavings.

Chavaree, Mark. "We Are a Riverine People: The Penobscot Nation of Maine." *Cultural Survival*, vol. 38, no. 2, June 2014, http://www.culturalsurvival .org/publications/cultural-survival-quarterly/we-are-riverine-people -penobscot-nation-maine.

Chickasaw Press. "Chickasaw Press." https://chickasawpress.com/About /Chickasaw-Press.aspx. Accessed 2 Aug. 2018.

Christen, Kimberly. "A Safe Keeping Place: Mukurtu cms Innovating Museum Collaborations." *Technology and Digital Initiatives: Innovative Approaches for Museums*, edited by Juilee Decker, Rowman & Littlefield, 2015, pp. 62–68.

Chunn, Ian. "'Preserving for the Sake of Handing Down': A Profile of Theytus Books." *Australian-Canadian Studies*, vol. 14, nos. 1–2, 1996, pp. 173–77.

Clark, William C., and Nancy M. Dickson. "Sustainability Science: The Emerging Research Program." *Proceedings of the National Academy of Sciences of the United States of America*, vol. 100, no. 14, July 2003, pp. 8059–61.

Clifford, James. *The Predicament of Culture: Twentieth-Century Ethnography, Literature and Art.* Harvard University Press, 1988.

———. "Varieties of Indigenous Experience: Diasporas, Homelands, Sovereignties." *Indigenous Experience Today*, edited by Marisol de la Cadena and Orin Stran, Berg Publishers, 2008, pp. 197–224.

Commuck, Thomas. *Indian Melodies.* Lane & Tippett, 1845.

———. "Sketch of the Brothertown Indians." *Wisconsin Electronic Reader*, 1859, http://www.library.wisc.edu/etext/WIReader/WER0439.html.

Cook, Terry. "Evidence, Memory, Identity, and Community: Four Shifting Archival Paradigms." *Archival Science*, vol. 13, nos. 2–3, June 2013, pp. 95–120, doi:10.1007/s10502-012-9180-7.

Cook-Lynn, Elizabeth. *Why I Can't Read Wallace Stegner and Other Essays: A Tribal Voice.* University of Wisconsin Press, 1996.

Coombs, Linda. "Hobbamock's Homesite." *Thanks, but No Thanks: Mirroring the Myth—Native Perspectives on Thanksgiving.* Plymouth MA: Wampanoag Indian Program, 9 Sept. 2000, pp. 2–3.

———. "*Mayflower: A Story of Courage, Community and War* by Nathaniel Philbrick [Book Review]." *Cultural Survival Quarterly*, vol. 31, no.

1, Spring 2007, http://www.culturalsurvival.org/publications/cultural
-survival-quarterly/united-states/mayflower-story-courage-community
-and-war-nat.

———. *Powwow.* Modern Curriculum, 1992.

———. "Thanks, but No Thanks." Introduction to *Thanks, but No Thanks: Mirroring the Myth—Native Perspectives on Thanksgiving.* Plymouth MA: Wampanoag Indian Program, 9 Sept. 2000, p. 5.

Cooper, Karen Coody. *Spirited Encounters: American Indians Protest Museum Policies and Practices.* AltaMira Press, 2008.

Corntassel, Jeff. "Re-Envisioning Resurgence: Indigenous Pathways to Decolonization and Sustainable Self-Determination." *Decolonization: Indigeneity, Education & Society*, vol. 1, no. 1, Sept. 2012, http://decolonization.org/index.php/des/article/view/18627.

Couldry, Nick. "The Social Foundations of Future Digital Politics." *Handbook of Digital Politics*, edited by Stephen Coleman and Deen Freelon, Edward Elgar Publishing, 2015, pp. 35–50.

Coulthard, Glen Sean. "From Wards of the State to Subjects of Recognition? Marx, Indigenous Peoples, and the Politics of Dispossession in Denendeh." *Theorizing Native Studies*, edited by Audra Simpson and Andrea Smith, Duke University Press, 2014, pp. 56–98.

Counihan, Carole, and Penny Van Esterik. *Food and Culture: A Reader.* Routledge, 2013.

Cronon, William. "The Trouble with Wilderness; Or, Getting Back to the Wrong Nature." *Uncommon Ground: Rethinking the Human Place in Nature*, edited by William Cronon, W. W. Norton, 1995, pp. 69–90.

Cruikshank, Julie. "The Social Life of Texts: Editing on the Page and in Performance." *Talking on the Page: Editing Aboriginal Oral Texts. Papers Given at the Thirty-Second Annual Conference on Editorial Problems, University of Toronto, 14–16 November 1996*, edited by Laura Murray and Keren Rice, University of Toronto Press, 1999, pp. 97–119.

Cushman, Ellen. *The Cherokee Syllabary: Writing the People's Perseverance.* University of Oklahoma Press, 2012.

———. *Literacy: A Critical Sourcebook.* Bedford/St. Martin's, 2001.

———. "Wampum, Sequoyan, and Story: Decolonizing the Digital Archive." *College English*, vol. 76, no. 2, Nov. 2013, pp. 116–35.

Dana, Carol. *Return to Spirit and Other Musings.* Bowman Books, 2014.

———. *When No One Is Looking.* Bowman Books, 2011.

Darnton, Robert. *The Case for Books: Past, Present, and Future.* PublicAffairs, 2010.

Davis, Heather, and Etienne Turpin. "Art & Death: Lives between the Fifth Assessment & the Sixth Extinction." *Art in the Anthropocene: Encounters among Aesthetics, Politics, Environments and Epistemologies.* Open

Humanities Press, 2015, pp. 3–30, http://openhumanitiespress.org/books
/download/Davis-Turpin_2015_Art-in-the-Anthropocene.pdf.

Dawnland Voices. "About." 2015, http://dawnlandvoices.org/collections/exhibits
/show/along-the-basket-trail/about.

———. "Tribal Archives: Untold Histories of Activism and Survival." 2016,
http://dawnlandvoices.org/collections/exhibits/show/tribalarchives.

DeLuca, Danielle. "What Do the Sustainable Development Goals Mean for
Indigenous Peoples?" *Cultural Survival Quarterly Magazine*, Dec. 2017,
https://www.culturalsurvival.org/publications/cultural-survival-quarterly
/what-do-sustainable-development-goals-mean-indigenous.

DeLucia, Christine. "Placing Joseph Bruchac: Native Literary Networks and
Cultural Transmission in the Contemporary Northeast." *Studies in American Indian Literatures*, vol. 24, no. 3, Fall 2012, pp. 71–96.

Den Ouden, Amy, and Jean M. O'Brien. *Recognition, Sovereignty Struggles,
and Indigenous Rights in the United States: A Sourcebook*. UNC Press
Books, 2013.

Derrida, Jacques, and Eric Prenowitz. "Archive Fever: A Freudian Impression." *Diacritics*, vol. 25, no. 2, July 1995, pp. 9–63, doi:10.2307/465144.

Destination Plymouth. "Plymouth Rock." 2012, https://www.seeplymouth
.com/things-to-do/plymouth-rock.

Dillon, Grace L., editor. *Walking the Clouds: An Anthology of Indigenous Science Fiction*. University of Arizona Press, 2012.

Dimaline, Cherie. *The Marrow Thieves*. DCB, 2017.

Din, Herminia Weihsin. *A History of Children's Museums in the United States,
1899–1997: Implications for Art Education and Museum Education in Art
Museums*. Ohio State University Press, 1998.

Discover St. John. "Discover Wolastoq Park." https://www.discoversaintjohn
.com/place/discover-wolastoq-park.

Donnelly, Sara. "After the Casino: A Conversation with Former Penobscot
Indian Nation Chief Barry Dana about Tribal Economic Development
in the Aftermath of Last Year's Failed Casino Proposal." *Mainebiz*, 27
Sept. 2004, http://www.mainebiz.biz/article/after-the-casino-a-conver
sation-with-former-penobscot-indian-nation-chief-barry-dana-about.

Dow, Judy. "Statement from Judy Dow about Vermont Eugenics Survey."
*Invisible/Visible: Emerging Contemporary New England Native American
Art*, 2010, https://cola.unh.edu/center-new-england-culture/judy-dow.

Dresser, Tom. *The Wampanoag Tribe of Martha's Vineyard: Colonization to
Recognition*. History Press, 2011.

Duarte, Marisa Elena. *Network Sovereignty: Building the Internet across Indian
Country*. University of Washington Press, 2017.

Ellis, Clyde, et al. *Powwow*. University of Nebraska Press, 2005.

English, James F. *The Economy of Prestige: Prizes, Awards, and the Circulation of Cultural Value*. Harvard University Press, 2009.

Enoch, Jessica, and David Gold. "Seizing the Methodological Moment: The Digital Humanities and Historiography in Rhetoric and Composition." *College English*, vol. 76, no. 2, Nov. 2013, pp. 105–14.

Erdrich, Heid E., editor. *New Poets of Native Nations*. Graywolf, 2018.

Erdrich, Louise, et al. *Conversations with Louise Erdrich and Michael Dorris*. University Press of Mississippi, 1994.

Ernest, Marcella. "Linguicide, Indigenous Community and the Search for Lost Sounds." *Sounding Out*, no. 40, 26 Mar. 2015, http://soundstudiesblog.com /2015/03/26/sounding-out-podcast-40-linguicide-indigenous-community -and-the-search-for-lost-sounds/.

Executive Order No. 502: Establishing the Plymouth, Massachusetts 400th Anniversary Commission. Office of Governor Deval L. Patrick, 10 June 2008, https://www.mass.gov/executive-orders/no-502-establishing-the -plymouth-massachusetts-400th-anniversary-commission.

Fahmy, Ziad. *Ordinary Egyptians: Creating the Modern Nation through Popular Culture*. Stanford University Press, 2011.

Fielding, Stephanie. *Mohegan Language Project*. http://www.moheganlanguage .com/. Accessed 6 Aug. 2012.

"First Thanksgiving: Boston City Hall Linda Coombs 4/4." *YouTube*, 2010, http://www.youtube.com/watch?v=FCTnaQU9X2g&feature=youtube _gdata_player.

Fitzpatrick, Kathleen. *The Anxiety of Obsolescence: The American Novel in the Age of Television*. Vanderbilt University Press, 2006.

Foster, Tol. "Of One Blood: An Argument for Relations and Regionality in Native American Literary Studies." *Reasoning Together: The Native Critics Collective*, edited by Craig Womack et al., University of Oklahoma Press, 2008, pp. 265–302.

Francis, David A., and Robert M. Leavitt. *A Passamaquoddy-Maliseet Dictionary / Peskotomuhkati Wolastoqewi Latuwewakon*. Bilingual edition. Goose Lane Editions, 2008.

Gabrys, Jennifer. *Digital Rubbish: A Natural History of Electronics*. University of Michigan Press, 2011.

Gagnon, Dawn. "Penobscot Nation, Allies Protest Federal Ruling on River Rights." *Bangor (ME) Daily News*, 10 July 2017, http://bangordailynews .com/2017/07/10/news/state/penobscot-nation-allies-protest-federal -ruling-on-river-rights/.

Gallagher, Nancy L. *Breeding Better Vermonters: The Eugenics Project in the Green Mountain State*. University Press of New England, 1999.

Garrard, Greg. *Ecocriticism*. Routledge, 2004.

Garroutte, Eva. *Real Indians: Identity and the Survival of Native America*. University of California Press, 2003.

Garvey, Ellen Gruber. *Writing with Scissors: American Scrapbooks from the Civil War to the Harlem Renaissance*. New York: Oxford University Press, 2012.

Ghosh, Amitav. *The Great Derangement: Climate Change and the Unthinkable.* University of Chicago Press, 2016.

Goddard, Ives, and Kathleen J. Bragdon. *Native Writings in Massachusett.* American Philosophical Society, 1988.

Gold, Matthew K., and Lauren Klein, editors. *Debates in the Digital Humanities.* University of Minnesota Press, 2012.

Gone, Joseph. "'We Never Was Happy Living Like a Whiteman': Mental Health Disparities and the Postcolonial Predicament in American Indian Communities." *American Journal of Community Psychology,* vol. 40, 2007, pp. 290–300.

Goody, Jack. *The Domestication of the Savage Mind.* Cambridge University Press, 1977.

Gould, Rae. "The Nipmuc Nation and a Case of Mistaken Identity." *Recognition, Sovereignty Struggles, and Indigenous Rights in the United States,* edited by Jean O'Brien and Amy Den Ouden, University of North Carolina Press, 2013, pp. 213–33.

Grace, Catherine O'Neill. *1621: A New Look at Thanksgiving.* National Geographic Children's Books, 2004.

Grant-Costa, Paul, et al. "The Common Pot: Editing Native American Materials." *Scholarly Editing,* vol. 33, 2012, http://www.scholarlyediting.org /2012/essays/essay.commonpot.html.

Gunderson, Jessica. *The Pilgrims' First Thanksgiving.* Nonfiction Picture Books, 2011.

Haas, Angela. "Wampum as Hypertext: An American Indian Intellectual Tradition of Multimedia Theory and Practice." *Studies in American Indian Literatures,* vol. 19, no. 4, Winter 2007, pp. 77–100.

Harris, Dylan M. "Telling the Story of Climate Change: Geologic Imagination, Praxis, and Policy." *Energy Research & Social Science,* vol. 31, Supplement C, Sept. 2017, pp. 179–83.

Harris, Verne. "The Archival Sliver: Power, Memory and Archives in South Africa." *Archival Science,* vol. 2, 2002, pp. 63–86.

Hawkes, Jon. *The Fourth Pillar of Sustainability: Culture's Essential Role in Public Planning.* Common Ground, 2001.

Heise, Ursula K. *Sense of Place and Sense of Planet: The Environmental Imagination of the Global.* New York: Oxford University Press, 2008.

———. "Unnatural Ecologies: The Metaphor of the Environment in Media Theory." *Configurations,* vol. 10, no. 1, 2002, pp. 149–68, doi:10.1353/ con.2003.0006.

Herndon, Ruth Wallis, and Ella Wilcox Sekatau. "The Right to a Name: The Narragansett People and Rhode Island Officials in the Revolutionary Era." *Ethnohistory,* vol. 44, no. 3, July 1997, pp. 433–62, doi:10.2307/483031.

Hobson, Geary, editor. *The People Who Stayed: Southeastern Indian Writing after Removal.* University of Oklahoma Press, 2010.

Hopkins, John Christian. *Carlomagno*. iUniverse, 2003.

———. *Rhyme or Reason: Narragansett Poetry*. Blue Hand Books, 2012.

———. *Twilight of the Gods*. CreateSpace Independent Publishing Platform, 2012.

———. *Writer on the Storm: A Collection of Columns*. Blue Hand Books, 2014.

James, Elizabeth. "Toward Alaska Native Political Organization: The Origins of *Tundra Times*." *Western Historical Quarterly*, vol. 41, no. 3, Oct. 2010, pp. 285–303, doi:10.2307/westhistquar.41.3.0285.

James, Frank. "National Day of Mourning." *Dawnland Voices: An Anthology of Indigenous Writing from New England*. University of Nebraska Press, 2014, pp. 455–58.

Johansen, Emily. *Cosmopolitanism and Place: Spatial Forms in Contemporary Anglophone Literature*. Palgrave Macmillan, 2014.

Johnson, Joseph, and Laura J. Murray. *To Do Good to My Indian Brethren: The Writings of Joseph Johnson 1751–1776*. University of Massachusetts Press, 1998.

Joubert, Joseph. *Nitami Podawazwiskweda: The First Council Fire*. Bowman Books, 2011.

Jurgenson, Nathan. "When Atoms Meet Bits: Social Media, the Mobile Web and Augmented Revolution." *Future Internet*, vol. 4, no. 1, Jan. 2012, pp. 83–91, doi:10.3390/fi4010083.

Justice, Daniel Heath. *Why Indigenous Literatures Matter*. Wilfrid Laurier University Press, 2018.

Katanski, Amelia V. *Learning to Write "Indian": The Boarding-School Experience and American Indian Literature*. University of Oklahoma Press, 2005.

Kates, Robert W., editor. *Readings in Sustainability Science and Technology*. CID Working Paper no. 213. Harvard University Center for International Development, 2010.

Kauanui, J. Kēhaulani. "Issues of Sovereignty in Indian Country." *Cross Paths*, Summer 2013, pp. 6–7.

Kaufman, Ned. "Places of Historical, Cultural and Social Value: Identification and Protection." *Environmental Law in New York*, vol. 12, no. 11, Nov. 2001, pp. 211–12, 224–33.

Keller, Lynn. "Beyond Imagining, Imagining Beyond." *PMLA*, vol. 127, no. 3, May 2012, pp. 579–85, doi:10.1632/pmla.2012.127.3.579.

Kidwell, Clara Sue. *Native American Studies*. University of Nebraska Press, 2005.

Kimmerer, Robin Wall. *Braiding Sweetgrass: Indigenous Wisdom, Scientific Knowledge, and the Teachings of Plants*. Milkweed Editions, 2013.

King, Lisa, et al. *Survivance, Sovereignty, and Story: Teaching American Indian Rhetorics*. University Press of Colorado, 2015.

Kino-nda-niimi Collective. *The Winter We Danced: Voices from the Past, the Future, and the Idle No More Movement*. ARP Books, 2014.

Kirshenblatt-Gimblett, Barbara. *Destination Culture: Tourism, Museums, and Heritage*. University of California Press, 1988.

Klopotek, Brian. *Recognition Odysseys: Indigeneity, Race, and Federal Tribal Recognition Policy in Three Louisiana Indian Communities*. Duke University Press, 2011.

Knight, Lauren. "Tomaquag Museum Ready to Teach Its Own Curriculum: RICentral.com." *Southern Rhode Island Newspapers*, 12 Mar. 2012, http://www.ricentral.com/content/tomaquag-museum-ready-teach-its-own-curriculum.

Koh, Adeline. "Introduction: Re/Collecting." *Verge: Studies in Global Asias*, vol. 1, no. 2, 2015, pp. 21–24.

Kosnik, Abigail De. *Rogue Archives: Digital Cultural Memory and Media Fandom*. MIT Press, 2016.

Krech, Shepard. *The Ecological Indian: Myth and History*. W. W. Norton, 1999.

Kreps, Christina. *Liberating Culture: Cross-Cultural Perspectives on Museums, Curation and Heritage Preservation*. Routledge, 2003.

LaDuke, Winona. *Recovering the Sacred: The Power of Naming and Claiming*. South End Press, 2005.

———. *The Winona LaDuke Reader: A Collection of Essential Writings*. Voyageur Press, 2002.

Latour, Bruno. *We Have Never Been Modern*. Harvard University Press, 1993.

Laurent, Joseph. *New Familiar Abenakis and English Dialogues: The First Ever Published on the Grammatical System*. 1884 ed. Bowman Books, 2010.

LeMenager, Stephanie, and Stephanie Foote. "The Sustainable Humanities." *PMLA*, vol. 127, no. 3, May 2012, pp. 572–78.

Lepore, Jill. *The Name of War: King Philip's War and the Origins of American Identity*. Vintage, 1999.

Lester, Joan A. *We're Still Here: Art of Indian New England. The Children's Museum Collection*. Moyer Bell, 1987.

———. "Working Together to Get It Right." *Boston Stories: The Children's Museum as a Model for Non-Profit Leadership*. Boston Children's Museum, 2013, pp. 1–22.

Levitt, Marc. *Stories in Stone*. Transformation Films, 2008.

L'Hirondelle, Cheryl. "Code Talkers Recounting Signals of Survival." *Coded Territories: Tracing Indigenous Pathways in New Media Arts*, edited by Steven Loft and Kerry Swanson, University of Calgary Press, 2014, pp. 147–68.

Lincoln, Kenneth. *Native American Renaissance*. University of California Press, 1985.

Littlefield, Daniel F., and James W. Parins. *American Indian and Alaska Native Newspapers and Periodicals*. Greenwood Press, 1986.

Liu, Alan. "Imagining the New Media Encounter." *Companion to Digital Literary Studies (Blackwell Companions to Literature and Culture)*, edited by Ray Siemens and Susan Schreibman, Blackwell Publishing Professional, 2007, pp. 3–25, http://www.digitalhumanities.org/companionDLS/.

Loew, Patty, and Kelly Mella. "Black Ink and the New Red Power: Native American Newspapers and Tribal Sovereignty." *Journalism & Communication Monographs*, vol. 7, no. 3, Sept. 2005, pp. 99–142.

Loewen, James W. *Lies My Teacher Told Me: Everything Your American History Textbook Got Wrong*. New Press, 2008.

Loft, Steven, and Kerry Swanson, editors. *Coded Territories: Tracing Indigenous Pathways in New Media Art*. University of Calgary Press, 2014.

Loring, Donna. *In the Shadow of the Eagle*. Tilbury House, 2008.

Lowenthal, David. *The Past Is a Foreign Country*. Cambridge University Press, 1985.

Lynch, Deidre, and William Beatty Warner. *Cultural Institutions of the Novel*. Duke University Press, 1996.

Mackay, Angus. "Climate and Popular Unrest in Late Medieval Castile." *Climate and History: Studies in Past Climates and Their Impact on Man*, edited by T. M. L. Wigley, M. J. Ingram, and G. Farmer, Cambridge University Press, 1985, pp. 356–403.

Magelssen, Scott. *Living History Museums: Undoing History through Performance*. Rowman & Littlefield, 2007.

Makepeace, Anne. *We Still Live Here (Âs Nutayuneân)*. DVD. Makepeace Productions, 2010.

Makepeace Productions and Cultural Survival. "Wampanoag." *Our Mother Tongues: Discover America's First Languages*, http://ourmothertongues.org/language/Wampanoag/12. Accessed 28 Aug. 2013.

Mann, Alana. *Global Activism in Food Politics: Power Shift*. Palgrave Macmillan, 2014.

Mann, Larry Spotted Crow. *The Mourning Road to Thanksgiving*. Word Branch Publishing, 2014.

Manning, Helen. *Moshup's Footsteps: The Wampanoag Nation, Gay Head/Aquinnah, the People of First Light*. Blue Cloud across the Moon Publishing, 2001.

Marmion, Maeve, et al. "'Heritage? What Do You Mean by Heritage?'" *Sharing Cultures*, 2009, pp. 575–83.

Marshall, Kate. "What Are the Novels of the Anthropocene? American Fiction in Geological Time." *American Literary History*, vol. 27, no. 3, Aug. 2015, pp. 523–38.

Marshall, Murdena, and David L. Schmidt. *Mi'kmaq Hieroglyphic Prayers: Readings in North America's First Indigenous Script*. Illustrated edition. Nimbus Publishing (CT), 1995.

Masta, Henry Lorne. *Abenaki Indian Legends, Grammar and Place Names*. 1932 ed. Bowman Books, 2008.

Maxwell, Richard, and Toby Miller. *Greening the Media*. New York: Oxford University Press, 2012.

McBride, Bunny. *Molly Spotted Elk: A Penobscot in Paris*. University of Oklahoma Press, 1997.

McGann, Jerome J. "Sustainability: The Elephant in the Room." *Online Humanities Scholarship: The Shape of Things to Come*, 2010, http://shapeofthings .org/papers/.

McLuhan, Marshall. *The Gutenberg Galaxy*. Centennial edition. University of Toronto Press, Scholarly Publishing Division, 2011.

Meadows, Donella. *Thinking in Systems: A Primer*. Chelsea Green Publishing, 2008.

Melamed, Jodi. *Represent and Destroy: Rationalizing Violence in the New Racial Capitalism*. University of Minnesota Press, 2011.

Mifflin, Jeffrey. "Saving a Language." MIT *Technology Review*, 22 Apr. 2008, http://www.technologyreview.com/article/409990/saving-a-language/.

Mihesuah, Devon Abbott. *Indigenous American Women: Decolonization, Empowerment, Activism*. University of Nebraska Press, 2003.

Million, Dian. *Therapeutic Nations: Healing in an Age of Indigenous Human Rights*. University of Arizona Press, 2013.

Mills, Earl. *Talking with the Elders of Mashpee: Memories of Earl H. Mills, Sr.* Mills, 2012.

Milz, Sabine. "Aboriginal Publishing in Contemporary Canada: Kateri Akiwenzie-Damm and Kegedonce Press." *Essays on Canadian Writing*, no. 84, Fall 2009, pp. 213–27.

Mohegan Tribe. "The Mohegan Tribe's History." 2017, https://www.mohegan .nsn.us/explore/heritage/our-history.

Moody, John. "'Absolute Republick': The Abenaki Nation in 1791." *Vermont Bicentennial Newsletter*, vol. 3, no. 4, Winter 1991, pp. 6–7.

Moore, MariJo, editor. *Genocide of the Mind: New Native American Writing*. Bold Type Books, 2003.

Morgan, Henry Louis. *Ancient Society or Researches in the Lines of Human Progress from Savagery through Barbarism to Civilization*. Charles H. Kerr, 1907.

Moriarty, Mairead. "New Roles for Endangered Languages." *The Cambridge Handbook of Endangered Languages*, edited by Peter K. Austin and Julia Sallabank, Cambridge University Press, 2011, pp. 446–58.

Mukavetz, Andrea Riley, and Malea Powell. "Making Native Space for Graduate Students: A Story of Indigenous Rhetorical Practice." *Survivance, Sovereignty, and Story: Teaching American Indian Rhetorics*, edited by Lisa King, Rose Gubele, and Joyce Rain Anderson, Utah State University Press, 2015, pp. 138–59.

Naguib, Saphinaz-Amal. "Museums, Diasporas and the Sustainability of Intangible Cultural Heritage." *Sustainability*, vol. 5, no. 5, 2013, pp. 2178–90.

Narragansett Indian Tribe. "Early History." 2018, http://narragansettindian nation.org/history/early/.

Native American Journalists Association. *Charter, Articles I & II: Name & Statement of Purpose.* http://www.naja.com/about/charter-bylaws/articles-i -ii/. Accessed 10 Dec. 2014.

Native Youth Sexual Health Network. "February 14 Women's Memorial Marches: Not Forgetting the Legacy and Honouring through Action." *Rabble,* 12 Feb. 2014, http://rabble.ca/blogs/bloggers/bwss/2014/02/february -14-womens-memorial-marches-not-forgetting-legacy-and-honouring-.

Newsom, Bonnie, and Martin Wobst. *Developing Policies and Protocols for the Culturally Sensitive Intellectual Properties of the Penobscot Nation of Maine.* Report of the Penobscot Nation Intellectual Property Working Group, Intellectual Property Issues in Cultural Heritage, Apr. 2014, http://www .sfu.ca/ipinch/outputs/reports?order=field_author_value&sort=asc.

Newton, Julianne Lutz, and Eric Freyfogle. "Sustainability: A Dissent." *Conservation Biology,* vol. 19, no. 1, Feb. 2005, pp. 23–32.

Nieves, Angel David. "Places of Pain as Tools for Social Justice in the 'New' South Africa." *Places of Pain and Shame: Dealing with "Difficult" Heritage,* edited by William Logan and Keir Reeves, Routledge, 2009, pp. 198–214.

O'Brien, Jean M. *Dispossession by Degrees: Indian Land and Identity in Natick, Massachusetts, 1650–1790.* Cambridge University Press, 1997.

———. *Firsting and Lasting: Writing Indians out of Existence in New England.* University of Minnesota Press, 2010.

Occom, Samson, and Joanna Brooks. *The Collected Writings of Samson Occom, Mohegan: Literature and Leadership in Eighteenth-Century Native America.* New York: Oxford University Press, 2006.

Oliveira, Katrina-Ann R. Kapa'anaokalaokeola Nakoa. *Ancestral Places: Understanding Kanaka Geographies.* Oregon State University Press, 2014.

Ong, Walter J. *Orality and Literacy: The Technologizing of the Word.* Routledge, 2002.

Ortega, Ernest. "Protecting a Diverse Heritage: Engaging Communities in Preserving and Interpreting That Which They Value." *Protecting Our Diverse Heritage: The Role of Parks, Protected Areas, and Cultural Sites.* Hancock MI: George Wright Society, 2003, pp. 259–62.

Ortoleva, Matthew. "'We Face East': The Narragansett Dawn and Ecocentric Discourses of Identity and Justice." *Environmental Rhetoric and Ecologies of Place,* edited by Peter N. Goggin, Routledge, 2013, pp. 84–96.

Parker, Robert Dale. *Changing Is Not Vanishing: A Collection of American Indian Poetry to 1930.* University of Pennsylvania Press, 2010.

Paul, Mihku. "Artist Statement." *Look Twice: The Waponahki in Image and Verse.* Bar Harbor ME: Abbe Museum, 2010.

———. *20th Century Powwow Playland.* Bowman Books, 2012.

Penobscot Cultural & Historic Preservation Office. "Tribal Timeline." 2019, https://www.penobscotculture.com/index.php/tribal-timeline.

Perley, Bernard C. *Defying Maliseet Language Death: Emergent Vitalities of Language, Culture, and Identity in Eastern Canada*. University of Nebraska Press, 2011.

Peters, Paula. "About the Mashpee Nine." *Mashpee Nine*, 2015, http://mashpeenine.com/about.html.

Peters, Russell M. *The Wampanoags of Mashpee: An Indian Perspective on American History*. Media Action, 1987.

Phillips, Ruth B. *Museum Pieces: Toward the Indigenization of Canadian Museums*. McGill-Queens University Press, 2011.

Pouliot, Paul. "Publishing the Cowasuck Band Newsletters." English 739 (American Indian Literatures) Lecture. University of New Hampshire, Durham, 25 Apr. 2013.

Powell, Malea. "Rhetorics of Survivance: How American Indians Use Writing." *College Composition and Communication*, vol. 53, no. 3, 2002, pp. 396–434.

Powell, Timothy, and Larry Aitken. "Encoding Culture: Building a Digital Archive Based on Traditional Ojibwe Teachings." *The American Literature Scholar in the Digital Age*, edited by Amy Earhart and Andrew Jewell, University of Michigan Press, 2010, pp. 250–74.

Prins, Harald. *The Mi'kmaq: Resistance, Accommodation, and Cultural Survival*. Wadsworth/Tomson Learning, 2002.

Quinn, William W., Jr. "The Southeast Syndrome: Notes on Indian Descendant Recruitment Organizations and Their Perceptions of Native American Culture." *American Indian Quarterly*, vol. 14, no. 2, Apr. 1990, pp. 147–54.

Ramirez, Renya. *Native Hubs: Culture, Community, and Belonging in Silicon Valley and Beyond*. Duke University Press, 2007.

Ranco, Darren. "The Indian Ecologist and the Politics of Representation: Critiquing the Ecological Indian in the Age of Ecocide." *Perspectives on the Ecological Indian: Native Americans and the Environment*, edited by Michael Harkin and David Rich Lewis, University of Nebraska Press, 2007, pp. 32–51.

Ranco, Darren, Amy Arnett, Erika Latty, Alyssa Remsburg, Kathleen Dunckel, Erin Quigley, Rob Lillieholm, John Daigle, Bill Livingston, Jennifer Neptune, and Theresa Secord. "Two Maine Forest Pests: A Comparison of Approaches to Understanding Threats to Hemlock and Ash Trees in Maine." *Maine Policy Review*, vol. 21, no. 1, Jan. 2012, pp. 76–89.

Rancourt, Suzanne. *Billboard in the Clouds*. Curbstone, 2004.

Red Eagle, Henry. *Aboriginally Yours, Chief Henry Red Eagle*. Moosehead Communications, 1997.

Reese, Debbie. "American Indians in Children's Literature (AICL): Joseph Bruchac's HIDDEN ROOTS Back in Print!" *American Indians in Children's*

Literature (AICL), 5 Jan. 2011, https://americanindiansinchildrensliterature
.blogspot.com/2011/01/joseph-bruchacs-hidden-roots-back-in.html.

———. "American Indians in Children's Literature (AICL): Scholastic, Joseph Bruchac, and the Out-of-Print Status of HIDDEN ROOTS."
American Indians in Children's Literature (AICL), 29 Sept. 2010, https://
americanindiansinchildrensliterature.blogspot.com/2010/09/scholastic
-joseph-bruchac-and-out-of.html.

———. "Native Literary Nationalism and Reinventing the Enemy's Language:
Simon Ortiz's Books for Youth." *American Indians in Children's Literature (AICL)*, 12 June 2009, http://americanindiansinchildrensliterature
.blogspot.com/2009/06/native-literary-nationalism-and.html.

———. "Review of Caleb's Crossing." *American Indians in Children's Literature (AICL)*, 9 Jan. 2012, http://americanindiansinchildrensliterature
.blogspot.com/2012/01/calebs-crossing.html.

Ridge, Mia. *Crowdsourcing Our Cultural Heritage*. Routledge, 2016.

Rifkin, Mark. *Settler Common Sense*. University of Minnesota Press, 2015.

Riley, Naomi Schaefer. "No, Native Americans *Weren't* the Original Envi-
ronmentalists." *New York Post*, 14 July 2015, http://nypost.com/2015
/07/13/no-native-americans-werent-the-original-environmentalists/.

Risam, Roopika. "The Race for Digitality." *Roopika Risam*, 27 Sept. 2014, http://
roopikarisam.com/2014/09/27/the-race-for-digitality/.

Roanhorse, Rebecca. *Trail of Lightning (The Sixth World Book I)*. Gallery/
Saga Press, 2018.

Rosier, Paul C. *Serving Their Country: American Indian Politics and Patrio-
tism in the Twentieth Century*. Harvard University Press, 2010.

Roy, Loriene, et al. *Tribal Libraries, Archives, and Museums: Preserving Our
Language, Memory, and Lifeways*. Scarecrow Press, 2011.

Ryan, John Charles. "Toward a Phen(Omen)Ology of the Seasons: The Emergence of the Indigenous Weather Knowledge Project (IWKP)." *Environment, Space, Place*, vol. 5, no. 1, 2013, pp. 103–31.

Sanders, Thomas Edward, and Walter W. Peek. *Literature of the American
Indian*. Glencoe Press, 1976.

Savageau, Cheryl. *Dirt Road Home*. Curbstone, 2005.

———. *Home Country*. Alice James, 1992.

———. "Looking for Indians." *Dirt Road Home*. Curbstone Press, 1995, pp.
19–20.

———. *Mother/Land*. Salt Publishing, 2006.

———. *Muskrat Will Be Swimming*. Tilbury House, 1996.

———. *Out of the Crazywoods*. University of Nebraska Press, 2020.

Scarce, Rik. *Creating Sustainable Communities: Lessons from the Hudson
River Region*. SUNY Press, 2015.

Schiffman, Richard. "Are Trees Sentient Beings? Certainly, Says German Forester." *Yale E360*, 16 Nov. 2016, e360.yale.edu/features/are_trees _sentient_peter_wohlleben.

Seale, Doris, and Beverly Slapin. *A Broken Flute: The Native Experience in Books for Children*. Rowman Altamira, 2006.

Senier, Siobhan. *Dawnland Voices: An Anthology of Indigenous Writing from New England*. University of Nebraska Press, 2014.

———. "Decolonizing the Archive: Digitizing Native Literature with Students and Tribal Communities." *Resilience: A Journal of the Environmental Humanities*, vol. 1, no. 3, 2014, pp. 69–85.

———. "Indigenizing Wikipedia: Student Accountability to Native American Authors on the World's Largest Encyclopedia." *Web Writing: Why & How for Liberal Arts Teaching and Learning*, edited by Jack Dougherty and Tennyson O'Donnell, University of Michigan Press, 2014, http:// epress.trincoll.edu/webwriting/chapter/senier/.

———. "Rethinking Recognition: Mi'kmaq and Maliseet Poets Re-write Land and Community." *MELUS: Multi-Ethnic Literature of the U.S.*, vol. 37, no. 1, 2012, pp. 15–34, Project MUSE, doi:10.1353/mel.2012.0003.

———. "Writing of Indigenous New England: Building Partnerships for the Preservation of Regional Native American Literature." White Paper Report no. 111894. National Endowment for the Humanities White Papers, July 2016, https://hcommons.org/deposits/item/hc:12663/.

Senier, Siobhan, and Clare Barker. "Introduction." *Journal of Literary & Cultural Disability Studies*, vol. 7, no. 2, 2013, pp. 123–40.

Shay, Charles Norman. "Joseph Nicolar and His Daughters." *Penobscot: Culture and History of the Nation*, 25 Sept. 2006, http://www.penobscotculture .com/?option=com_content&view=article&id=97&Itemid=72.

Short, Damien, and Corinne Lennox. *Handbook of Indigenous Peoples' Rights*. Routledge, 2016.

Silko, Leslie Marmon. "An Old-Time Indian Attack Conducted in Two Parts." *The Remembered Earth: An Anthology of Contemporary Native American Literature*, edited by Geary Hobson, University of New Mexico Press, 1981, pp. 211–16.

Silverman, David J. *Faith and Boundaries: Colonists, Christianity, and Community among the Wampanoag Indians of Martha's Vineyard, 1600–1871*. Cambridge University Press, 2005.

Simmons, William S. *Spirit of the New England Tribes: Indian History and Folklore, 1620–1984*. University Press of New England, 1986.

Simpson, Audra. *Mohawk Interruptus: Political Life across the Borders of Settler States*. Duke University Press, 2014.

Simpson, Leanne. "Can Fracking Showdown on Native Land Help Break Canada's Cycle of Colonialism?" *YES Magazine*, 23 Oct. 2013, http://www

.yesmagazine.org/peace-justice/can-fracking-showdown-on-native-land
-help-break-canada-s-cycle-of-colonialism-elsipogtog.

————. "Land as Pedagogy: Nishnaabeg Intelligence and Rebellious Transformation." *Decolonization: Indigeneity, Education & Society*, vol. 3, no.
3, 2014, pp. 1–25.

————, editor. *Lighting the Eighth Fire: The Liberation, Resurgence, and Protection of Indigenous Nations.* Arbeiter Ring Publishing, 2008.

Sinclair, Niigaanwewidam James. "The Power of Dirty Waters: Indigenous
Poetics." *Indigenous Poetics in Canada*, edited by Neal McLeod, Wilfrid
Laurier University Press, 2014, pp. 203–16.

Siperstein, Stephen, et al., editors. *Teaching Climate Change in the Humanities.* Routledge, 2016.

Smith, Andrea. *Conquest: Sexual Violence and American Indian Genocide.*
South End Press, 2005.

Smith, Laurajane, and Natsuko Akagawa, editors. *Intangible Heritage.* Routledge, 2009.

Speck, Frank G. "Penobscot Tales and Religious Beliefs." *Journal of American
Folklore*, vol. 48, no. 187, Jan. 1935, pp. 1–107.

Spotted Crow Mann, Larry. *Tales from the Whispering Basket.* CreateSpace,
2011.

Srinivasan, Ramesh, et al. "Diverse Knowledges and Contact Zones within
the Digital Museum." *Science Technology Human Values*, vol. 35, no. 5,
May 2010, pp. 735–68.

Steffen, Will, et al. "The Trajectory of the Anthropocene: The Great Acceler-
ation." *Anthropocene Review*, vol. 2, no. 1, Apr. 2015, pp. 81–98.

Sterne, Jonathan. "The Theology of Sound: A Critique of Orality." *Canadian
Journal of Communication*, vol. 36, 2011, pp. 207–25.

Steuert, Patricia A., Aylette Jenness, and Joanne Jones-Rizzi. *Opening the
Museum: History and Strategies.* Children's Museum, 1993.

Stoler, Ann Laura. *Along the Archival Grain: Epistemic Anxieties and Colonial
Common Sense.* Princeton University Press, 2010.

Street, Brian V. *Literacy in Theory and Practice.* Cambridge University Press,
1984.

Striphas, Ted. *The Late Age of Print: Everyday Book Culture from Consumer-
ism to Control.* Columbia University Press, 2011.

Sunray, Cedric. "Blood Policing." *Native Studies Keywords*, edited by Stephanie Nohelani Teves, Andrea Smith, and Michelle H. Raheja, University
of British Columbia Press, 2015, pp. 209–20.

————. "'Federally Recognized' Often Misused." *Indian Country Today Media
Network*, 21 Oct. 2012, http://indiancountrytodaymedianetwork.com
/2012/10/21/federally-recognized-often-misued.

Tallbear, Kim. *Native American DNA: Tribal Belonging and the False Promise of Genetic Science*. University of Minnesota Press, 2013.

Tantaquidgeon, Gladys. *Folk Medicine of the Delaware & Related Algonkian Indians*. Pennsylvania Historical & Museum Commission, 2000.

Tantaquidgeon Zobel, Melissa. "The Accomac Business Model." *Anchorage Daily News*, 4 Nov. 2009, https://www.adn.com/commentary/article/accomac-business-model/2009/11/05/.

———. "Algonquian Naming, Power, and Relationality in a Rare Native Love Poem." *Papers of the Forty-Sixth Algonquian Conference*, edited by Monica Macaulay and Margaret Noodin, Michigan State University Press, 2017, pp. 213–22, http://www.jstor.org/stable/10.14321/j.cttlr33qlv.16.

———. "Butterfly." *Charles River Journal*, no. 8, Autumn–Winter 2017, http://penandanvil.com/crj/8/tantaquidgeon-zobel/.

———. *Fire Hollow*. Raven's Wing Books, 2010.

———. "The New York Times Can Do Better: Book Reviews of Native American Literature." *Dawnland Voices 2.0*, no. 3, 11 Oct. 2016, http://dawnlandvoices.org/melissa-tantaquidgeon-zobel-issue-3/.

———. *Oracles: A Novel*. University of New Mexico Press, 2004.

———. *Wabanaki Blues*. Poisoned Pen Press, 2015.

Tantaquidgeon Zobel, Melissa [as Melissa Jayne Fawcett]. *Medicine Trail: The Life and Lessons of Gladys Tantaquidgeon*. University of Arizona Press, 2015.

———. "Mohegan Women's Sociocultural Leadership." *Rooted Like the Ash Trees*, edited by Richard Carlson, Eagle Wing Press, 1987, pp. 153–54.

Taylor, Graham D. *The New Deal and American Indian Tribalism: The Administration of the Indian Reorganization Act, 1934–45*. University of Nebraska Press, 1980.

Teves, Stephanie Nohelani, et al., editors. *Native Studies Keywords*. University of Arizona Press, 2015.

Theimer, Kate. "What Is the Meaning of Archives 2.0?" *American Archivist*, vol. 74, no. 1, Apr. 2011, pp. 58–68.

Throsby, David. "Cultural Sustainability." *A Handbook of Cultural Economics*, edited by Ruth Towse, Edward Elgar Publishing, 2003.

Tigerman, Kathleen. *Wisconsin Indian Literature: Anthology of Native Voices*. University of Wisconsin Press, 2006.

Titon, Jeff Todd. "Music and Sustainability: An Ecological Viewpoint." *World of Music*, vol. 51, no. 1, 2009, pp. 119–39.

Todd, Zoe. "Indigenizing the Anthropocene." *Art in the Anthropocene: Encounters among Aesthetics, Politics, Environments and Epistemologies*, edited by Heather Davis and Etienne Turpin, Open Humanities Press, 2015, pp. 241–54.

———. "An Indigenous Feminist's Take on the Ontological Turn: 'Ontology' Is Just Another Word for Colonialism." *Journal of Historical Sociology*, vol. 29, no. 1, Mar. 2016, pp. 4–22, Wiley Online Library, doi:10.1111/johs.12124.

———. "An Indigenous Feminist's Take on the Ontological Turn: 'Ontology' Is Just Another Word for Colonialism." *Urbane Adventurer: Amiskwacî*, 24 Oct. 2014, https://zoeandthecity.wordpress.com/2014/10/24/an-indigenous-feminists-take-on-the-ontological-turn-ontology-is-just-another-word-for-colonialism/.

Toensing, Gale Courey. "Passamaquoddy Tribe Amends Fishery Law to Protect Its Citizens from State Threat." *Indian Country Today Media Network*, 8 Apr. 2014, http://indiancountrytodaymedianetwork.com/2014/04/08/passamaquoddy-tribe-amends-fishery-law-protect-its-citizens-state-threat-154365.

"Tornado in Connecticut." *New York Times*, 28 Sept. 1899, p. 1.

Torres, Gerald, and Kathryn Milun. "Stories and Standing: The Legal Meaning of Identity." *After Identity: A Reader in Law and Culture*, edited by Dan Danielson and Karen Engle, Routledge, 1995, pp. 129–42.

Trettien, Whitney Anne. "A Deep History of Electronic Textuality: The Case of *English Reprints Jhon Milton Areopagitica.*" *Digital Humanities Quarterly*, vol. 7, no. 1, 2013, http://digitalhumanities.org/dhq/vol/7/1/000150/000150.html.

Trexler, Adam. *Anthropocene Fictions*. University of Virginia Press, 2015.

United Nations. *Declaration on the Rights of Indigenous Peoples*. Mar. 2008, http://www.un.org/esa/socdev/unpfii/documents/DRIPS_en.pdf.

United Nations Educational, Scientific and Cultural Organization. "Text of the Convention for the Safeguarding of the Intangible Cultural Heritage." 2003, http://www.unesco.org/culture/ich/en/convention.

Uy, Mary Jean Sia. *The Narragansett Indians: Race and State, 1880–1983. A Senior Thesis*. Brown University, 1998.

Vaidhyanathan, Siva. *Antisocial Media: How Facebook Disconnects Us and Undermines Democracy*. New York: Oxford University Press, 2018.

Vallance, Suzanne, et al. "What Is Social Sustainability? A Clarification of Concepts." *Geoforum*, vol. 42, 2011, pp. 342–48.

Vecco, Marilena. "A Definition of Cultural Heritage: From the Tangible to the Intangible." *Journal of Cultural Heritage*, vol. 11, no. 3, 2010, pp. 321–32.

Vizenor, Gerald. *Manifest Manners: Narratives on Postindian Survivance*. University of Nebraska Press, 1999.

Wanamaker, Tom. "Wanamaker: Maine Casino Plans Go Up in Flames, New York Tax Deadline Extended." *Indian Country Media Network*, 14 Nov. 2003, https://newsmaven.io/indiancountrytoday/news/wanamaker-maine-casino-plans-go-up-in-flames-new-york-tax-deadline-extended/.

Warrior, Robert Allen. *Tribal Secrets: Recovering American Indian Intellectual Traditions*. University of Minnesota Press, 1994.

Waziyatawin. "The Paradox of Indigenous Resurgence at the End of Empire." *Decolonization: Indigeneity, Education & Society*, vol. 1, no. 1, 2012, pp. 68–85.

Weaver, Jace. *Other Words: American Indian Literature, Law, and Culture*. University of Oklahoma Press, 2001.

Wessels, Tom. *Reading the Forested Landscape: A Natural History of New England*. Countryman Press, 2005.

Wherry, James. "Of Micmacs and Maliseets: Maine's Other Indians." *Indian Truth*, Apr. 1980, pp. 1–3.

White, Hayden. *The Content of the Form: Narrative Discourse and Historical Representation*. Johns Hopkins University Press, 1990.

White, Kyle Powys, et al. "Indigenous Lessons about Sustainability Are Not Just for 'All Humanity.'" *Sustainability: Approaches to Environmental Justice and Social Power*, edited by Julie Sze, NYU Press, 2018, pp. 149–79.

Wiget, Andrew. *Handbook of Native American Literature*. Routledge, 2013.

Wigley, T. M. L., et al. *Climate and History: Studies in Past Climates and Their Impact on Man*. Cambridge University Press, 1985.

Williams, Dana A., and Marissa K. Lopez. "More Than a Fever: Toward a Theory of the Ethnic Archive." *PMLA: Publications of the Modern Language Association of America*, vol. 127, no. 2, 2012, pp. 357–60.

Williams, Roger. *A Key into the Language of America* (1643). Rhode Island Historical Society, 1827.

Wisecup, Kelly. "'Meteors, Ships, Etc.': Native American Histories of Colonialism and Early American Archives." *American Literary History*, vol. 30, no. 1, pp. 29–54.

Wiseman, Frederick Matthew. *The Voice of the Dawn: An Autohistory of the Abenaki Nation*. University Press of New England, 2001.

Wolfe, Patrick. *Settler Colonialism and the Transformation of Anthropology. The Politics and Poetics of an Ethnographic Event*. Cassell, 1999.

Woodard, Colin. "As Reservation's Rule of Law Erodes, Abuses Thrive." *Central Maine*, 19 July 2014, http://www.centralmaine.com/2014/07/19/as-reservations-rule-of-law-erodes-abuses-thrive/.

Wôpanâak Language Reclamation Project. "Fun with Words." 2018, http://www.wlrp.org/fun-with-words.html.

———. "Home." 2018, http://www.wlrp.org/.

Wright, Alexis. "Deep Weather." *Meanjin*, vol. 70, no. 2, Winter 2011, pp. 70–82.

———. *The Swan Book: A Novel*. Atria Books, 2016.

Wzôkhilain, Pial Pol, and Jesse Bowman Bruchac. *The Gospel of Mark Translated into the Abenaki Indian, English and French Languages*. Bowman Books, 2011.

Yazzie, Melanie K., and Nick Estes. "Guest Editors' Introduction: Essentializing Elizabeth Cook-Lynn." *Wicazo Sa Review*, vol. 31, no. 1, July 2016,
pp. 9–26.

Young-Ing, Greg. "An Overview of Aboriginal Literature and Publishing in
Canada." *Australian-Canadian Studies*, vol. 14, nos. 1–2, 1996, pp. 157–71.

Zuck, Rochelle Raineri. "'Yours in the Cause': Readers, Correspondents, and
the Editorial Politics of Carlos Montezuma's Wassaja." *American Periodicals*, vol. 22, no. 1, 2012, pp. 72–93.

Index

CPSIA information can be obtained
at www.ICGtesting.com
Printed in the USA
LVHW112020250320
651177LV00008B/109